THE LANGUAGE OF FLOWERS
A History

VICTORIAN LITERATURE AND CULTURE SERIES

Karen Chase, Jerome J. McGann, *and* Herbert Tucker, *General Editors*

THE LANGUAGE
OF FLOWERS
A History

Beverly Seaton

UNIVERSITY PRESS OF VIRGINIA
Charlottesville and London

THE UNIVERSITY PRESS OF VIRGINIA
Copyright © 1995 by the Rector and Visitors
of the University of Virginia

First published 1995

Library of Congress Cataloging-in-Publication Data
Seaton, Beverly.
      The language of flowers : a history / Beverly Seaton.
            p.   cm. — (Victorian literature and culture)
      Includes bibliographical references and index.
      ISBN 0-8139-1556-2 (cloth)
            1. Flowers—Literary collections.   2. Flower language.   I. Title.
      II. Series: Victorian literature and culture series.
      PN6071.F5S43   1995
      398'.368213—dc20   94-29337
                                                                                    CIP

Printed in the United States of America

Dedicated to my husband, John A. Seaton
Ivy, Myrtle, Periwinkle, Rosemary
Following Mme de Latour

Contents

Illustrations

Acknowledgments

During the years I have been studying the language of flowers, I have become indebted to many people and institutions. Foremost among these is my own university, the Ohio State University at Newark. The Research Committee of the Faculty Assembly has supported my research with many grants to pay for travel, photocopies, and microfilm, while the administration provided me with a much needed sabbatical to write. Mary Kay Yaus of Faculty Services helped me convert the manuscript from MultiMate to WordPerfect. Colleagues in the university library worked with me in tracking down elusive biographical data and exotic volumes that we gathered, through Interlibrary Loan, from every conceivable library in the country. Here I would like especially to acknowledge the guidance of Eleanor Devlin of the OSU Library, who started me off in the right direction.

Naturally I had to have the cooperation of other libraries and librarians. The Hunt Institute for Botanical Documentation at Carnegie Mellon University in Pittsburgh was the starting point of my research, where Bernadette Callery, head librarian (now at the New York Botanical Garden Library), and other helpful folk made me welcome. My files are stuffed with photocopies of flower books from the Hunt collection, some with hand and thumb prints of Hunt librarians to remind me of the hours I spent reading the language of flowers beneath the benevolent gaze of Linnaeus. Other libraries also welcomed my visits: the New York Botanical Garden Library, Sterling Morton Library at the Morton Arboretum, Pennsylvania Horticultural Society Library, Eleanor Squire Library at the Garden Center of Greater Cleveland, Kingwood Center Library, Longwood Gardens Library, Eleutherian Mills Historical Library,

National Agricultural Library, Library of Congress, Princeton University Library, and Cornell University Library. Without the supportive interest of librarians at these institutions, I would not have been able to complete my work.

It has also been my pleasure to encounter many helpful individuals. Anne B. Shteir provided me with microfilm from the British Museum; Charles van Ravenswaay helped me make contact with John Francis McDermott; and Charles Boewe invited me to investigate Rafinesque's flower language. James Moretz, director of the American Floral Art School in Chicago, has shared information (and photocopies) with me from his own personal collection of the language of flowers. The late Elisabeth Woodburn of Booknoll Farm welcomed me to her home and business to discuss the language of flower books. The encouragement of the late Professor Emanuel Rudolph of the Ohio State University Department of Botany was especially helpful, for he shared his collection with me as well as his enthusiasm for the topic. Throughout the years that I have been studying the language of flowers I have published a number of papers on the language and related topics, and I thank the usually anonymous but knowledgeable referees for their suggestions. And then there were the many individuals over time who asked me questions about the language of flowers, sometimes after a lecture, sometimes in a letter or telephone call.

Finally, I must thank the staff at the University Press of Virginia for their careful consideration of my work and their many helpful suggestions.

To all those who have a part in my work, a spray of wisteria (following Mme de Latour).

THE LANGUAGE OF FLOWERS
A History

Introduction

TO MODERN enthusiasts, no feature of Victorian popular culture appears more charming, more cozy, or more absolutely *Victorian* than the language of flowers. But, in reality, none is more obviously misunderstood. The purpose of this study is to explain the language of flowers, recount its history, and discuss its relationship to other aspects of Victorian popular culture.

My own interest in the language of flowers began as a minor research project, associated with my reading of Victorian garden autobiography. In the course of this research, I discovered Rachel M. Hunt's collection of language of flower books at the Hunt Botanical Institute in Pittsburgh. What was intended for a brief study has turned into a long-term project, for the more I looked into the language of flowers the more books there seemed to be and the more complicated the pursuit of them, for most have either been discarded as literary ephemera or are currently housed in rare book libraries. The sheer numbers of such books offered me the opportunity any historian of culture should be seeking: the identification of material that has not been seriously studied but that exists in plenty. My related work in nineteenth-century garden history confirmed the idea that flowers were something different in that period than they are today, for they took on great significance in the domestic, social, and intellectual lives of the people, and found full expression in the arts and the literature of the period.[1]

There is a great deal of misinterpretation of the nineteenth-century language of flowers in today's cultural history. Let me define what, in the minds of many persons interested in Victorian styles and manners, the language of flowers *seems* to have been. These people think that the language of flowers was a socially agreed-upon symbolic language which men and women actually used to communicate with one another concerning matters of love and romance. Thus, they picture the Victorian lady receiving a bouquet of flowers which she can easily "translate" into a coherent message.

First of all, as will be abundantly shown in the text of my study, there was no agreed-upon set of meanings. Instead of a universal symbolic language, the language of flowers was a vocabulary list, matching flowers with meanings, differing from book to book. Originating among the journalists catering to the genteel reader in Napoleonic France, the language of flowers was almost certainly a creation of writers of popular books. Belonging to the genre of literary almanacs and their offspring, the gift annuals, language of flower books were intended as suitable gifts, perhaps to entertain the genteel female reader for a few dull afternoons. There is almost no evidence that people actually used these symbolic lists to communicate, even if the parties agreed upon what book to use for their meanings. In all the popular and serious fiction I have read, especially relating to the lives of women and domestic matters, I have found only one reference to the use of the language of flowers. Nor have I found any references in memoirs or diaries, although I have not searched extensively for such evidence. Furthermore, the books themselves do not show any marks of use as practical dictionaries, although some I have seen have little comments or notes. All of these points will be explained in much more detail.

The books in which the floral vocabularies and related matters are to be found, which I call language of flower books, belong to a larger class of sentimental flower books. The sentimental flower book is one that does not treat flowers in botanical (scientific) or horticultural (practical) terms, but rather in terms of sentiment, feeling, and association. Next to the language of flower book, the most popular type of sentimental flower book was the prose work with religious and moral themes. Other types of sentimental flower books—anthologies of flower poetry, flower folklores, and sentimental botanies—are fewer in number, but their contents are often represented in the more eclectic language of flower books. The sentimental flower book can usually be identified by its illustrations and its bindings, since most of them were intended as gift or reward books.

In order to explain the language of flowers in its proper context, my study includes material on the importance of flowers in nineteenth-century domestic and social life, as well as a fuller discussion of the entire class of sentimental flower books. Since women were the intended audience for the language of flower books, chapter two discusses the issue of audience in terms of the culturally approved connection between women and flowers. There is a general discussion of floral symbols in earlier times and other cultures before I approach the language of flowers specifically. The origins of the language of flowers is traced, so far as has been possible, to popular themes and concepts of the late eighteenth century. Then, since the language of flowers as we know it began in France, the study turns to its development in France, going on to England and America in chapter five. I conclude with some cross-cultural readings in the language of flowers and a chapter on its literary and artistic aspects. Following the text are a chart of flower meanings from various important language of flower books and a complete bibliography of language of flower titles. In most cases I have not quoted French writers in French, but in my own translations; when the French text is essential, my translation directly follows.

Thus my topic is both the history of the concept of a language of flowers and the history of a popular genre, the language of flower book. This study is intended for Victorian scholars in all fields—academic researchers in literature and the visual arts, museum personnel, and historians of popular culture. As the nineteenth century recedes ever farther from our collective memories, we can begin to look more objectively at even its most sentimental aspects.

I

Flowers in the Nineteenth Century

The matron fills her chrystal vase
* With gems that Summer lends,*
Or groups them round the festal board
* To greet her welcome friends,*
Her husband's eye is on the skill
* With which she decks his bower,*
And dearer is his praise to her
* Than earth's most precious flower.*

(Lydia H. Sigourney, "The Ministry of Flowers")

IN HENRY WARD Beecher's novel *Norwood*, the hero, Rev. Dr. Wentworth, compares the unsentimental view of flowers to the way in which the moles in his garden regard his hyacinths.

> *The moles see the bottom and nothing else. Imagine a mole forming a philosophical theory of my bulbs. In mole's language, whatever that is, he would say: "a hyacinth is a vegetable creation put underground for the benefit of moles. It is round, of a sweetish taste, quite juicy, and whole-some for moles. It has been held by some moles that the hyacinth has an existence above ground, and speculatists have gone so far as to say that this root is only a kind of starting point, while the best part of the plant is above ground. But there is no evidence of that, and it is doubtless a vagary of the imagination."*

(55)

Nineteenth-century persons like Beecher saw nothing wrong with a practical view of nature—Beecher himself wrote a horticultural column for many years—just as long as the practical view was not the only one. But just as the moles cannot visualize the above-ground manifestation of the hyacinth, so twentieth-century readers have great difficulty understanding, let alone appreciating, the sentimental view of flowers so common in the nineteenth century. We have many prejudices that can restrict us to the mole's-eye view of the subject, including a general lack of sympathy with nineteenth-century sentiment (which we call "sentimentality") and a vastly different view of nature. In order to understand the Victorian sentimentalization of flowers, we must consider the status of actual flowers in nineteenth-century social, intellectual, and spiritual life.

Flower Gardens

The nineteenth century was the great age of the flower garden; that is, a garden featuring as many blooms as possible. While there are differences in styles of gardening in the period, the importance of flowering plants cannot be overemphasized. In France, Josephine's well-documented love of flowers not only created an artistic industry (to which the language of flowers ultimately belongs) but also inspired the gardens of Malmaison, whose blooms were memorialized by Pierre-François Redouté, the famous illustrator. Ordinary Frenchmen loved flowers as well. Early in the century Lady Sydney Morgan, writing of her 1816 visit to France, commented specially on the spread of flower gardening to the lower classes:

> There was a day in France, when flowers seemed only to breathe their odours for noble senses, or to expand their beauties to carpet the steps of royalty: the road was strewed with jonquils, over which Louis XIV passed on his celebrated visit to Chantilly; and Madame de Montespan hid out the unseemly earth, which nourished her orange groves at her "Armida palace" of Clugny, with the rarest plants. The finest flowers in France are now to be found in the peasants' gardens—the native rose de Provence, the stranger rose of India, entwine their blossoms and grow together amidst the rich foliage of the vine, which scales the gable, and creeps along the roof of the cottage.

(France 1:42)

The urban lower classes also had their gardens, as Thomas Meehan's observation from *The Gardener's Monthly* much later in the century shows. Writing from Paris in the June 1878 issue, he said, "The roofs, the windows, the backyards—wherever it is possible to stow away a flower, a flower is found." He tells of visiting a shoe-mending shop which was also the man's home. While the furniture consisted of a small cot, there were windows and shelves full of flowering plants (188).

Flower gardens were equally popular in England and America. As in France, the enjoyment of flowers in gardens and homes transcended class lines. One of the most influential of horticulturists during the century was John Claudius Loudon, who popularized the *gardensque* style in his books and those of his wife, as well as his influential *Gardener's Magazine* (1826–34) and *Gardener's Magazine, and Register of Rural and Domestic Improvement* (1835–43). The basic premise of the gardenesque is that a garden is a work of art, not merely an imitation of nature; thus, the garden should be an embellishment, an ornament to the house. This style of garden design was involved in the rise of bedding-out, one of the most controversial garden schemes of the period. Simply put, bedding-out is the practice of keeping the garden beds bare for most of the year, then in the late spring planting them thickly with colorful annual plants. These beds could be of any shape, of course, but were often cut in circles, crescents, stars, and diamonds in a background of either gravel or turf. An extreme (and expensive) version of bedding-out is carpet-bedding, which is the art of imitating carpeting in pattern-cut beds designed to be looked at as a whole, perhaps from above or from a distance. These fashions caused the destruction of many old gardens of hardy perennials and flowering bulbs, a fact often lamented in both the gardening press and in other popular material. The demise of bedding-out came sooner in England than America, of course, under the leadership of William Robinson, but in both countries the century is marked by the rise and fall of gardensque styles.

Naturally, the flowers grown for bedding-out were different from the old-fashioned favorites. The most popular bedding plants were geraniums, especially the scarlet ones, and lobelia and calceolaria. Not much sentiment was attached to such plants or such gardens, however, and the major garden flowers of sentiment remained the traditional ones, in England following the floral procession beginning with the snowdrop and the primrose, progressing through the bluebell, the violet, the daffodil, and the pansy, to the lily, hollyhock, and rose of midsummer, and the aster of the autumn garden. American floral sentiment was as often attached to wildflowers as to garden favorites; but Americans gardened enthusiastically as well, guided to carpet-bedding by the horticultural writers who were also seed sellers (such as Peter Henderson and James Vick), while also treasuring the associations of the more venerated flowers.

While flowers and flower gardening were associated with the enlightenment of the lower classes in Europe, in America flowers often symbolized the very civilization of the wilderness. It was commonplace in nineteenth-century popular literature that if a character rode through rude frontier regions and arrived at a cabin with a rose bush by the door, he knew before he got off his horse that a good woman lived there. The rose bush was a token of the old home in the East, a pledge that schools, churches, and other amenities would soon materialize. Writers showed readers that flower gardening is both financially and spiritually profitable. A good example of flowers as a civilizing force can be found in Mrs. Henry Ward Beecher's 1859 semiautobiographical novel, *From Dawn to Daylight: By a Minister's Wife*. A minister and his wife take a church in an Indiana town, where there are many problems associated with their parishioners' lack of culture. However, the couple plant and tend a large garden, including a flower garden. The husband uses his flower garden to educate his flock. "He began their course of education by being almost always seen with a rose or rare flower in his hand, which he gave, in the course of his walks and calls, to such as appeared most likely to appreciate them" (195). The result of these efforts was, after a time, that "few small cities could be found, where ornamental shrubs and trees were so abundant, or selected with greater taste" (196).

Flower gardening, whether gardenesque or naturalistic, was seen as an important aspect of domestic life in the nineteenth century. Flower gardens were allied with the arts, literature, and other civilizing and cultured pursuits. But the enjoyment of flowers was not confined to gardens and woodlands, for flowers were featured indoors in many ways, not only as pot plants or as cut and arranged flowers but also as models for craft work such as artificial flowers, picture frames carved in flower shapes, or needlework. The point of view of Dickens's Utilitarian Mr. Gradgrind of *Hard Times,* who criticized Sissy Jupe for liking a flowered carpet, was definitely not shared by most people.

Indoor Flowers

The popularity of flowering plants in the home grew throughout the century, in part related to the increased availability of cheaper glasshouses for the affluent classes. In 1823 Leigh Hunt's sister-in-law Elizabeth Kent published a small guide to growing "plants in pots," *Flora Domestica,* which advised the homemaker to grow roses and stocks on her balcony. Most visitors were entranced by the flower markets of Paris, which apparently moved about the city to make it easier for all residents to buy from them at least once a week. The markets sold potted plants, bouquets, and a huge variety of flowers and foliage. The markets were elaborately arranged, and they were patronized by all classes of people. Victorian housewives had a wide range of choice in plant "furniture," such as window boxes, hanging baskets, plant stands, Wardian cases, and the like in which to grow their flowers. Sophia Orne Johnson's "Daisy Eyebright," the heroine of a popular serial in the *Country Gentleman* (1869–71), had seventy houseplants, including twenty geraniums and fifteen varieties of fuchsia. Among the most popular of nineteenth-century flowering houseplants—along with geranium and fuchsia—were flowering maple (abutilon), Chinese primrose, Jerusalem cherry, wax plant, cape and Holland bulbs, and nasturtium vines. These were all widely available and not very expensive, compared to camellias and other exotics for the conservatory or glasshouse. Whether she owned an elaborate glasshouse, a small conservatory, a walk-in bay window, or just a sunny kitchen widow sill, the nineteenth-century woman was expected to love and tend her indoor flowers.

Cut flowers, too, were a prominent feature of interior decoration. Home manuals of the time illustrate elaborate arrangements suitable for the dinner table, with centerpieces, arrangements around each place, and draped tablecloths. Parisians decorated their rooms with flowers, and American log cabin homes (the ones with good women in them) had bunches of goldenrod and wild aster on the hearth. There were definite trends in flower arrangement, too. Lady Sydney Morgan comments sarcastically on floral fashions in her essay "French Dandies," from *France in 1829–30:* a woman loses her chance "of getting into the *coterie du petit chateau*" because she used a jardiniere for her cut flowers rather than having them arranged in the latest fashion, in baskets (1:166). A writer in the May 1863 issue of Thomas Meehan's *The Gardener's Monthly* commented that the French, "who are ever foremost in matters of elegant taste and social refinements," originated the principles of modern flower arrangement, but that the English have brought it "to its greatest perfection" because of their fine gardens. The article then lists many arrangements from the prizewinning Misses March, of England (143). Annie Hassard's book, *Floral Decorations for Dwelling Houses,* shows a dinner table with a hole cut in the center leaf so that plants can come "up through the table," as well as high flower stands, in which flower arrangements can tower over the diners, or arches, with flowers arranged on a wire arch running the length of the table (30–36). Frequently in fiction the heroines spend a great deal of time arranging the flowers in their homes; when one sees the illustrations of what was expected in middle- and upper middle-class homes, one can see why. No doubt there were many homes in which cut flowers were simply put into vases of water and set around the rooms, but not, apparently, in fashionable society. When flowers were out of season, nineteenth-century homemakers used dried and otherwise preserved flowers in their place.

Besides simply using everlasting flowers, there were many other popular ways to preserve flowers and leaves for winter use. Regular garden flowers could be dried by sulphur vapor, sand, or acid treatment; they could be coated with wax or spermaceti; leaves could be skeletonized, dyed, bronzed, or crystallized; and pictures could be made of fern leaves, mosses, and the like (Kresken). Dried flowers were limited, though, in color and variety, and some tastes turned to the making of artificial flowers. The French were particularly good at artificial flower making, as it had a long history of being an acceptable pastime for gentlewomen. Victorine de Chastenay-Lanty, for example, wrote in her *Mémoires* that she supplemented her daytime preoccupation with flowers with an evening habit of making artificial flowers: "I have never seen a spring so beautiful as that of 1794; one would have said that nature wished to console the world for the crimes of society. I have made, with some perfection, many branches of fruit trees and stems of beautiful hyacinths; this was my evening work" (1:191).

In addition to flowering plants, bouquets of cut flowers, arrangements of preserved flowers, and various types of artificial flowers, nineteenth-century homes often had flowered china, flowered fabrics, and flowered wallpapers. It is no accident that a common twentieth-century visual token of the nineteenth century is a bunch of flowers.

Social Uses of Flowers

Flowers played a role in nineteenth-century social life much as they do in today's society, but to a greater extent. Flowers were worn on many more occasions than they are today, and the gift of flowers in a romantic context was much more complicated. Flowers were used for occasions of celebration, such as weddings, and of consolation, such as illness and death, just as they are today.

Nineteenth-century men and women often wore flowers. Men did not just wear flowers at weddings; many businessmen and men of fashion routinely wore a flower in the buttonhole of their coat, or even a small bouquet. I do not know when this custom began, but it appears in fiction in mid-century. Later, in the 1870s and 1880s, we can tell from the horticultural press what was being worn. Annie Hassard shows how to make several kinds of buttonhole bouquets for men to wear, and from the *American Florist* (which began publication in 1885) we can learn what flowers were in fashion for American men. For example, in February 1886 the New York reporter to the *American Florist* described the latest in floral ornament for men: "Freesia is very fashionable for boutonnieres, which are worn very large for evening dress and weddings. They are also made of Roman hyacinths, lily of the valley and narcissus. But one kind of flower is permissible. A few violets are the most preferred for the buttonhole daytimes. White violets are only so worn evenings, unless it is an occasion where a dress-coat is demanded" (February 1, 1886: 1). On May 15, 1886, the New York reporter advised that "White flowers are unfashionable for street or driving boutonnieres," explaining that, for coaching, men should wear "two or three roses in their buttonholes" or "two or three trusses of hyacinths" (May 15, 1886: 318).

If men wore corsages and boutonnieres, what did women wear? They also wore flowers on their shoulders and in the buttonholes of their winter coats, but then they could wear flowers at the waist of their coats as well. Flowers were routinely worn in the hair, often in an elaborate spray from the florist. Dresses were ornamented with garlands, and sometimes flower clusters dotted the large skirts of evening dresses, pinned on at the folds of the draped overskirt. Early in the century, flowers were kept fresh in posy bouquet holders, which could be pinned on and sometimes set down at the dinner table (Moretz). These were usually gold, silver, or other metal, some with pearl handles. Later, other methods of keeping flowers fresh were used. A well-dressed belle would often have flowers in her hair, pinned somewhere on her dress, either at the waist, the bodice, or on the skirt; and she might have flowers on her wrists, or she might be carrying a bouquet as well. Evening parties and weddings, of course, required the wearing of flowers. French brides pioneered the use of orange blossoms for bridal wreaths, but all sorts of flowers were used in all three countries. In May 1886, according to the *American Florist,* one New York bride "had all the drapery of her white satin gown held by clusters of arbutus. In her hand-bouquet, breast-bunch, and tiara composed of this wild flower, were a few orange blossoms" (May 15, 1886: 341). Other New York June brides the same year wore dresses trimmed with white orchids, snowballs, or sweet peas, and carried bouquets of the same flowers.

The giving of flowers to women during courtship became particularly elaborate during the century. The handheld bouquet was the gift mentioned most often, and it was symbolic of the young man's chances if the girl carried his flowers rather than those of another admirer. Bouquets went through many changes in fashion, many "improvements" over past methods of arrangement; a writer in the *Ladies' Floral Cabinet* in April 1886 commented that "a funeral design of 1876 would pass muster now, a bouquet of the same date, never!" (96). The French were especially noted for their leadership in bouquet design. Apparently, too, the giving of bouquets to women was quite an expense to the active Parisian man about town, at least to judge from the satire on bouquets written in the late 1840s by Taxile Delord, who especially ridiculed the complicated etiquette of bouquets (2:283). Hassard, the English floral expert, wrote, "Nothing requires more taste or skill in its arrangement than a well-made hand bouquet" (76). She explained that the flowers should be mounted on wire stems and surrounded by lace. One of the best bouquets she ever made, she claimed, was as follows: "In the centre was a white Camellia, then white Azaleas, Stephanotis, Gardenias, Asperula odorata (woodruff), and a rich mauve-shaded Cineraria, Lily of the Valley being spiked over the whole, together with blooms of Dendrobium nobile Orchis and fronds of Adiantum cuneatum Fern, a fringe of the latter being formed round the edge" (81).

Flowers were considered indispensable in the sickroom. The fiction and poetry of the period gave ample evidence of this, although there was some notion that flowers were unhealthy in sleeping rooms, especially at night. In *Le langage des fleurs,* Charlotte de Latour cites a story from a German source of two young girls who had just gathered a bunch of flowers as part of their botanical studies; they fell asleep in their room with the windows closed, the bouquet at their feet. The next morning they were found dead (119). While this is presented as a fanciful story, it was widely believed that flowers "decompose the air" and kill by suffocation.

The ill person would be given flowers by his friends and visitors in modest amounts; but if and when he died, flowers assumed much greater importance (Morley). The floral funeral designs of the period were elaborate and contrived for those served by professional florists; but even the poor had flowers if possible. A cliché of fiction and poetry was the gift of flowers to a poor child to lay on the coffin or place in the dead hand of baby sister. Flowers, especially aromatic ones, played a hygienic role in handling of the dead in those days before embalming, but floral tribute went far beyond such matters. Bodies were covered with flowers as they lay in their coffins, and flowers were placed on the grave after burial. Just a few examples of funeral arrangements might give the general idea. A striking funeral design for an infant's funeral mentioned in the March 1, 1886, *American Florist* is as follows: "The little white casket was surrounded with tall daisy plants the blossoms of which had to be pushed aside to look at the waxen-like baby" (234). Most funeral arrangements had symbolic meaning, such as crosses, sickles, lyres, or open books, or, after the popularity of Elizabeth Stuart Phelps's novel about the afterlife, *The Gates Ajar,* open gates. In 1876 Hassard recommends wreaths and crosses for home manufacture, and gives color advice: white for the young or unmarried, violet or mauve preferred for a married or elderly person. Bright colors are to be avoided, of course, but the choice of flowers depends on the season (92–93). However, an American writer in the *Ladies' Floral Cabinet* ten years or so later recommended the use of brightly colored flowers in funeral designs, including scarlet. The same writer deplored some of the excesses in funeral arrangements, one example of which, from the funeral of General Hancock, was "a bleeding heart of heliotrope, with a long graduated garland of Jacqueminot roses to represent the blood" (14:96). Maria Theresa Earle also criticized floral excesses at funerals in England, but felt that the French were even worse: "I shall never forget once in Paris going up to the Père-Lachaise cemetery on a fine morning to visit the grave of a young and much-lamented woman. The wreaths were so numerous that they had to be taken up in a cart the day before. The night had been wet, and the surroundings of the grave were a mass of unapproachable corruption and decay" (35).

Flower Use in Churches

Among the many civilizing graces brought by Sophia Johnson's Daisy Eyebright to the small town where she lives with her physician husband is the custom of placing flowers on the communion table. Since one of the main themes in "Daisy Eyebright's Journal" is the superiority of liberal Christianity over Calvinistic gloom, this action is not insignificant.

Throughout the nineteenth century in America the rising popularity of flowers fought the puritanical idea that flowers in the sanctuary signaled the beginnings of Romanism. Early Christians such as Tertullian who worried about pagan associations with flowers had their counterparts in nineteenth-century Protestants, who grouped flowers with incense, special vestments for the clergy, and candles as signs of the overthrown religion. Writing in *The Gardener's Monthly* in May 1871, Rev. P. S. Davis ridiculed such ideas, characterizing such a person as having a "scrofulous mind," and he did so in the words of John Calvin himself. Flowers should be associated with God and his creation; as such, how could they be objected to? Rev. Davis cited the recent examples of floral decorations seen at the "late centenary celebration of Methodism" and "the meeting of the united Assemblies of the Presbyterian Church, just held in Philadelphia." He went beyond the gentle ridicule of Daisy Eyebright (who, nevertheless, received some letters of criticism), calling anyone who objected to flowers in church a "long-faced croaker" or a "donkey that had been feeding on thistles all his life" (138).

While I have not found anything in my French sources about flower use in churches, I assume that in Catholic France the issue was nonexistent. But England was the same as America in the nineteenth century in regard to the controversiality of flowers in the sanctuary. In fact, in 1869 a case was brought against Rev. John Purchas of St. James's, Brighton, to the

Ecclesiastical Court; his crime was decorating his church with flowers. The court ruled in his favor, and so did public opinion, if one can judge by the general popularity of flowers in popular religious literature. Use of flowers in the sanctuary was a minor point of dispute in the high and low church battles of the time. Writing of flower use in churches in *Nineteenth Century* in 1880, Agnes Lambert, quoting from the *Pall Mall Gazette,* told of the great numbers of customers buying flowers at Covent Garden on the day before Easter Sunday. "As early as 4 A.M. well-known Churchmen and delicate ladies were standing outside the entrance anxious to have the first bid; for so great a profit do the growers as well as the shopkeepers make of the decoration of churches that of late years they have refused to book orders in advance" (815). There were all sorts of ideas as to just how flowers should be displayed in churches; a good source for English arrangements is W. A. Barrett's *Flowers and Festivals or Directions for the Floral Decoration of Churches,* published in 1868 by Rivington, the Tractarian publisher, which gives a calendar of saints and their flowers: just the sort of thing that worried Evangelicals. Floral decoration was accepted, though, in most middle-of-the-road churches, where the use of vestments or incense would have been anathema.

Flowers were used in churches in many other ways than just decoration. According to an article in *The Garden* (June 2, 1877), sometime in the mid-century the rector of St. Katherine Cree in London began a long-lasting and often mentioned tradition, a children's flower service on Whitsunday. The children carried flowers to the service, the church was decorated with flowers, and the sermon took a flower text, such as "Although the fig tree shall not blossom, . . . yet I will rejoice in the Lord" (Habakkuk 3:17–18). Many ministers in both England and America loved flowers and when preaching used them as examples. Lay persons did not just limit themselves to supplying flowers for the church and helping to decorate it, either. One of the most flourishing charitable enterprises of many nineteenth-century churches during the 1870s and 1880s was the flower mission, the spreading of the gospel through the distribution of flowers to the poor and the sick.

I have not been able to discover whether the concept of the flower mission originated in England or America.[1] Clearly, though, by the 1870s flower missions were very common in both countries. Some flower missions were allied with churches, while others appear to have been independent. The main idea of a flower mission is that unfortunate people need more than just physical care, they need inspiration as well. What better way to express love and concern for those less fortunate, or to send a religious message? For nineteenth-century Christians believed that flowers spoke God's language; thus, sending flowers to the sick and the poor was a way of testifying to them of God's love. In England flower missions were so organized that flowers were sent by train from country homes to a distribution center in the city; some of the railways transported boxes of flower mission materials at half price. Among the recipients of flowers were the inhabitants of homes for the aged, public hospitals, and orphanages. Sometimes the flowers were handed out to individuals on the streets as well. While most flower missions felt that flowers alone could handle the job, the Bible Flower Missions attached Bible verses to each flower or bouquet. Of course, care had to be taken to make the verses suitable to the person receiving it. In a short story printed in the *Ladies' Floral Cabinet* in January 1883, a little girl named Bessie helps gather flowers in her home garden and joins others at the school building to make up bouquets. She inserts little messages in each bouquet, "With Bessie's dear love." One of these is taken to a sick girl in a hospital, who cannot seem to understand Christ's love for her. The flowers please her, but then when she reads the message she is brought to know Christ. The efficacy of flowers in saving souls is also claimed in a short story by Olive Dana, "A Flower Mission," in which a sick girl cures herself by growing flowers, then saves souls by sending the flowers to the unfortunate. A remnant of the flower mission in present-day American churches is the practice of taking the altar flowers to shut-ins on Sunday afternoon.

The flower mission flowers were usually home grown, but in most other social uses of flowers, the professional florist was involved. The florist business as we know it today—supplying flowers for personal wear and decoration, in arrangements and corsages for special occasions—began in the nineteenth century. No history of the florist industry has been written, but all observers agree that the business gained in importance throughout the nineteenth century. Such is the testimony of many observers, including Peter Henderson, speaking of New York City, and Thomas Meehan, observing English growth.[2] The Parisian flower business was well established early in the century, and continued in popularity. Toward the end of the century, florists prided themselves on the complexity of their creations, especially in America, and most especially in California. *The Gardener's Monthly* for June 1887 describes what they called "a Californian floral fete," a sort of ancestor of the Rose Bowl Parade of today. In Los Angeles impressive floral designs were put on public display to earn money for charity. Among the displays were a floral ship, an

American flag, and a huge shield. The hit of the show, though, was a representation of the old woman in the shoe and her many children, made of geraniums, marigolds, and smilax. While flowers are not as indispensable in our domestic and social lives today as they were in the lives of our ancestors 100 years ago, we do still have the Californian floral fete every New Year's Day.

II

The Sentimental Flower Book and Its Audience

Flowers speak a separate language to the botanist, the poet, and the moralist. Some there are who may disdain this elegant intercourse; and I once recollect mentioning it to a lady of some note for her writings, who observed that she should ever prefer "the human face divine," and the conversation of rational men, before the presence and the language or sentiment of flowers; but she was one whose masculine understanding, and intrepid nerves, fitted her for the society of men. You, my dear Anne, are very differently constituted.

(*The Queen of Flowers,* 1841)

THE LANGUAGE of flowers found its eventual home in the broad category of sentimental flower books so popular in the century, some of which were focused on the language of flowers while others were peripheral—religious prose works using flowers, collections of flower poems, various literary studies of flowers, and sentimental botanies. All of these books were mainly intended for female readers, the "fair readers" of so many prefaces like this one, from the most popular of all English language of flower books, Frederic Shoberl's *The Language of Flowers; With Illustrative Poetry* (1834): "We shall do no more than rove through the European Garden, to cull its beauties, to arrange them into odoriferous significance, and to teach our refined and purifying science to those fair beings, the symbols of whose mortal beauty are but inadequately found in the most glorious flowers, and whose mental charms cannot be duly typified, till we shall have reached those abodes where reigns everlasting spring, and where decay is unknown" (6–7). Remarks like this one (and including this one) are many times part of a longer explanation that the material to be found in the book is not too difficult for female readers, who are also often linked with children. Shoberl's identification of flowers with women is typical, with its carefully managed division into physical ("mortal beauty") and spiritual.

In modern centuries Western culture has typically identified women with nature, as opposed to society, or the world; this has been a subtopic of the country-city opposition, with further subdivision into good women (country) and bad women (society). The sentimental flower book, including the language of flowers, from its beginnings in Napoleonic France through its last feeble appearance in late Victorian England, has upheld this formula. Flowers, in fact, were seen as the most suitable aspect of nature to represent women, or to interact with them, reflecting as they do certain stereotypical qualities of the female being: smallness of stature, fragility of mind and body, and impermanence of beauty. The primary associations of flowers, developed in the sentimental flower book based on traditional aspects of flower personification, are love and death, both of which are intimately involved with the nineteenth-century woman. Marriage and children were her typical fate as well as her most cherished goal; marriage should bring love, and, unfortunately, children all too often brought death, either hers, in childbirth, or their own. These associations of flowers are primary, as seen in this sentence, from the preface to Anna Elizabeth's *Vase of Flowers* (1851): "The hand of affection twines the rosy wreath for the brow of the fair bride; and the cherub child, who passes away to the spirit-land, bears on its bosom, to its silent resting-place, as the last sad offering of love, a stainless flower,—fit emblem of its unsullied purity" (iv). Further, the personification of flowers used for devotional purposes relates to the woman's main work outside her home—her church work and her religious duties. Thus we see that flowers were regarded as a properly edited form of nature for women, personalizing the landscape as can be seen in Anna Peyre Dinnies's prefatory remarks to *The Floral Year* (1847). Writing from St. Louis, she explains that there is no botany in her book (a collection of flower poems), and even no original language of flowers, merely her own expression of her love for flowers. "I love flowers! They have been the friends and companions of my whole life. I owe to their gentle influences much that has soothed and brightened the hours of an unusually monotonous existence; and so tranquilizing and refining have I ever found their power, that I never see another engaged in their cultivation that I do not feel attracted towards her, and experience an innate conviction that she is pure in her tastes, and amiable in her disposition" (viii). Dinnies expands on her characterization of women gardeners by giving the example of the woman who cares for indoor plants in the winter:

I am apt to moralize sometimes, and seek for traits of character where few would expect to discover them; hence, when I see flowers blooming so cheerfully within doors, and hear the storm whistling without, I know that the cold which has made me shiver would soon wither and destroy those fragile offerings of Nature, and am led to the reflection, that their
(ix–x)   *feebleness and dependence have touched some tender chord in the sympathizing heart of woman, and awakened that propensity to cherish and to love, so instinctively excited in her bosom by the weak or suffering. I learn, thence, how natural it becomes for such a being to soothe the careworn, and console the disappointed man; and I see how truly she may become a helpmate in his hour of trial.*

In such passages as these we see that love of flowers is a touchstone of true femininity, an outward expression of woman's finest feelings.

But all three cultures involved in my study of the language of flowers did not regard the identification of women with nature quite the same way. The English and American books were apt to take the country ideal for women for granted, assuming that all good women love flowers, perhaps not wanting to acknowledge any other type of woman. The French works are much franker, much more willing to discuss both types. Also, while the goal of the English or American woman in her love of flowers was to purify her soul, to make herself more of a "helpmate" for a "disappointed man," the French woman's goal was to further feminize herself, making herself more attractive for her lover(s). This is clearly expressed throughout the preface to Latour's *Le langage des fleurs* (1819), beginning with her image of the lovely young woman at home in the country: "Happy the young girl who ignores the foolish joys of the world, and knows no sweeter occupation than the study of plants! Simple and naive, she demands from the fields her most affecting finery: each spring brings her new delights, and each morning a harvest of flowers repays her cares with new pleasures" (1). The motivation for her nature study is to educate her emotions, to broaden her repertoire of feelings: "These studies, in giving her a taste for nature, fill her soul with delightful emotions and open before her the enchanted avenues of a world full of marvels" (2). The mingling of spiritual and romantic associations so common in French flower books, but so shocking to English and American readers, is well put in this explanation of why the country life is superior for the woman who expects to triumph in love:

(4)   *It is not in the heart of the city, but in the countryside, surrounded by flowers, that love has all of its power; it is there that a heart truly in love*

raises itself to its Creator; it is there that eternal hopes come to mix with transitory sentiments, transfiguring the lovers, and giving to their looks, to their attitudes, those celestial expressions which touch even the indifferent. It is thus especially for those who know love and who live in the country, far from the tumult of the world, that we have collected some syllables from the language of flowers.

The contrast between these passages from Latour and those from Dinnies is typical of the different interpretation put on the rapprochement of women and flowers by the French and the English-American cultures.

While we can find the identification of women with nature and especially flowers in the sentimental flower books, we do not know that women actually read these books to any great extent. Obviously some were read, but many of them were better adapted to desultory reading or conspicuous display than to sustained, concentrated reading. Most of the sentimental flower books were intended as gifts, either for the New Year or Christmas, or as Sunday School reward books. They were part of the publishing phenomenon of the gift annual, and their uses were about the same as those of *The Forget-Me-Not* or *The Rose of Sharon*. This advertisement, for Laura Greenwood's *The Rural Wreath; or, Life Among the Flowers*, expresses both the literary purpose and the social function of the work:

(Greenwood 1854, end papers)

It is not pretended, in a work like this, to treat upon the science of Botany, but it is designed merely as a Table Book for the Parlor, of a sentimental character, to diversify the monotony of a long winter evening, being comprised of prose and poetry, containing the Language of Flowers and Sentiments of the Heart. Floral Names and Classifications are given. The whole work forms a delightful Gift-Book for any and all seasons of the year, particularly when God's choice and beautiful ornaments adorn our land, and fill the air with their fragrance.

Most sentimental flower books were intended for the center table, that institution of cultural respectability in nineteenth-century homes. Books for the center table were not only there so that the family could amuse themselves on winter evenings; they were there to signify the gentility of the women of the family.

A gift chosen for someone often states, more clearly than words, our attitudes toward that person. The sentimental flower books, produced and purchased for women, tell us that nineteenth-century society viewed women in certain ways. The ideal woman is one who is close to nature, practicing her role in life by working with her flowers, whether she be a

French girl rehearsing her emotions with bouquets of field flowers or a young American tending a bed of verbena. Later chapters in this book will go into more detail on the depth of this cultural convention, analyzing the cross-cultural differences as they appear in the language of flower books.

Botany for Women

In the eighteenth century botany was a common pastime of gentlemen. It is tempting to consider that the popularity of botany in the nineteenth century was merely a trickling down of elite tastes, but, while patrons of botany like the earl of Bute and Jean-Jacques Rousseau naturally sanctioned the study of flowers, there is much more to it. First, there were many practical concerns—such as the Apothecaries Act of 1815—which are explained in David Allen's *The Naturalist in Britain* (107). Allen's discussion of the popularity of study of the natural sciences is the most complete I have seen, and there is no need to repeat his material here. The medical connection with botany was strong in America, too; for example, the French-American botanist Constantine Rafinesque earned a precarious living for seven years on the American frontier teaching medical botany at Transylvania University in Lexington, Kentucky, between 1819 and 1826.

But there were also more general reasons for the popularity of botanical study in the century, and these were related to the great increase of middle-class individuals throughout the period. If we define the middle class as those who work for a living but not at manual labor, the growth in their numbers occurred in all three countries. While maintaining and improving their financial status was plainly their highest priority, they also were concerned to increase their social status through education, particularly in England and America. David Allen likes to relate the popularity of the study of natural science to Evangelical religion and Utilitarian thought, but he ignores the fact that interest in the natural sciences crossed religious and philosophic lines. Susan Cannon, in *Science in Culture,* her study of science in early nineteenth-century England, proposed the notion that in the first half of the century natural science provided "a norm of truth," which satisfied the early Victorian craving for order and security (2). I find this explanation more satisfactory. And, while this perception of science as a norm of truth changed for the intellectual elite after Darwin, for the middle and lower classes it seemed to hold throughout the century. For most of the century, study of the natural sciences was a standard way for the middle-class person or the ambitious working-class individual to improve himself mentally. Its very lack of controversy was its attraction; the average person seemed to have no great problem holding whatever religious views he pleased and also studying botany, conchology, or ornithology. The great intellectual battles of the century were not viewed in the same way by the intellectual classes and the class of common readers.

A good example of the appeal of natural history to average persons can be seen in a lecture delivered at Reading in 1846 by Charles Kingsley, later published as "On the Study of Natural History." Kingsley takes it for granted that "young men" want to improve themselves mentally, want to be "wide-minded and wide-hearted" (349). But they usually start by studying the humanities, which involve them right away in personal feelings, political issues, and the like. How much better it would be to begin with studies in which "no personal likes or dislikes shall tempt them out of the path of mental honesty; a study in which they shall be free to look at facts exactly as they are, and draw their conclusions patiently and dispassionately" (351). The study of natural history will educate young men out of any "loose, sentimental tone of mind" (352) and make them masters of handling facts. But Kingsley also feels that natural history will help develop the imagination, for it will "excite wonder, reverence, the love of novelty and discovering, without heating the brain or exciting the passions" (357). One can find material for study just outside one's own home, just down the lane. And a further practicality: knowledge of science is useful in business life—"How many a mine is sought for where no mine could be" (361).

But Kingsley was thinking (and speaking) of "young men." David Allen relates the following anecdote about Kingsley: that when his botanical classes were infiltrated by women students, he was once heard to remark, "These good ladies quite spoilt my day—but what *can* you do? When they get to a certain age you must either treat them like duchesses or sh-sh-shoot them!" (168). In fact, botany had been considered the most suitable of the sciences for women to study since the late eighteenth century. Some historians of science imply that this ruined botanical study for males, but there seems to me to be no lack of male interest in botany in the century. After all, botany is a *science*. No interest on the part of women can take that away. The professionalization of science, including botany, was pretty much in place by mid-century, and the very fact of scientific professionalism helped botany retain a masculine image.

There have been several recent studies of women seriously involved in botany during the nineteenth century. Ann Shteir, in her "Linnaeus's Daughters: Women and British Botany," notices that most women who had any professional connection with botany at all (and there were not many) were usually related to male botanists. Emanuel Rudolph, in "Women in Nineteenth Century American Botany," shows that, while a large number of American women were somehow involved in botany, few were professional botanists. The scientific establishment, as is well known, did not encourage female participation. Many nineteenth-century upper-class women were interested in science, following a tradition of the female amateur in science begun in the seventeenth century (Meyer). However, a far greater number of middle-class women made a hobby of botany with the aim of self-improvement, just as Charles Kingsley urged young men to do. Yet girls were seldom approached the same way as boys. A typical late-century admonition to girls to study nature appears in Annie Ryder's *Hold up Your Heads, Girls!* (1886). She encourages them to study nature for the inspiration it gives, for the improvement to the health gained from walking, and, finally, for its very subjectivity: "Remember that, in learning to know Nature, you are learning to know yourselves" (44). This contrasts directly with Kingsley's recommendation, "The earnest naturalist is pretty sure to have obtained that great need of all men, to get rid of self" (357). The way in which botany was packaged for female readers in the nineteenth century needs to be examined specially.

Dr. John Newman, an American author of several popular flower books for women, named one of them *Boudoir Botany; or, The Parlor Book of Flowers* (1847). His title indicates well the special nature of the proper woman's botanical inquiries—amusement for the boudoir (private space) or the parlor (the social sphere). To be fair, many nineteenth-century American women studied botany in school from the enormously popular *Familiar Lectures on Botany* (1829) by Almira Lincoln Phelps of the Troy Female Seminary, but those who did not were encouraged to sample scientific learning in all sorts of miscellaneous publications. The same was true in France and England. While Phelps's book emphasizes the science of botany with only a glance at related topics—short lectures on seasons of bloom and habitats, flower history, comparisons between animals and plants, and a language of flowers vocabulary—most flower books for women went at it the other way around. Little bits of botany were sandwiched in among the more genteel aspects of flower study, including, of course, the language of flowers.

The idea that women had to be taught botany in publications just for women was based on the notion that, since the female intellect was weak, women had to be approached from a different perspective than male students. This worked to the advantage of some women, who wrote botanical books. French women were taught botany in a romantic setting:

Victorine de Chastenay-Lanty's 1802 *Calendrier de Flore*, for example, is set forth as a series of letters from a woman in the country. According to her memoirs, these letters were practically unchanged copies of private letters to her lover Pierre-François Réal, who had told her he was trying to study botany to amuse himself during her absence. She promised to help him, and did so by studying herself and then writing him letters about flowers. In the printed version, however, she changed her correspondent to a fellow female, "Fanny" (1:441). The letter form was popular in French botanical material, for it was used not only by Chastenay-Lanty but also by Rousseau in his *Lettres sur la botanique* (1781) and Louis Aimé-Martin in his popular verse work covering various sciences, *Lettres à Sophie* (1810). English and American women were approached in a less romantic way, as might be expected; many of the English botany books for young women were very didactic and related the study of botany more to good health, good sense, and religion. Yet the level of application was about the same—much more sentiment than science. The formula for this approach to women's education in science is clearly put forth in this sham apology by Aimé-Martin in letter 33 "Des Végétaux et des Animaux Venimeux" ("Concerning Vegetables and Venomous Animals"):

> Je sais que nos jeunes docteurs,
> Bouffis d'orgueil et de science,
> Auront pitié de mes erreurs,
> Et riront de mon innocence.
> Hélas! telle est mon ignorance,
> Qu'en voyant les berceaux de fleurs
> Dont Zéphire embellit la terre,
> Qu'en voyant le fruit salutaire
> Et le moisson du laboureur,
> Je crois alors au Créatur,
> Comme l'enfant croit à sa mère,
> Et l'adolescent au bonheur;
> Ou comme on croit à l'innocence,
> A l'esprit, l'amabilité;
> Ou comme on croit à la beauté
> Lorsqu'on est en votre présence.

(2:95–96)

(I know that our young doctors, puffed up with pride and science, will take pity on my errors, and laugh at my innocence. Alas! Such is my ignorance that, when seeing the arbors of flowers with which Zephyr embellishes the earth, when seeing the wholesome fruit and the harvest of the laborer, I then believe in the Creator, as an infant believes in his mother, and the adolescent in happiness; or as one believes in innocence, spirit, amiability; or as one believes in beauty when one is in your presence.)

A very popular form of botanical instruction for women in the early nineteenth century was the dialogue, sometimes in the form of a rather dull catechism, often in story form. According to Gerald Meyer, in his book *The Scientific Lady in England 1650–1760,* use of a story-form dialogue to teach science can be traced back to the popularity of Bernard de Fontonelle's *Pluralité des mondes* (1686), which was translated into English and appeared in many editions. Beginning in the late eighteenth century this form was often used to teach botany to young women (Rudolph 1978). A typical example is *The Young Botanists* (1810), in which Agnes, Rachel, and Arthur, three children living in a country village, study botany in outdoor settings. The first of thirteen dialogues, on the buttercup family, takes place on a fine May morning in a meadow with a stream running through it. But letter form or dialogue, the message was clear: women need an informal approach to mental improvement. Thus, we find snippets of botany in most of the language of flower books. For instance, Sarah Josepha Hale's *Flora's Interpreter* opens with four pages of botanical instructions, then at each flower the reader is told its class and order:

HAWTHORN.	Class 12. Order 2. Principally a North	
Crataegus.	American genus, but found in Europe,	
	the Levant, and India.	
	Flowers scarlet.	

(81)

After this information the meaning of the flower and poetry follow. Thus, even in the most sentimental of works, botanical information appears, representing mental culture in all its respectability.

For nineteenth-century women, then, botany was an acceptable form of scientific learning, even if they were not welcome in professional circles (or even Charles Kingsley's botany classes). As a fashionable subject for females, it was subject to all the vagaries of fashion. Emanuel Rudolph points out that only in America was botany presented as the only science girls should study, which is borne out by the introductory works in other sciences that were published for female readers in late eighteenth-century France and England (Rudolph, "How It Developed" 92). This issue relates to the cultural differences among the three countries, and perhaps serves to illustrate the close association between flower gardening and women in America. While in Europe flower gardening has always been an acceptable pastime for men, in America the flower garden has, from earliest times, been the ladies' province. Perhaps it is a question of strength of influence: the French encouragement to study flowers was imitated by the English but really taken to heart by the Americans, ever anxious to be refined and genteel.

Literary, Historical, and Religious Studies

In the sentimental mode literary, historical, and religious study was much more important than science, and was seen as a most worthwhile expansion of the knowledge of plants. True learning might begin with botany, but must go beyond it for completion. The middle-class audience for studies of flowers in the Bible, the Holy Land, and the works of great writers as well as devotional works on flowers was quite large in England and America, but not in France, where these aspects of "botany" never got past the superficiality of the almanacs. This reflects the religious differences in the cultures as well as the different intellectual orientation of the French middle classes.

One popular manifestation of nineteenth-century Protestantism was interest in the Bible as history, including natural history. Many books and articles on Jewish history, the geography of Palestine, and such topics were published for the common reader. This development occasioned many publications on the plants of the Bible or the plants of the Holy Land. Two interesting early Victorian books about plants of the Bible are *The Scripture Garden Walk* (1832) and Maria Callcott's *A Scripture Herbal* (1842), both of which give information about Bible plants in a form accessible to the average person. Readers were interested to discover just what flower Christ might have meant in the famous passage, "Consider the lilies of the field," or just exactly what plant, translated as "the rose of Sharon," might have been referred to in the Song of Solomon. Likewise, readers were interested in the flora of the Holy Land in general. An American book, Henry Osborn's *Plants of the Holy Land* (1861), presents a view of plants which could be found in nineteenth-century Palestine and discusses changes in the flora over the centuries since Old and New Testament times. The study of Bible plants neatly combined religious, literary, historical, and botanical concerns. As one would expect, the study of plants associated with the Virgin Mary and the saints played little role in this type of literature, but instead found its place in folklore collections.

While Bible study was more important than the Greek and Roman classics in middle-class life, there were a number of studies of flowers in the classics published for a slightly more learned audience. Most of these books were not intended for the common reader, but extracts were sometimes found in the sentimental flower books. One authoritative work was German, Johan Dierbach's *Flora Mythologica* (1833), and another French, J.-B. Du Molin's *Flore poétique ancienne* (1856). To identify the plants in Homer, Virgil, and other classical poets was considered a significant historical task. A related subject appears in Richard Deakin's *The Flora of the Colosseum of Rome* (1873). Knowledge of the classics was the highest form of genteel learning in the century, the mark of the gentleman (and of the overambitious female scholar); while the middle classes showed some appreciation for this fact, they did not go so far above their station as to prefer such studies over more relevant ones. In England the literary works most suited to middle-class aspirations were those of the great native writers such as Shakespeare.

In his biography of the Cowden Clarkes, Richard Altick characterizes the Victorian version of Shakespeare.[1] "At one and the same time he was an unapproachable genius and a perfectly knowable human being, endowed with all the traits which the everyday Victorian held most dear: earnestness, domesticity, modesty, wholesomeness, personal simplicity" (130). Among his admirable accomplishments was a love for flowers and knowledge of them. This impressed Victorian writers, for they saw love of flowers as a universal symptom of wholesomeness and simplicity. During the nineteenth century a number of studies of Shakespeare's flowers appeared, none more significant than that by the famous gardener Rev. Henry N. Ellacombe, *Plant-Lore and Garden-Craft of Shakespeare,* first published in 1878 and appearing in several other editions, including a beautifully illustrated one in 1896. Ellacombe listed the plants named in Shakespeare's works, identified them or discussed the issue of identity, and added historical and other information about the plant. In the introduction to his 1896 edition he mentioned favorably *The Shakspere Flora* (1883) by Leo Grindon, the popular science writer from Manchester, England, which is a collection of essays on various flower topics rather than a dictionary-style work. Grindon's "Shakspere" is just such a person as Altick described. In "The Garden Flowers" Grindon writes, "Keenly alive to the charms of wild and untrimmed nature, Shakspere could not fail to love a well-furnished and well-kept garden. How he delighted in the contemplation of the little enclosures which Taste, in all ages, has devoted to choice flowers and fruits" (149). There were other Victorian studies of Shakespeare's flowers also, including some gift-book types, that contained illustrations and passages arranged together. One of these, Jane Giraud's *The Flowers of Shakespeare* (1850?), appeared with a companion volume on the flowers of Milton. There are also publications on the flowers of Tennyson (by Leo Grindon) and Burns. The little pamphlet on Burns, called *Burns's Bouquet* (1875), written by William Elder, tells that the book is the offshoot of the Paisley flower show. There had been prizes offered for a display of flowers named in Shakespeare, Milton, and Burns, and apparently the author had entered each category and then published pamphlets on all of his endeavors. All of these literary studies were done in the spirit of uncritical adulation of the great writer, expressed nicely by Elder in a dedicatory poem: "Each floral gem thou nam'st I'll bring, / And on thy shrine with rev'rance fling" (3).

Toward the end of the century a number of writers published semi-scholarly books on the folklore of plants. The tradition of these books developed early in the century in France, and saw steady popularity throughout the period. Under the titles of "folklore," "legend," "mythology," "lore," "history," or "association," writers in all three countries presented their readers with what is, essentially, popular history. Today, plant folklore is studied by specialists in folklore, while the history of plants is a task for botanists and historically minded horticulturalists (although books for the average reader still appear). But in the nineteenth century these early scholars did not always scruple to examine sources or to identify plants carefully. In reality it is very difficult to know just which variety of a particular plant played a role in historic events. Standards of scholarship rose during the century, but, even so, the major flower folklorists were not particularly concerned with accurate scholarship. Their audience of middle-class readers was even less concerned.

When the topic of flowers became fashionable in publications for genteel French women early in the century, journalists needed material to fill the pages of their flower books. One category of content was often called "history," and included randomly organized remarks on flower use in ancient times, flower customs in the Near East, flowers in religious services, appearances of flowers in modern history, and unusual plants. The topic was given added respectability by the publication, in 1810, of Stéphanie de Genlis's *La botanique historique et littéraire*. Genlis was widely regarded in both France and England as an authority on education, and her publications were considered wholesome reading for the young (Hazard 14–22). Her title page description gives as good a summary of this material as one can find: "Containing all the Traits, all the Anecdotes and Superstitions relative to Flowers which are mentioned in History both sacred and profane, and the details on some singular Plants, or those which carry the names of celebrated persons, and on those which are used in religious

Cults and in the civil Ceremonies of diverse People and Savages; with the Emblems, the Proverbs, and so forth, which vegetables have occasioned." The almanac editor Charles Malo also used a quantity of such material. In his *Guirlande de Flore* (1814) he included a twenty-eight page "Histoire des Plantes," with subsections on the origin of agriculture, gardens in the ancient world, and marvelous plants. The superficiality of his treatment is explained in a preface by his acknowledgment that he was writing for "dames" and "gens du monde," but even so he expected that "Women will find me perhaps a bit erudite, the men, a bit frivolous" (vi). In Genlis, Malo, and other such French works the reader would find the dream symbolism of plants according to the Greek soothsayer Artemidorus (a popular study in nineteenth-century France) beside the introduction of the dahlia to cultivation and the wonders of the carnivorous Venus flytrap.

Three popular writers introduced English readers to plant history, Henry Phillips (1775–1838), Anne Pratt (1806–93), and Robert Tyas (1811–79). Phillips was a horticultural writer who systematically published works on the history of fruits, vegetables, trees, and flowers: *Pomarium Britannicum* (1820), *History of Cultivated Vegetables* (1822), *Sylva Florifera* (1823), and *Flora Historica* (1824). His *Floral Emblems* (1825) is an important early language of flower book. Phillips's plant history contains much more botanical and horticultural knowledge than that of the popular French writers, but the general aspect of the material is about the same. A typical entry in *Flora Historica* is the one on the lily of the valley. Phillips begins by giving its botanical classification, followed by a poem celebrating the flower by J.L.S. He tells us its meaning in the floral language, quotes a number of poems which mention the flower, explains where the plant was found in "its natural state," gives the derivation of its Latin name, tells how to grow it and how to use it, describes the major varieties of it currently available in commerce, and introduces its close relatives. In the case of flowers with mythological or historical associations, such as the hyacinth, Phillips explains the legend or historical event. When a flower does not have a floral meaning, he gives it one based on its history; for example, the *Fritillaria Meleagris* was, he claims, discovered by Noel Capron, who was murdered in the massacre of St. Bartholomew. So Phillips assigns the meaning "persecution" to the flower, and adds an admonition: it is "recommended . . . to fill a situation in all gardens, as a memento, that by persecuting others we lessen our own portion of happiness" (243).

Anne Pratt was an amateur botanist and popular writer who began her career working for the inexpensive book publisher Charles Knight. Her contribution to the folklore and history of plants was *Flowers and Their Associations* (sometimes *The Associations of Flowers*), which first appeared in 1840. Her work is less horticultural than Phillips's and was considered as a companion to the study of wildflowers, as is made clear in her introduction:

(1)

> *There certainly was never a time when the love and study of flowers was more general than at present. Not only is the number of botanists annually increasing, but flower-shows and horticultural societies are frequently inviting public attention to the beautiful ornaments of the garden or conservatory. Many who will not study plants scientifically, or who care little to rear them, are disposed to listen to any general information to be obtained respecting them. To those who value the study of nature, it is matter of congratulation that wild-flowers are now regarded with so much interest, that they who wander abroad in the meadows wish to know their names and properties, and to learn the old legends connected with many of them, and which have brought down to us so much of the feelings and habits of other days.*

Pratt's first published work was a flower guide and so was her most influential book, *Flowering Plants and Ferns of Great Britain* (1855). In her chapter on the primrose in *Flowers and Their Associations,* she describes the delight people find in the flower because of its early bloom, then tells what species are native to England and what species are common in gardens. This information is not presented in a straightforward way, but very casually. She provides the primrose's former names, explains some of its uses by country people, and then gives its botanical classification. The chapter ends with a long poem which tells the story of a traveler far from home who is cheered by the sight of a primrose. Maria Theresa Earle received *Flowers and Their Associations* as a Christmas gift when she was a child, from "a serious old uncle." She describes the book, in her *Potpourri from a Surrey Garden,* as containing "much desultory information" (235). Since Pratt's work was more accessible than Phillips's, we do find that she was copied fairly often by the compilers of flower gift books.

Also active in mid-century was Robert Tyas, a publisher, popular flower writer, and clergyman, whose many titles are almost an index to the demands of his middle-class audience. His various publications on the language of flowers were among the most popular in the century, and he also wrote a wildflower guide which included many associations and other relevant material: *Favourite Field Flowers; or, Wild Flowers of England Popularly*

Described (1848–50). He wrote a special work in a field which combined association and history, *Flowers and Heraldry* (1851), and two botanical-historical works on foreign flowers, *Flowers from the Holy Land* (1851) and *Flowers from Foreign Lands* (1853). *Popular Flowers* (1843–54) gave cultivation advice on favorites such as the geranium. Tyas's titles show how a good popularizer could combine imitation and slight innovation in presenting plant history and related materials to his audience.

The popular history of flowers continued to appear throughout the century, including several studies that mark the decline of such flower books. Many later writers—like "Miss Carruthers," whose *Flower Lore: The Teachings of Flowers Historical, Legendary, Poetical and Symbolical* (1879) is a hodgepodge of the topics already introduced under this heading— were compilers of a secondary type, drawing heavily on earlier work. Plant history and folklore books were not popular in America, at least to judge from the lack of American titles and American editions of English titles. In the twentieth century, however, a number of American popular plant histories appeared, perhaps indicating the slowed tide of cultural influence.[2]

Beginning in the late 1870s a number of more serious studies of flower folklore and history appeared. These self-conscious works were seen by their writers as complementing the anthropological scholarship of men such as F. Max Müller, professor of comparative philology at Oxford. The most important of these is Angelo de Gubernatis's *La mythologie des plantes ou les légendes du règne végétal* (1878). Gubernatis was a professor of Sanskrit and comparative mythology at the Institut des études supérieures at Florence. This work, published in two volumes, is organized into two parts; the first has short essays on topics such as garlands, while the second and far more substantial part is an alphabetical listing of plants detailing the legends attached to each one. While Gurbernatis (184?–1913) was Italian, it appears that this book was only published in French. The three major British writers on plant folklore, all of whom published in the 1880s, follow his lead. The least important British work is T. F. Thiselton-Dyer's *The Folklore of Plants* (1889), which claims to be nothing more than "a brief systematic summary" of previous work. More complete work was published by two writers whose books appeared about the same time, Rev. Hilderic Friend and Richard Folkard, Jr. Friend's *Flowers and Flower Lore* (1883) appears to be the most often reprinted of the flower folklores. It is also probably the best, in that Friend seems the closest to modern scholarship—which does not mean that his work is not popular and sentimental. Richard Folkard's *Plant Lore, Legends, and Lyrics* (1884) covers all plants not just flowers, and is arranged the same way as Gubernatis's book, from which he drew much of his material. The Cleveland Garden Center owns Hilderic Friend's copy of Folkard, with his notes for review purposes. The only review I could find, that in *Notes and Queries* (November 22, 1884: 420), is not necessarily by Friend; it points out how much Folkard owes to Gubernatis, but also credits Folkard with material gathered in his career as a horticultural journalist. Friend dedicated his book to Max Müller, and throughout his work one can trace the late Victorian concern for systematization of culture so characteristic of early folklorists. (Gubernatis, for example, wanted his work to be a unit in a grand dictionary of world mythology.)

Despite its popularity, Friend's *Flowers and Flower Lore* has the appearance of a scholarly work, with a bibliography of some length preceding the introduction. In the text Friend cites many sources from a wide variety of cultures, many of them Eastern. A brief description of his chapter topics gives a good overview of the state of flower folklore studies in the period. He gives good coverage to flower names, explaining the origins of many, describing various rural names for popular flowers, and discussing place and personal names taken from flowers. The symbolic use of flowers in heraldry and the much more modern system of the language of flowers is explained, as is the social use of flowers for weddings, funerals, and other celebrations. The uses to which witches, sorcerers, and herbalists put flowers is briefly covered, and many flower superstitions and proverbs are explained. Popular legends about flowers, so prevalent during the nineteenth century, have their place, such as the legend of the forget-me-not or how the moss rose came to be. Flowers that foretell the weather or tell the time of day are covered; this material was first popularized by Linnaeus. Those flowers associated with fairies, the devil, heroes, saints, gods, and the Virgin Mary are described; and the various Mary plants of medieval garden history are routinely taken up as matters of superstition in Protestant England and America. While Friend owed many details to Gubernatis, the work is the result of years of collecting lore in rural England and elsewhere. What is most apparent to the modern scholar is the mixing of material gathered from rural informants with the stuff of the modern popular press, most notably the language of flowers, about which he is not critical. In his chapter on the language of flowers he adds to the literature of the subject himself by collecting a number of random flower meanings from various sources. For example, in his paragraph on the White Julienne (rocket) he takes almost word for word the anecdote about Marie Antoinette being brought bouquets of the flower while in prison told in Alphonse Karr's *Voyage autour de mon jardin* (1845). To the Karr anecdote he adds the meaning of "love that cheers in adversity," for obvious reasons. These works of flower folklore, including these late century examples, are both sentimental flower books themselves and books that try to study flower sentiment.

Besides these sentimental folklores, there were books indicative of a more scientific attitude toward plant history. Grant Allen's *Flowers and Their Pedigrees* (1883) brings together a number of essays first published in various popular magazines on topics of botanical evolution. John Ellor Taylor's *Flowers: Their Origin, Shapes, Perfumes and Colours* (1878) is a more ambitious attempt to inform the general reader on the place of flowers in the history of the earth. A work which in some ways brings together the aims of these two works and those of the sentimental folklores is Mordecai Cubbit Cooke's *Freaks and Marvels of Plant Life; or; Curiosities of Vegetation*, published in 1882 by the Society for Promoting Christian Knowledge (SPCK). This is essentially a popularization of some of Darwin's most recent work on flowers along with other unusual botanical topics, including "Mystic Plants" and "Flowers of History." Cooke explains the aim of his work in his introduction: "This work has been undertaken for the purpose of presenting in a popular form, devoid as much as possible of technical language, some of the most prominent features in the investigations which have of late years contributed so much to our knowledge of the phenomena of vegetable life" (1). He later apologizes for the "miscellaneous character" of his topics, but argues that this is done to please the common reader. It is interesting that the SPCK found it important to make the research of Darwin available to such readers. It is equally interesting to me that it was done in a mixture of popular botany, flower lore, and flower history.

In the sphere of action, both English and American Victorian Christians communicated their love and goodwill through the flower missions, letting actual flowers carry their messages. Of course, they considered that the flowers conveyed messages from God himself. Many works of prose and many poems that specifically explained the moral and religious teachings of flowers were published for the popular audience, sometimes directly relating to the language of flowers but most often only linked indirectly. In the view of nineteenth-century Protestantism there was no real difference between morality and religion, especially for the middle class. Nineteenth-century writers tended to subsume the term *religious* under *moral,* while modern commentators on the period often favor *religious* over *moral,* correctly indicating the consistent religious basis of the times. Flowers were frequently used to teach moral lessons invested with the authority of their creator.

The popular devotional writer James Hervey (1714–58) set the tone for a number of nineteenth-century flower writers on religious topics in his "Reflections on a Flower Garden," which first appeared in his *Meditations and Contemplations* (1745–46). Hervey's garden meditation is not much like the later flower books except in purpose, for the work is much lacking in specific detail—the hallmark of many of the flower evangelists of the Victorian period such as Charlotte Tonna and John Kitto. Tonna (1790–1846), who wrote as "Charlotte Elizabeth," published a series of little essays, variously called "Floral Biography" or "Chapters on Flowers," in the magazine she edited, *Christian Lady's Magazine*. In 1836 these pieces began to appear in book form under various titles in both England and America. Another popular Evangelical flower writer was John Kitto (1804–54), a self-educated printer whose *Thoughts Among Flowers* (1843) was first published by the Religious Tract Society; this work, unusually appearing without his name, as was common in RTS publications, had many editions, again in both England and America. Many religious flower books were intended for children, such as Mary Roberts's *Wonders of the Vegetable Kingdom Displayed in a Series of Letters* (1822). Less religious than moral and didactic were the flower stories of Margaret Gatty and her daughter Juliana Horatia Ewing. Gatty's *Parables from Nature* (a series appearing 1855–71) are unremarkable moral fables, but Ewing's stories, most of which appeared in *Aunt Judy's Magazine*, founded by her mother, are quite interesting. "Mary's Meadow," the most famous story, concerns children who improve their little world by garden principles. In all these books, whether intended for adults or children, flowers are used to teach moral and religious lessons; flowers were seen as natural allies in the socialization and religious indoctrination of the young and the unchurched.

The impact of Darwin and all those scientific advances associated with his name, both before and after the publication of *On the Origin of Species* (1859), was only indirectly reflected in religious flower books, for they were usually addressed to the class of people who rejected Darwinism out of hand. One scientist, John Hutton Balfour (1808–84) attempted to avoid conflict between science and religion by placing science under the authority of religion. His *Phyto-Theology* (1851) shows many parallels between scripture and botanical observations. Balfour's special target for criticism in *Phyto-Theology* is the pantheist, who sees a God in nature but not necessarily the God of the Bible. One such writer, Leo Grindon, a popularizer of science with no credentials in the field, set aside both Darwin and conservative religionists as irrelevant, for nature reveals the existence of God regardless of our philosophies. Three of his books—*Life: Its Nature, Varieties, and Phenomena* (1856), *Phenomena of Plant Life* (1866), and *Echoes in Plant and Flower Life* (1869)—are a mixture of botany, plant observation, and vague religiosity very similar to that found in much popular flower poetry. John Ruskin's eccentric "botany" for young people, *Proserpina,* might also be categorized as a moralistic flower study which pits the didactic flowers against the "nasty" scientists, although there is much more to be said about the book.[3]

Probably the most widely read flower preacher was Hugh Macmillan, a leading minister in the Free Church of Scotland and a trained botanist, whose most popular book, *Bible Teachings in Nature* (1867) sold thousands of copies in England and America and was translated into French, German, Italian, Norwegian, and Danish. Many of his essays are actually flower sermons, making detailed and involved points combining Scripture, botany, and morality. The major theme throughout his work is a call to the higher life, the spiritual life in Christ that is generally symbolized by the wonders of the visible world, particularly flowers. He cites both "Dr. Balfour" and Darwin with approval, secure in the notion that the "light of natural science" would not outshine the scriptural Christ, "the light of the world."

Most of the English moral and religious flower books were popular in America as well as England, but there were also such books created in America for specific American needs. The exigencies of nineteenth-century American life gave flowers a different role than they played in Europe, as we have previously seen. They were a civilizing influence, a sign of the advance of enlightenment and gentility, carrying associations of virtuous lives and liberal religious sentiments. One such work, Sarah F. Smiley's *Garden Graith; or, Talks Among my Flowers* (1880), mixes talk about her actual garden near Saratoga Springs with religious meditations suggested by the making of the garden. A collection of short stories using flowers as moral and religious messages is Rose Porter's *The Story of a Flower and Other Fragments Twice Gathered* (1883). In these stories flowers save souls, most often being pictured in the hand of a dying but repentant sinner. Such stories as these were common in the women's periodical press of the time. Flowers can recall a lost soul to his better self, or unite lovers, or influence a young boy to lead a sanctified life.

Naturally, then, flowers also appear in American Sunday School literature such as the American Sunday School Union's five-part series

The Wonders of Vegetation (1845) or Margaret Coxe's *Floral Emblems; or, Moral Sketches from Flowers* (1845). In the latter volume the author explains that, if she could, she would "*baptize* science, so that it might be made a useful assistant in the cultivation of the moral natures of children" (6). She follows the traditional form of children on an outing with a teacher, who instructs them in the flowers. The same structure is used in Jane Gay Fuller's *Uncle John's Flower-Gatherers* (1869) and Ella Rodman Church's *Flower-Talks at Elmridge* (1885).

Louisa May Alcott's *Flower Fables* (1854) belongs to the genre of more fanciful flower stories teaching moral lessons to children. In this work the flower fairies are the teachers, showing children like Little Eva, in "Eva's Visit to Fairy-Land," that good behavior will be rewarded. Eva also learns a lesson on the importance of flowers. She is taken to a poor home where a "pale, sad-eyed child" mourns a drooping plant; the fairies restore it to health and make it bloom for her because, as they explain, "through this simple flower will we keep the child pure and stainless amid the sin and sorrow around her. The love of this shall lead her on through temptation and through grief, and she shall be a spirit of joy and consolation to the sinful and the sorrowing" (49). Similar lessons are taught in Anna Warner's *Pond Lily Stories* (1857) and Mary Mason's *A Wreath from the Woods of Carolina* (1858), both of which were published for Sunday School use.

While many of these sentimental flower books have a greater claim to intellectuality and usefulness than does the language of flowers, they were almost equally talismans of gentility and femininity. Whether she studied botany or the more literary and historical aspects of flowers; whether she read devotional flower books or saw that her children received them as Sunday School rewards; whether she consulted her language of flower books or played at one of the floral fortune-telling games; or whether she just received such books graciously when they were given to her, the Victorian woman was clearly aware that her society believed the floral kingdom to be essentially the domain of Woman.

III

Floral Symbolism

Flowers are the sylvan syllables,
  In colors like the bow,
And wise is he who wisely spells
The blossomed words where beauty dwells,
  In purple, gold, and snow.

(George W.
Bungay,
"Thoughts
in My
Garden")

IN WRITING their own "histories" of the language of flowers, nineteenth-century editors often referred to the floral symbolism of earlier periods as proof that flowers are a universal language. Some wrote as if every flower and leaf simply possesses a meaning in itself—not from some association created by human culture—which is just out there for the compiler to read, as easily as picking a bouquet from the garden. This type of thinking recalls the medieval doctrine of signatures, in which the appearance of the plant was thought to carry a clue to its uses. Others wrote as if there has been a standard set of floral emblems throughout human history. This second idea is more commonly found than the first, but both are equally mistaken, for the flower meanings as developed by the Victorians were dependent on both tradition and contemporary associations. Furthermore, there is not much similarity between Western and Eastern floral symbolism, although many of the editors seemed to believe that flower symbolism was born in the East.

A fictionalized history of the language of flowers by Thomas Miller, "Love and the Flowers," from his *Poetical Language of Flowers* (1847), typifies several key elements in the period's understanding of floral emblems. Miller explains that the real origin of the language of flowers is a language spoken by the flowers among themselves:

(17–18)

It was in that age when the golden mornings of the early world were unclouded by the smoke of cities; when the odor from thousands of untrodden flowers mingled with the aroma of old forests, and the gentlest wind that ever tried its wings, flapped its way through vast realms of sleeping fragrance—that Love first set out to discover the long-lost

*Language of Flowers. For there had been rumors in the olden world that,
before the winged lovers of Earth's first daughters left their watch beside
the star-beaconed battlements of Heaven, and gave up all their glory for
the heart of woman,—the buds and blossoms held sweet converse together; and that many a time when the nightingale ushered in the twilight
with her song, voices from the flowers had made low response, among the
glades and rose-girded pastures, in the Garden of Paradise.*

At first Love was unsuccessful in his quest, but ultimately he met his sister
the Rose, who taught him to speak with all the flowers. Then when he
continued on, each flower he met told him its emblem from "olden times"
until he found that he had learned the complete language of flowers. But
his next problem was whether or not to teach it to Woman, who already
possessed a powerful weapon in her beauty. His decision was to test her
out by letting her know a few of the emblems, to see what she made of
them. His first stop was the "burning East," where he "dropped a few
flowers in the guarded turett," from which a "white hand" gathered them
and created a secret language of the heart to console her lover. "Ages" later
Love "entered the flowery fields and velvet valleys of merry England," and
as he spread around his flowery messages he discovered that "man grew
more refined, and woman every day bore a closer resemblance to the
angels" (25). He considered his mission accomplished when he saw how
the language of flowers was honored in England, so he made it possible (it
does not say how) for everyone to learn it.

This little narrative identifies the language of one flower speaking to
another with emblems having meaning for human beings; nature's meanings and human meanings appear to be related in some way. Love's victo-
rious quest is again shown to relate to the past in one final point: "Thus
Love restored a language which for undated centuries had been lost—
which the sweet tongue of Woman had made music of before the beauty of
the early world was submerged beneath the waters" (27). Miller's story
shows both the notion that the language of flowers existed in some form in
prehistory and that it is the same language then as now, in England and
Turkey alike. The fact that other cultures, past and present, had floral
emblems seemed enough evidence to declare a universal language.

Perhaps the most frequently mentioned source of flower symbolism
is the *sélam,* a Turkish language of objects supposedly used in communication between harem girls and their lovers on the outside. Since this idea is
even today brought forth as reliable, however, I am postponing discussion
of it until chapter four. This is especially prudent since the *sélam* is, after all,

neither floral nor symbolic. But the editors and commentators of the nineteenth century joined the *sélam,* the flower symbolism of China (about which they knew very little), and the religious flower emblems of the Christian Middle Ages into a type of Indo-European floral language which was never specifically set forth but was widely accepted. It gave the language of flowers a worthy ancestry—which, in reality, it has; but not in the way in which they presented it.

Flowers have been employed to represent our ideas and emotions as far back as we can trace our artistic heritage, Eastern or Western. My purpose in this chapter is to discuss floral symbolism prior to the nineteenth century, in order to assess the notion of flowers as a universal language or a set of traditional associations which could validate a *language* of flowers. In chapter six I will discuss derivation of flower meanings in detail, but here a brief sketch of the ways in which the meanings are attached to specific flowers is called for.

One way of approaching floral symbolism is through the symbolism of colors. If white is the emblem of purity, and a specific lily is white, it can be used to represent purity; but never a red or yellow lily. Other qualities of the plants and flowers are also called on to furnish correspondences—habit of growth, time of bloom, and fragrance or lack of it. The uses to which plants are put, whether medicinal or ceremonial, call forth meanings, as do any traditional associations, such as the connection between Buddha and the lotus. There are also language-based correspondences, especially in Chinese floral symbolism. Both the Eastern and Western artistic traditions assign meanings to flowers based on observation and tradition, but the meanings they have derived are not universal. Actually, floral symbolism is quite strongly rooted in the specific culture and its ideals.

Chinese and Japanese Floral Symbolism

Victorians writing of the language of flowers, and some twentieth-century commentators as well, like to point to the flower-loving Chinese and Japanese as evidence of the universality of flower meanings. What is actually universal, of course, is the love of flowers, the use of them in ceremonies, and the association of them with seasons and rites of passage. While I am not familiar with much scholarly discussion of Oriental flower symbolism, what I have seen is consistent with my understanding of other aspects of Eastern art, including garden styles. Japanese culture has some differences with that of China over specific flower customs, but Chinese tradition dominates the issue. The arts of the Sung dynasty (960–1279) focused on landscape and nature, including flowers, and the artistic heritage of this dynasty is strongly felt in later periods as well.

The major similarity between Eastern and Western floral symbolism is the method of derivation (or explanation) of the flower's significance. For instance, the peach blossom, flowering in the spring, the season of many marriages, symbolizes matrimony (Koehn, *Chinese Flower Symbolism* 10). Since bamboo stems are hollow, which can represent a hollow or empty heart in a person, the bamboo is the emblem of modesty (Koehn, *Chinese Flower Symbolism* 14). However, the written and spoken complexities of the language create many more meanings based on the pronunciation of the plant name, especially in connection with other symbolic elements. For example, the chrysanthemum, an emblem of autumn, symbolizes joviality and a life of ease and retirement. Yet since one of its other names, "flower of the ninth month" (or *chiu hua*) suggests another *chiu,* meaning "enduring," a chrysanthemum can be combined with other symbolic elements to add the concept of endurance to the message. Likewise, sometimes the regular name of the flower, *chü hua,* can be used for *chü,* or wholeness. Thus, a chrysanthemum and an oriole pictured together can mean "May the whole house be happy" (Koehn, *Chinese Flower Symbolism* 23). In fact, these combinations of elements suggest a language beyond just a list of words, which was one of the goals of the Victorian language of flowers, although it seldom managed to be intelligible.[1]

The most obvious difference between Eastern and Western floral emblems is that the flowers chosen are different, which is hardly surprising but does create problems for a universal language. The rose, our Western queen of the flowers, is not an important symbolic flower in China; her counterpart is the king of the flowers, the tree peony. In fact, just as our rose is usually the emblem of femininity or feminine values, the tree peony symbolizes masculinit;, along with the qualities of brightness, good luck, and distinction. It is often called the "Flower of Riches and Honours," suitable for celebrating the achievements of ambitious males (Koehn, *Chinese Flower Symbolism* 13). Oriental flower symbolism is not so involved with females as in Western tradition.

The most important religious flower symbol of China and Japan is the lotus, associated with Buddha. The emblem of truth, perfection, and immortality (Koehn, *Japanese Flower Symbolism* n.p.), it is represented in many ways in images of Buddha or references to him. It stands especially for purity, as it rises beautiful and white out of the mud (Clement 40). A number of other meanings are formulated from other circumstances; for example, since the seed pods, open flowers, and buds are found at the same time on the plant, it can be used to show the past, present, and future. Victorian flower writers often made a point about rising out of the mud concerning the water lily, but the plant is not an important emblematic one in Western symbolism.

The blossoms of early flowering trees are especially significant in Oriental flower traditions. The plum is emblematic of perseverance (since it blooms so early) and womanly virtue and sweetness (Clement 10–13). But by far the most important flowering tree in Japan is the flowering cherry, which represents all that is high-minded and honorable in life (Clement 20; and Koehn, *Japanese Flower Symbolism* n.p.). In the West the flowering cherry is a negligible symbolic flower, while its importance in Oriental life and customs is matched by the import of its symbolic meanings.

Just a listing of the important emblematic plants of the Orient will reveal the variance of Oriental floral symbolism with that of the West: pine, bamboo, plum, peach, cherry, narcissus, wisteria, iris, morning glory, lotus, maple, chrysanthemum, camellia, willow, peony, gourd, orchid, daylily, pomegranate, fragrant olive, and persimmon. Of these flowers, only the narcissus is prominent in Western symbolism, although some of the others are to be found in the longer vocabulary lists of the developed language of flowers in the nineteenth century.

The other major difference between Western and Eastern floral emblems is found in the meanings themselves. The Victorian language of flowers is the language of the love affair, while earlier Western flower symbols deal with religion. Religion and love are the two major aspects of life communicated in the sets of meanings in Western culture, but the same is not true in China and Japan. Instead of many religious meanings, there is the one association of the lotus with Buddha and qualities such as purity and truth, while there are very few meanings that relate to love affairs per se. In China the flowering cherry can represent female chastity and marital happiness, and the peach blossom can represent matrimony. There is no emblem for love, although there is one for modesty (bamboo) and one for feminine meekness (willow). Fertility is stressed, however; the pomegranate and the daylily represent fertility, especially the notion of bearing sons (Koehn, *Chinese Flower Symbolism*). In Japanese customs a young woman might send a young man a group of coloring maple leaves to express the idea that her love has changed, while the flowering plum signifies womanly virtue (Clement 47).

Most of the Oriental meanings concern living a long and prosperous life. In China the fruit of the peach represents longevity, as does the bamboo, the chrysanthemum, and the pine. There are a number of plants which signify riches and honors, most notably the tree peony. The fra-

Table 1. Eastern and western flower symbols

Flower	Eastern	Western
cherry	loyalty, patriotism, a life lived joyfully	a good education
narcissus	good fortune, happiness	egoism
lotus	purity, truth	eloquence
willow	meekness, femininity, good luck	melancholy
peony	masculinity, brightness, prosperity	boldness
pomegranate	fertility	fatuity
olive	honors	peace
pine	longevity, prosperity, friendship in adversity	hardiness
wistaria	youth	your friendship is sweet and agreeable to me
maple	my love has changed	reserve
morning glory	mortality	coquetry

grant olive is given for success in literary endeavors or other studies, while the persimmon suggests good fortune in business. Along with such worldly success comes personal accomplishment, such as friendship in adversity (pine) or general happiness (narcissus). The Chinese meanings associate flowers with matters of general concern in life (Koehn, *Chinese Flower Symbolism*). The same is true of the Japanese, as can be seen in the meanings of the three emblematic flowers of the New Year: pine (prosperity), bamboo (longevity), and plum (loveliness). The flowering cherry can represent a life lived joyfully, while the camellia signifies a beautiful life brought suddenly to an end (Koehn, *Japanese Flower Symbolism;* and Clement). Clearly, Oriental flowers have a more masculine fragrance than those of the West.

Furthermore, specific flowers that appear in the floral symbolism of both East and West have very different meanings. Table 1 shows the meaning from Oriental sources (Clement; Koehn, *Japanese Flower Symbolism;* and Koehn, *Chinese Flower Symbolism*) and meaning from *Le langage des fleurs* (1819). The major similarities are in the meanings of pine and peony, although I must add that the more traditional early Western meaning of peony is shame. Clearly, the flowers do not speak the same language in the East and the West, although the Eastern flower symbolists saw the same qualities in specific plants as did Westerners.

But if there has been a major difference between East and West in floral symbolism, has there not been a consistent tradition of Western flower meanings? Certainly, there has been a sustained usage of literary flower personification since Greek and Roman times, although there were many changes throughout the centuries.[2]

Early Floral Symbolism in the West

Many of us are familiar with the flowery garlands of Greek poetry, at least through *The Oxford Book of Greek Verse in Translation* (1938). In Greek and Roman times plants had many symbolic uses, fashioned into garlands and chaplets for specific occasions. Pliny's *Natural History* deals with these uses and others in great detail (volumes 6, 7, books xx–xxvii). In Greek poetry dewy garlands of violets, narcissus, and anemones were presented to lovers, sometimes symbolizing the fragility of physical beauty but often just being appropriate to love and its season—spring. The rose, the lily, and the violet are all important flowers in the literature, along with many others, such as the iris, crocus, sweet myrtle, cyclamen, anemone, and snowdrop. The most serious sort of flower meaning is expressed in the metamorphic stories, which became an important part of Western flower symbolism. Narcissus, the youth who is changed into the flower as he admires his reflection in a pool, is perhaps the most familiar. Then there is Hyacinthus, who becomes the purple hyacinth when he is killed while playing games; and Adonis, killed by a wild boar, is turned into a crimson anemone by Venus. More complicated is the story of Clytie, who loved the sun but was not loved in return; she caused the death of Leucothoe, beloved of the sun, then pined away just as Narcissus did, turning into a flower "like a violet" which "turns to the sun" (Ovid, *Metamorphoses* 101). This flower is certainly not the sunflower of modern times, but commentators from the Middle Ages onward have identified Clytie with the sunflower rather than its original, which appears to be the heliotrope. The Narcissus legend created the pervasive meaning of narcissus—egoism—but the Clytie legend, while the flower chosen is different from the original, is not associated with any one popular meaning.

During early Christian centuries, the pagan use of flowers in worldly and sensuous ways—they were dressed in garlands and chaplets at banquets and civic affairs or rewarded with crowns for military achievements—caused the church fathers to distrust flowers used in symbolic ways. The offering of flowers to pagan gods also troubled early Christian writers. This suspicion of flowers can be seen in the *De corona* of Tertullian, the third-century Christian apologist. Tertullian does not oppose Christian use of flowers in ordinary ways—for example, to strew over a bed. But in ceremonial uses flowers are forbidden for Christians because of their pagan associations. Other early Christian writers agreed with him— Clement of Alexandria, for one—but this view of flowers did not prevail. Flowers became common in religious and ceremonial uses for Christians by the fourth century, being used for weddings, funerals, and church decoration (Cabral and Leclerq 1923: 1693–99; 1932: 1889–90). And by the Middle Ages flowers were an established part of Christian worship, their symbolic meanings having been developed as well. Christian writers took the three great ceremonial flowers of the classical period—the lily, the rose, and the violet—and turned them to major symbols of the Christian religion.

Two biblical gardens and their necessary interpretations by early Christian writers gave flowers their chance to symbolize aspects of the new religion. Both the Garden of Eden and the garden of the Song of Songs were used to describe Paradise, and flowers, being important in real gardens, had to become part of the furnishings of this important spiritual garden. Teresa McLean, in her *Medieval English Gardens,* explains that the two gardens were merged to form the enclosed garden that came to represent both divine and secular love (120–25). Each plant had its burden of meaning in these symbolic gardens; Rabanus Maurus (in *De universo*) explained the Christian meaning of many plants, as did Hugh of St. Victor.

Much has been written about the symbolic meanings of the rose in Western culture (Gordon). From classical times, when it was the paramount flower in relationship to love and pleasure, down to the present century, the rose has been and still is our major symbolic flower. Early Christians could not resist its appeal, and all the disapproval of Tertullian and other church fathers could not diminish it. Besides being used, then, for church decoration and other aspects of religious life, it began to attract meanings, at first associated with Mary (an easy transition from its connection with Venus). Later, color symbolism (the traditional rose is red) correlated the flower with the passion of Christ. Likewise, the white lily became associated with Mary because white is the color of purity. Lilies (not necessarily white ones) are another important literary flower of pre-Christian times, often associated with fertility or royalty, again making an easy transition to the new religious concepts. The third great symbolic flower of the Middle Ages is the violet, its color, stature, and fragrance communicating the qualities of humility and modesty. These three great allegorical flowers are not only color coded (red for passion, white for purity, and purple for humility) but also fragrant. Fragrance in plants was of extreme importance in their symbolism, stemming from the importance of scent in everyday life in the period.

The popularity of allegory in medieval literature assured symbolic flowers an important place in poetry and prose alike.[3] Other common flowers also held significance based on virtues abstracted from their qualities—color, odor, growth habits, and uses. For instance, the daisy, through the centuries the symbol of innocence, was used in medieval garlands and chains, being suitable for youthful celebration because of its color (white) and other meanings that could be developed from its appearance (McLean 161). The wallflower figured in many legends of faithful love and was used by both monks and disappointed lovers to symbolize their faithfulness and devotion (McLean 152). The medieval tendency to consider all sorts of objects and actions to be more important symbolically than otherwise resulted in flower meanings that have been faithfully gathered by later writers concerned with flowers, especially in the nineteenth century.

But the Victorian language of flowers was the language of love. True, as we shall see, there were significant differences in the vocabularies thought essential to the love affair between the French and the English (and American) versions. Yet most of the religious significance of the medieval flowers had to be secularized for this purpose. This was done in the Renaissance.

When the beginnings of the Renaissance were felt in Europe, the association of flowers and love took place in poems imitating devotional hymns, especially those addressed to the Virgin Mary (Wilhelm 105–39). Flowers began to take on the symbolic uses they had held during the classical period, as writers sought to reestablish Greek and Roman concepts. Also, there was an emphasis on observation, stemming from the rise of science and scientific botany in this period. This situation moved the primary basis of flower meanings in the Renaissance from religious to secular, especially to love poetry. Renaissance poetry from different literatures—from Petrarch to Ronsard, Daniel von Lohenstein to Thomas Carew—relates flowers to love, to the woman being addressed or described. She is clearly *not* the Virgin Mary. The allegorical enclosed garden representing Paradise becomes the earthly Paradise that can be attained here on earth (see John Parkinson's *Paradisi in sole paradisus terrestris* or

"Earthly Paradise of the Park in the Sun," a gardening classic of 1629). Strictly emblematic or allegorical usage of flowers begins to disappear, as poets create more personal meanings—Ronsard finds a marigold (whose French name, *souci,* means anxiety) with snow on it a fitting image for the state of his emotions in one of his *Sonnets pour Helene* (238). In "The Rapture" Thomas Carew compares his mistress's body to a "delicious Paradise" in which he, the bee, fills his "bagge with honey." Her various charms are seen as flowers: "the Rosebuds in their perfum'd bed," "Violet knots," and finally the "vale of Lillies"—his last stop, need we say exactly where he is? The rose, the lily, and the violet are back among the hills of Greece, formed into fragrant garlands to remind young lovers that their beauty is mortal.

Two important flower books of the early seventeenth century can be used to show the changes from flowers as religious symbols to flowers regarded objectively and scientifically. One, the *Partheneia Sacra* of Henry Hawkins (1633), is almost medieval in its content; the other, the *Jardin d'hiver* by Jean Franeau (1616), looks ahead to the next century with its botanical appearance and its concentration on description. The two works share a concern with realistic detail, however, which is a major step in bringing flowers from abstractions to physical objects (which then can be attached to human beings, whether in the love poems of the Renaissance or the moral fables of the next period).[4]

Henry Hawkins was an English Jesuit priest who was educated at the English College at Rome, imprisoned for a short time in England, and then exiled to the continent. However, he spent most of his life in England, where the marriage of Charles I to Henrietta Maria gave English Catholics some freedom. His other published works are mainly translations or adaptations, but the *Partheneia Sacra* seems to be original (Freeman 177–78). Considered an emblem book by Rosemary Freeman, albeit a very complex one, it was addressed to members of a devotional organization, the Parthenian Sodality of the Immaculate Conception.

The overall plan of the book is to present devotion to the Virgin through consideration of symbols associated with her. The general symbolism is that of the enclosed garden, the *hortus conclusus*—she, Mary, is the garden, as he explains in his introductory Epistle: "I, knowing the sympathie of harts, between the Mother and the Sonne, the Blessed JESUS, flower of Nazareth, and his sacred Stem, presume heer to personate, and make her appeare to your viewes, not in the habit or fashion of a Gardener, which office she rather yealds (as proper) to her Sonne, but of a *Garden,* under the veyle of Symbols, to deliciate a while with her Devotes, You,

deerest Parthenians" (n.p.). The twenty-four symbols associated with
the Virgin form the basis of twenty-four complex interpretations. The
twenty-four are the Garden, Rose, Lillie, Violet, Heliotropon, Deaw, Bee,
Heavens, Iris (the rainbow), Moone, Starre, Olive, Nightingal, Palme,
House, Hen, Pearl, Dove, Fountain, Mount, Sea, Ship, and—outside the
garden proper—the Phoenix and the Swan. All are represented in the
emblematic frontispiece, which shows the principal flowers, the rose, lily,
violet, and heliotropon (sunflower) as outsize blooms. Then each symbol
is presented in various ways—the Devise (a picture), the Character, the
Morals, the Essay, the Discourse, the Embleme (another picture), the
Poesie, the Theories, and the Apostrophe.

The Devise always shows the flower itself, and on the same page the
Character is given. The Rose, for instance, is characterized as the Queen of
the Flowers, while the Lillie is "the Scepter of the chaste Diana" and "a
Silver-Bel, without sound to the eare, but ful of sweets to the brim." The
Violet, elsewhere identified with the Virgin herself, is characterized in
relation to the Rose and the Lillie: "Where if the Rose and Lillie, be the
Queene and Ladie of Flowers, she will be their lowlie hand-mayd, lying at
their feet" (39). In the Morals, as one would expect, the morality of the
symbol is examined. In the case of the rose the virgin blush is mentioned.
The Essay is a full description of the flower, with an emphasis on close
observation. In the Discourse the specific relationship between the Virgin
and the flower is explained in detail. The Embleme, another picture, has a
narrative meaning—the Embleme of the Violet, for example, shows the
eye of God looking down on the Violet. The Poesie (poem) on the Rose
tells how the rose became red. The Violet is directly compared to the
Virgin:

In Heaven the humble Angels God beheld:
And on the earth, with Angels paralel'd,
The lowlie Virgin view'd; her modest eye,
Submissive count'nance, thoughts that did relye
On him, that would exalt an humble wight,
And make his Mother, Alma, ne're in sight,
(45)   With vertures, fragrant odours, round beset,
Close to the earth lay like the Violet,
Which shrowded with its leaves, in covert lyes,
Found sooner by the sent, then by the eyes.
Such was the Virgin rays'd to be Heavens Queene,
Who on the earth neglected, was not seene.

In the Theories there are direct comparisons of the flower and various religious truths, reviewing points made elsewhere in the chapter. The last portion is the Apostrophe, a direct appeal to the Virgin in her emblematic guise (the Rose and the Lillie, for examples).

In the chapter on the Garden, other flowers are mentioned, and their emblems are provided, along with the four flowers that figure in their own chapters:

lillie	spotless and immaculate chastity
rose	shamefastness and bashful modesty
violet	humility
sunflower	contemplation
gillyflower	patience
marigold	charity
hyacinth	hope
tulip	beauty and gracefulness

Hawkins's *Partheneia Sacra* is a fascinating combination of backward-looking medieval symbolism and forward-looking observation and comment.

Jean Franeau, who was probably an academic associated with the University at Douay, published his collection of flower poems, *Jardin d'hiver,* in 1616; illustrated with carefully detailed drawings of flowers or plates showing several varieties, this book is a sharp contrast to the *Partheneia Sacra.* Traditional medieval symbols, while present, do not dominate the presentation. The plan of the work is that, in these twenty-six flower "elegies," one can have a garden of flowers even in winter. The body of the book is preceded by a group of poems addressed to Franeau concerning his flower poems from various friends and admirers.

The first poem, "Alliance du Printemps avec Flore, et leur progres," personifies Spring as a male and Flore as a female, who are separated for three months but then get together and finally marry. The poem discusses gardening styles and has two footnotes on where to see especially attractive gardens. The flowers chosen for complete poems are the hepatica, saffron, primrose, dogtooth violet, hyacinth, anemone, spring iris, frittilaria, narcissus, crown imperial, Persian lily, tulip, peony, ranunculus, Martagon lily, lily, iris, gladiolus, colchicum, cyclamen, rose, wallflower, and carnation. The poems are mostly descriptive, although those on the hyacinth, the anemone, and the narcissus do mention the classical metamorphic legend attached to each. His poem on the tulip is long and detailed, with many footnotes; the tulip was a new and very fashionable

flower in the seventeenth century (and so interesting that Hawkins introduced it into his enclosed garden). Franeau's lily is not concerned with the
Virgin Mary, but rather he mentions the milk of Juno as the origin of the
flower and presents the notion that the lily was presented to Clovis, the
first Christian king, by an angel. The violet does not appear in a prominent
position, and the rose only comes after Elegy 22, "Complainte et d'oleance
des fleurs anciennes," in which old-fashioned flowers complain that they
have been left out of his literary garden. The rose is then celebrated in
Elegy 23, in which he discusses the varieties of the rose and gives the queen
of flowers her proper attention.

The final poem, Elegy 24, "Les doctes lecons, et beaux enseignemens,
que nous font les fleurs, et les jardins," considers the symbolism of flowers,
"de bons documens" that Nature has hidden under the beautiful masks and
mantles of flowers. Franeau uses many different approaches to the subject;
Christ is the "grand Jardinier" in whose red fountain we bathe ourselves to
find refreshment. The enclosed garden is mentioned, representing Mary:

> Marie est tout l'enclos, aussi la Lis pucelle,
> (16–17)   Elle est des aultres fleurs, et le bausme, et l'odeur,
> La Thresoriere encor de vertu, et d'honneur.

(Mary is the entire enclosed garden, also the chaste Lily; She is the other
flowers—their healing powers, their fragrance; The Treasurer of virtue
and honor.) But the central symbol of the poem, and the flower illustrated,
is a newly discovered plant from Central or South America, the *Passiflora*
or passion flower, which reached Europe in the early seventeenth century
and was interpreted symbolically in a treatise on the cross by Jacomo Bosio
in 1610 (Alice Coats, *Garden Shrubs and Their Histories* 238). Franeau found
it to be a much more interesting symbol than the older ones, and he gives a
detailed picture of the flower and the meanings of its various parts,
symbolizing the crucifixion. At the end of this poem he asks God, the
"Roy des fleurs," to help the poet and "tous humains" to find the religious
truths in flowers. In contrast to Hawkins, throughout his poems Franeau
seems to present the more modern notion of finding God in his creation
rather than from the exacting interpretations of nature so valued in the
Middle Ages. It is perhaps significant that the most sustained religious
symbol in the poems is the new flower, the *Passiflora*.

These two Renaissance flower books together reveal the transition
from flower personification based on religious correspondences to that
based on physical and scientific description. Hawkins mixes the medieval
style of flower personification with new ways, while Franeau practically

turns his back on the Middle Ages, giving more place to classical flower legends or recent flower fancies than to the older flowers of the *hortus conclusus*. Renaissance flower literature as a whole is important, not for its creation of new symbolic meanings but rather for setting aside the medieval symbols, going back to the Greek and Roman associations of flowers, preparing for new ways of using flowers to represent human concerns.

The Eighteenth Century

All across Europe, as the Renaissance evolved into the Enlightenment, literary flowers were disenfranchised by the newly grandiose humanism. The larger elements of nature were those associated with men and their ideas, just as the landscape gardens of the period delegated flower gardening to women and the artisan class. But by the end of the eighteenth century the status of flowers had changed, so that flowers could take on literary and artistic importance once again and thus be suitable for a language of flowers.

The shift that occurred during the period can be seen in some of the French and English long nature poems. In France René Rapin's famous *Des jardins* (1665), a Latin poem describing gardens, lists many flowers in a narrative which finds Flora, whose hair was unkempt, learning to dress it with box; that is, the proper flower garden is set into beds edged with box. But in his *Les jardins* (1782), the eighteenth-century poet Jacques Delille does not get so specific; he was out of sympathy with the old-fashioned, box-bordered flower beds, and he mentions Rapin's list of flowers and declines to repeat it. He must get on to other important elements—rocks and water (he has already done trees in the previous section). Likewise in seventeenth-century England, Abraham Cowley, in Latin verse, personified Flora and listed the flowers of the English season in great detail, as the flowers campaign for leadership positions (*Sex libri plantarum* or *The History of Plants,* 1662). But the very popular nature poem of the eighteenth century, James Thomson's *The Seasons* (1727–30), gives most of its attention to the larger elements of landscape and weather. These contrasting poems mirror the different fashions in gardens between the two centuries, as flowers were displaced by arrangements of trees, fields, rocks, and water.

In most eighteenth-century poetry flowers were very stiff and conventional. The exceptions can be found in purely descriptive poetry, in which little symbolism is present, such as these lines from John Scott of Amwell's *Amoebaean Eclogues* (*Eclogue I*):

(97)

> In shady lanes red foxglove bells appear,
> And the golden spikes the downy mulleins rear;
> Th'inclosure ditch luxuriant mallows hide,
> And branchy succory crowds the pathway side.

The exuberant use of flowers in love poetry went the way of exuberance itself; in the eighteenth century the *jeux floraux* of Toulouse, which from their beginnings in the fourteenth century had awarded a golden violet as its highest award for poetry, changed the top flower to the golden amaranth, a flower of uncertain identity, probably some sort of everlasting. The amaranth was chosen over the fragrant, fleshy violet for its emblematic qualities: it easily symbolized eternity. Although a twentieth-century historian of the floral games described the amaranth as "fleur banale et sans parfum," its choice typifies the period's attitude toward flowers (Gélis 167).

Before flowers regained their expressive power, certain scientific and horticultural events converged to bring flowers back into fashion, and some popular trends in literature late in the century helped create the cultural background for the language of flowers.

The great public interest in the scientific achievements of botanists led by Linnaeus is one reason for Flora's change of status; there are so many studies of the popularity of botany in the eighteenth century that such material does not need to be repeated here, even briefly. Botanists in both Europe and America, headed by Linnaeus, were engaged in the major project of classifying and naming plants, and the excitement that their activities generated in the educated public is expressed in the increased number of amateur botanists. The lives and letters of such botanists as Mark Catesby, John Clayton, Alexander Garden, the Bartrams, André Michaux, John Fothergill, and Peter Collinson reveal the cultural integration of botany in eighteenth-century thought. Many of these men made gardens, too, that were famous for their exotic plants, especially those in England—Collinson's Mill Hill is one example. Members of the nobility and the royal family in England were interested in exotic plants, and the gardens at Kew were begun under the patronage of Augusta, dowager princess of Wales. These gardens were not the same as the botanic gardens of the past, which had a more medical emphasis; these new gardens featured unusual plants, so flowers began to gain some prominence in the gardening sense.[5] The discoveries of the plant collectors and the organization of these discoveries by eighteenth-century botanists thus contributed to the prominence of flowers in nineteenth-century gardening.

As we have seen, in the eighteenth century the landscape garden was the dominant type of ideal garden. The arrangement of water, stone, trees, and buildings was the main consideration of the men who planned and planted large estates. Early in the century flowers were the province of the botanist, as they had been the province of the apothecary in the seventeenth century. Aside from men of science, women and artisans were the major flower gardeners early; but as the century progressed, the flower garden became increasingly important in garden thinking. While the flower garden dominated garden styles in the next century, Richard Gorer has written, "The flower garden as we know it today, had to all intents and purposes been envisaged by the 1770s" (63). During the last part of the eighteenth century, horticulture and botany were closely linked in both the popular mind and the work of landscape gardeners such as Repton (Thacker 227). These events in garden history show a gradual change in attitudes toward flowers in gardens.

Another important garden type in the eighteenth century was the picturesque garden, and both France and England had their distinctive variations.[6] In such gardens the elements of the garden were required to bear associations. People expected their gardens to express the pleasures and sorrows of life, through ruins, hermitages, storm-wracked trees, and the like. Yet these associations were not emblematic, as in the past, but expressive; in other words, not allegorical but symbolic. If flowers gained prominence in gardens, and they did, then they must have attracted proper associations; it is not enough that they became prominent because of botanical advances alone. What these connotations were, and how they got them, is an historical question of the most difficult kind, especially so since most of us assume that, sentimentally speaking, flowers have always been what they are today outside of their garden presence, a conventional expression of feeling as exemplified by Hallmark Cards and FTD florists. In one sense it is true that flowers have been associated with love affairs and holidays, religious celebrations and mourning customs throughout history. But that very identification with convention and domesticity made them seem unacceptable when "higher thoughts" and "nobler feelings" were at issue. There is a missing link here, a connection between being noticed, being popular, and being considered expressive of humanity's finest feelings. I think that the popular sentimental literature about flowers can supply some of the answers to this historical question, beginning with the popularity of Oriental culture in the eighteenth century.

The vogue for Eastern culture influenced the fine arts, as we all know, and has a minor presence in the literature of the century. Since the East was often regarded more as a landscape than a culture—attention being given to the appearance of the East rather than to Eastern ideas—flowers were regarded as an important aspect of the Eastern mode. Westerners were fascinated by the flowers of the East and the glimpses they were afforded, in travelers' tales, of actual "gardens of love" in their own times. There are some specific relationships between this interest in the East and the language of flowers, which will be discussed later, but here we can acknowledge that the romantic aspects of a land where exotic flowers grow along the rivers and lovers converse in flowers helped to identify flowers with romantic love once again. I say once again because, in reaction to the prevailing clichés of rose-red lips and lily-white bosoms, so characteristic of Renaissance poetry, the love poems of the eighteenth century let the garden of Venus grow up to weeds. The new blood infused by the Eastern diaries and romantic tales brought flowers back into the literature of love.

In addition, the scientists of the Enlightened Age, following Linnaeus, brought sex and the flowers back together in a different way, by studying and popularizing their reproductive methods. The most famous literary exposition of this is, of course, Erasmus Darwin's *The Botanic Garden* (1791, 1789). It is easy to be irreverent about this poem, which is, after all, an inglorious hash of gods, goddesses, classical groupies of all sorts, and startling floral personifications. The great popularity of this poem astonished its author, and surely says something about the period's thinking about flowers. Linnaeus's theory that plants could best be classified sexually, that is according to their method of reproduction, naturally fascinated many readers, not only those seriously interested in botany. The classes of flowers in the Linnaean sexual system, which are characterized as "one male," or "nine males," or "feminine males," or "clandestine marriage," to name a few of the more amusing titles, led to a personification of plants based on biological rather than associational materials.

Part 1 of Darwin's poem, "The Economy of Vegetation," relates plants to other aspects of the natural world and surrounds the Goddess of Botany with such celebrities as notable scientists and the British royal family. In part 2 of the poem, "The Loves of the Plants," Darwin calls on the "hovering Sylphs" to listen as he tells how the various plant forms "woo and win their vegetable loves." Then he proceeds right through the orders, choosing an exemplary plant from each group, characterizing its mating in human terms. The ingenuity of this plan can be well illustrated by his example of the gloriosa lily (six males, one female, and two mating periods):

When the young Hours amid her tangled hair
Wove the fresh rose-bud, and the lily fair,
Proud Gloriosa led *three* chosen swains,
The blushing captives of her virgin chains.
(140)
—When Time's rude hand a bark of wrinkle spred,
Round her weak limbs, and silver'd o'er her head,
Three other youths her riper years engage,
The flatter'd victims of her wily age.

Despite the somewhat naughty sex, the generally lofty tone of the poem, added to the word "loves" in the title, quite romanticizes the subject and allies flowers with romantic love once again. The same sort of romanticization of flower reproduction appeared in a Latin poem of 1727, *Connubia florum* or "The Marriage of the Flowers" by "Demetrius de la Croix," who was possibly a British physician; this poem was first published in the preface to a work of Sébastien Vaillant, a French botanist who also wrote about the sex lives of flowers.

Another primary association of flowers has to do with social moralities and cultural conventions. We find these brought out in the English writers Langhorne, Wynne, and Montolieu in their floral fables. Early in the century fables were used for serious social and political comment, but, according to Stephen H. Daniel, later in the century they were used to convey "the social amenities and sentimental personification" (171), which we see in these floral verse fables addressed to women and children. While these fables are very conventional in form, and clearly show the vegetable philosophers in the eighteenth-century mode, they are suggestive in the connotations they relentlessly attach to flowers. They show flowers as human beings, exemplifying qualities such as pride, greed, or faithfulness.

John Langhorne (1725–74) was a clergyman who was more successful as a writer of sentimental fiction and light poetry than as a clergyman.[7] The sure instinct he had for public taste made a great hit of his epistolary tales about two star-crossed lovers, Theodosius and Constantia, which went through many editions. Likewise, his translation of Plutarch's *Lives,* done with his brother, was a financial success. His *Fables of Flora* (1771) created a minor fashion for floral fables, and appeared in many editions in both England and America.

Langhorne's *Fables,* eleven in all, were very popular. In the first fable, "The Sun-flower and the Ivy," some nuns openly admire the devotion that the Sunflower shows the sun (see Figure 1). The Ivy jealously describes the

FABLE I.

THE SUN-FLOWER AND THE IVY.

As duteous to the place of prayer
  Within the convent's lonely walls,
The holy ſiſters ſtill repair,
  What time the roſy morning calls:

Fig. 1. Dr. Langhorne, *The Fables of Flora.* (Courtesy of the Hunt Institute for Botanical Documentation, Carnegie Mellon University, Pittsburgh, PA.)

Sunflower as a sycophant, to which the Sunflower replies that it represents gratitude, not flattery. We should all be like the Sunflower, showing gratitude wherever due, rather than like the Ivy, which strangles and kills in its possessiveness. One of the young nuns finds some painful personal recollections coming to mind upon hearing this moral; her own love affair had more of the Ivy about it than the Sunflower. This fable shows traditional symbolism, with the Sunflower representing devotion to the sun— in this case interpreted as gratitude—worked in with symbolism based on plant habit (the Ivy's strangling of the tree it climbs), while human beings learn a lesson from plant behavior. The other fables make other connections between people and plants: the evening primrose's habit of opening only in the evening is made to represent the retired life; scent in the violet indicates virtue, as contrasted to the showy but scentless pansy. In a comment on the superiority of nature to humanity, the river complains when the reed, normally a musical instrument, is used to kill a shepherd; the forest also has a complaint, that laurel is disgraced by being put on the brows of killers. The final comment: "They are men." Throughout the *Fables,* speaking flowers are surrounded by scenery typical of the most allusive gardens—rivers and forests and ruins, peopled by nuns, shepherds, "hinds," and even—in the last fable—a hermit.

Two years after its publication, Langhorne's *Fables* was copied by another thirsty and impecunious writer, John Huddleston Wynne, in his *Fables of Flowers for the Female Sex.*[8] Early apprenticed to a printer, Wynne edited magazines and turned out "histories" for the booksellers; the same year he published his *Fables* (1773) he also published an imitation of Thomson's *The Seasons,* called *The Four Seasons.* His most popular work, judging from the number of editions, was *Choice Emblems* (1772), an emblem book for young people. In hopes of royal patronage, he dedicated the first edition of his *Fables* to Princess Charlotte. Wynne's fables are far worse poetry than Langhorne's and, although they are obvious imitations of Langhorne's work, in his introduction Wynne recognizes a debt to Marianne de Fauques, the author of *The Vizirs,* a three-volume Oriental tale concerning flowers published by Wynne's own publisher, George Riley. Riley had a considerable commercial interest in flowers, as the back pages of the *Fables* advertise editions of William Mason's *The English Garden* and Richard Weston's *The Universal Botanist and Nurseryman.*

Wynne's *Fables of Flowers for the Female Sex,* thirty in number, are set in a frame story; the narrator falls asleep in the vale of the Clyde and dreams of a visit to a magical garden ruled by Zephyrus and Flora. In his vision he gains the ability to listen in on conversations of the plants, so, when he wakes up, he tells us what the plants had to say. His poems are set in a variety of locations—fields, forests, riverbanks, graveyards, and gardens. The settings within the gardens are often specific—along the walk, beside the wall, or next to the fence. All of the fables have simple morals, many of them dealing with pride, for his talking flowers are a most contentious lot, quarreling over anything conceivable. The favorite arguments concern precedence or position, as when the climbing nasturtium tries to get the wallflower to let her have the wall to herself. The "gaudy Tulip" in Fable 12 boasts of her beauty and complains about the proximity of the dull-looking amaranth:

> Behold me, first and fairest known,
>   Still lov'd and valu'd most;
> Soft daughter of the vernal hour,
>   The cultur'd garden's boast.

(83)

> Why deign I then so long with *these*
>   To dwell without reserve;
> That scarce, though vulgar eyes they charm,
>   The name of FLOW'R deserve.

The Amaranth, that favorite of the period, replies with a boast about her own longevity compared to the tulip's brief season. The last verse of the poem, always the pointed moral, is typical:

> A fleeting joy, a fading bloom,
>   May charm the ravish'd sight;
> That only which is truly good,
>   Is lasting, as 'tis bright.

(86)

The same concentration on moral virtues is found in Maria Montolieu's *The Enchanted Plants*. Montolieu was the translator of Delille's *Les jardins*. These poems, twenty-two in number, are titled by qualities they seek to explain, such as "Adversity" and "Vulgarity." Although intended for children, and much humbler in perspective than the earlier fables, these poems are much more accomplished in both versification and content than the work of Langhorne and Wynne. There is playfulness in them, along with a good amount of humor and grace, which is missing from the other works. In each poem the flowers' behavior displays the quality named in the poem's title. "Contention," for instance, shows the hyacinth, the laburnum, and the chestnut debating whether mankind loves the flower, the shrub, or the tree best. The hyacinth, a female, speaks up:

(76)
> The Flower, as a Lady, spoke first,
>   And (illiberal Satire says) most,
> Sweets, garlands, charms, emblems rehearsed,
>   And made lovers, and sonnets, her boast.

However, the male shrub and tree will not allow her claims; she is put down for her democratic inclinations:

(77)
> "Thy delights," added he, "are confessed,
>   Truly nature has made thy race fair,
> But thy beauties by monarchs caressed,
>   Thy favors e'en cottagers share."

This identification of the flower with woman and the lower classes reflects the eighteenth-century status of flowers, but the hyacinth's list of evidence is suggestive of later importance.

By the early nineteenth century flower personification in books for children was a commonplace. In 1808 John Harris, one of the successors to Newbery, printed a little book called *Flora's Gala* in his Cabinet of Amusement and Instruction. This poem was copied by two Philadelphia firms the next year. It tells of a gala held at the Royal Botanic Garden at Kew by Flora, to which she invites all her flowers to appear, in ranks in the Linnaean orders. A prose work also published by Harris in 1808 and copied in Philadelphia, *The Rose's Breakfast,* describes a breakfast party given by Madame Rose, at which the flowers, characterized in ways satirical of social types, are served "heaps of various soils." No vulgar fruits or vegetables are invited: only flowers, those "in Ton." The same year, 1808, saw the publication of the most popular of these poems by the well-known writer for children, Ann Taylor Gilbert, *The Wedding Among the Flowers* (between Lord Sunflower and Lady Lily). Rev. Arthur Crichton published in 1818 an illustrated poem called *The Festival of Flora;* in his preface he acknowledged his debt to Ann Gilbert, but he copies whole lines from *Flora's Gala* (see Figure 2). These poems, all similar in type to the famous *The Butterfly's Ball and the Grasshopper's Feast* by William Roscoe, first published in *Gentleman's Magazine* in 1806, are humorous and mildly satirical of society, characterizing the flowers as different social types. This passage, from *The Wedding Among the Flowers,* is typical:

(348)
> There was one city lady, indeed, that the bride
> Did not wish to attend, which was MISS LONDON PRIDE;
> And his lordship declar'd he would rather not meet
> So doubtful a person as young BITTER SWEET.

"The Gnomes and the Sylphs, little comical elves,
Are charged with a budget of tickets to bear
To all the great families through the parterre.'

page 3.

Published April 12, 1819, by N. Hailes. Piccadilly.

Fig. 2. Rev. Arthur Crichton, *The Festival of Flora: A Poem*. (Courtesy of the Hunt Institute for Botanical Documentation, Carnegie Mellon University, Pittsburgh, PA.)

> SIR MICHAELMAS DAISY was ask'd to appear,
> But was gone out of town for best part of the year:
> And though he was sent for, NARCISSUS declin'd
> Out of pique, and preferr'd to keep sulking behind.

Two poems by Elizabeth Steele Perkins—who published a botany text for women in 1837—combine the appeal of these earlier poems and the language of flowers. *The Botanical and Horticultural Meeting, or Flora's and Pomonas's Fete* (1834) tells of a party with the usual procession of flowers, fruits, and vegetables, while its sequel, *Flora's Fancy Fete* (1839) describes a party in which the procession includes floral emblems:

(30)
> Next came the proud *Hollyhock* waving its head,
> With the bright *Amaryllis* array'd in her red,
> For *Ambition* is still the attendant of *Pride,*
> And if not her sister, is nearly allied!
> Till the *Broom* as *Humility* swept them away,
> Saying, "flowers and honors endure but a day!"

These children's poems follow the lead of the earlier floral fables and go far beyond traditional floral emblems like the rose and the lily, showing a familiarity with flowers typical of eighteenth-century botany and horticultural advances. That they had an educational purpose is seen in the Linnaean order kept by the flowers in *Flora's Gala*. But usually the educational purpose was moral rather than scientific. One charming work for children published in 1775 shows the rapprochement between flowers and morality more obviously than the personified blossoms: *The Florist or Poetical Nosegay and Drawing Book*. While essentially a coloring book, with plates of flowers arranged alphabetically and directions for mixing colors, this work accompanies each plate with a five-quatrain poem illustrating a moral virtue. For example, the jessamy (jasmine), because it takes a good deal of care, calls forth this:

(18)
> And thus a lesson to us all
>   Kind nature seems to speak,
> Let either good or ill befall
>   The strong shou'd help the weak.

In this book we see flowers being used to teach children moral lessons along with their alphabet and their painting.

The fables of Langhorne and Wynne, and all these flower books expressly intended for children, show over and over again that plants can convey the moral persuasions of society.[9] The fact that flowers were so used in children's literature tells us that it was a commonplace idea, for children's literature is an area always reserved for the tried and true, the totally acceptable. My thesis is that the domestic, conventional aspect of flowers—their nonliterary connotations in the eighteenth century—was finally found suitable to express human ideas of morality, surely a "noble" or "high" aspect of social philosophy. This connotation allowed flowers to take on an expressive function in the literature of the new century or, expressed another way, it played a part in the cluster of connotations that gave flowers their new dignity.

When we consider the associations of flowers, then, at the beginning of the romantic period, we see that flowers were prepared for the changes in their literary treatment in several ways. First, their scientifically based sexuality reintroduced them to the contexts of romantic love, while the connotation of morality they gained helped them achieve a proper nineteenth-century respectability in England and America. Second, their association with women and the lower classes was transformed into gentility and democracy in the expressive modality of the new floral personification.

Looking back over flower symbolism from classical times through the eighteenth century, we see that there is a strong tradition of using flowers in figurative ways. However, there is no consistent pattern of meanings attached to specific flowers beyond general connotations. Each culture uses flowers to express its own perspectives on life. The Greeks and Romans associated flowers with the joys and pleasures of life and with the Gods they worshipped. So did the early Christians, after they had emptied the flowers of their pagan meanings and related them to the Virgin Mary and Christ. Renaissance artists saw flowers as expressive of erotic love, following the Greek and Roman examples and enriched by the amatory Mary gardens of the Middle Ages. In the eighteenth century, writers concerned with social issues saw that flowers could express aspects of human behavior. The violet of the lover's garland found herself, in Christian times, a symbol of spiritual humility. Then in the Renaissance she was back in the garland, her earthiness and sweet scent even more appreciated, only to find herself replaced in the *jeux floraux* by the dry, unattractive amaranth in the next age. Her nineteenth-century image was no doubt much more gratifying: the symbol of modesty in the context of romantic love. While we can see patterns in this little flower history, there is no single theme. Every age writes its own language of flowers in its literature and its customs.

IV

The Origins of the Language of Flowers: France

For there is no Height in which there are not flowers.
For flowers have great virtues for all the senses.
For the flower glorifies God and the root parries the
    adversary.
For flowers have their angels even the words of
    God's creation.
For the warp & woof of flowers are worked by
    perpetual moving spirits,
For flowers are good both for the living and the
    dead.
For there is a language of flowers.
For there is a sound reasoning upon all flowers.
For elegant phrases are nothing but flowers.

(Christopher Smart, *Jubilate Agno* 105–6)

THE OBVIOUS WAY to begin a history of the language of flowers is to consider the history of the phrase that names it "the language of flowers." I have been unable to document its use in the eighteenth century, with the exception of Christopher Smart's line in *Jubilate Agno* (1759–63), but I think that the phrase began to be used sometime in the last half of that century. At any rate, there was a commonly understood referent of the phrase in Europe by 1809, as evidenced by a very important essay written on the language of flowers by Joseph Hammer-Purgstall, the great German Orientalist. The burden of his article is to make it clear that the *sélam* of travelers to the Orient in the eighteenth century is not a language of flowers, nor is it really a secret language of lovers. From this essay we learn two things of importance in the history of the language of flowers: by 1809 there was a meaning conveyed to readers by the phrase, and most Europeans thought it originated in the *sélam,* a method of communicating with flowers (and other objects).

    Oriental culture was a popular topic with eighteenth-century readers, as travelers' accounts and fictional tales alike testify (B. Sprague Allen). Hammer-Purgstall complained that there was not really much difference between fiction and nonfiction, in that the travelers did not really understand what they were witnessing and were as apt to mislead readers as were writers of the Oriental romances. Popular accounts of the history of the language of flowers from later in the nineteenth century usually credit two European visitors to Turkey, Lady Mary Wortley Montagu and Seigneur Aubry de la Mottraye, with the introduction of the language of flowers into Europe through their explanations of the Turkish *sélam*. Hammer-Purgstall says that, while other travelers discussed the *sélam*, it owed its popularity to Lady Mary, who described the phenomenon in one of her *Turkish Embassy Letters*. These letters, which describe Turkish life as she saw it in 1717 and 1718, were published in 1763, one year after her death. While the original letters on which the edited manuscript of letters is based were circulated among her friends, her remarks on the *sélam* were not made public before 1763 as far as can be determined. In her letter dated March 16, 1718, she describes a typical "Turkish Love-letter" and then writes a sentence which, according to Hammer-Purgstall, caused all the confusion. "There is no colour, no flower, no weed, no fruit, herb, pebble, or feather that has not a verse belonging to it; and you may quarrel, reproach, or send Letters of passion, friendship, or Civillity, or even of news, without ever inking your fingers" (389). A similar account of the *sélam* was given by Mottraye in his *Voyages du Sr. A. de la Motraye en Europe, en Asie et en Afrique* (1727), a well-known work which was translated into English at the time of its appearance. Mottraye, however, a visitor to the court of Charles XII of Sweden in exile in Turkey, seems to better understand the nature of the *sélam*, although he did considerably romanticize it by placing his example in the context of a love story.

These two writers and others described the *sélam* as a secret language of lovers, the girl in the harem, the lover outside. The message would be conveyed by a group of objects bound up in a handkerchief. As Mottraye correctly indicates, the significance of the objects is not symbolic, but relates to words that rhyme with the object's name. In his critical essay Hammer-Purgstall first attacks the most obvious weakness of this description: if the passage of communication between the lovers is dangerous, a group of objects tied up in a scarf would be much more difficult to conceal than a scrap of paper. The language of objects would be known to all, of course, not just the two lovers, and thus the crime would be amply documented. If, however, the language of the objects was secret between the girl and the boy, however could they have arranged it, since she was immured in the harem and had never been able to see him in person to set up such a language? In fact, says Hammer-Purgstall, the *sélam* is merely a harem game, an amusement invented by the women of the harem to pass the time. Anyone knowledgeable of the situation of real harems would know that such a method of communication would not be viable. Hammer-Purgstall reported that his efforts to get information about the *sélam* from Oriental scholars were met with rudeness, as they were insulted to be asked about such women's pastimes.

The nature of the *sélam* language is not symbolic, but relates to well-known sayings that rhyme with the name of the object. It is clear from Hammer-Purgstall's explanations that Europeans thought that the *sélam* contained a symbolic language: "Its genius does not consist, as one would naturally suppose, of perceiving the rapport which the imagination can find between flowers and fruits, and the ideas or sentiments which it is a question of expressing" (34). The example he gives explains the system: the pear (*armoude*) is not studied for what ideas it might suggest, but rather for other words that rhyme with its name, such as *omoude* (hope). Then a phrase, ending with the rhyming word, is sought for among the common sayings of the language, such as *vir bana bir omoude* (give me some hope). This constitutes an item in the dictionary of the *sélam*. At the end of his essay Hammer-Purgstall appends a "Dictionnaire du langage des fleurs," as in so many popular works, but his dictionary contains far more objects such as wire, dragon's blood, silver, bread, and jewels than flowers, and he tries to make the saying and the word, both in French, rhyme, so as to more truly represent the actual *sélam*. The floral examples are shown in Table 2. The issue of the practical use of this method of communication is perhaps put to rest by the inclusion of the pumpkin among the significant objects!

Both Mottraye and Montagu give examples of such "Turkish Love-letters," telling what was wrapped in the handkerchief and what it meant. They both present the material as if these were actual communications. However, neither of the two calls the *sélam* a language of flowers, nor do they suggest the development of any Western equivalents. Apparently, this was left to others, who must have abstracted from the *sélam* those objects that Westerners find romantic, especially flowers. Jewels as well as flowers have romantic connotations in Western culture, and they also have a history of associated meanings. But while there were a few attempts to create a language of precious stones, these did not have the mass appeal of

Table 2. Floral examples from Joseph Hammer-Purgstall's
    "Dictionnaire du langage des fleurs"

Jonquille (Jonquil	Guéris moi, ma fille Heal me, my daughter)
Tubereuse (Tuberose	Crève, malheureuse! Die, unhappy one!)
Des lys (Lilies	Je l'embrace, regarde, et ris I kiss her, look at her, and laugh)
Des jacinthes (Hyacinths	Nous exhalons en rossignols nos plaintes We express our complaints with flutes)
Violette (Violet	Nous sommes de la même taille We are the same in stature)
Rose (Rose	Je pleure, ris, toi! I weep, laugh—you!)
Rose (Rose	Tes torments m'on réduit en cendres Your torments have reduced me to cinders)
Du myrthe (Myrtle	Que le Seigneur vous donne à moi If only the Lord would give you to me)
Grenade (Pomegranate	Mon coeur brule My heart burns)
Jasmin (Jasmine	Aimez-moi bien. Mon amour est égal au tien Love me well. My love is equal to yours)

the flower language. Thus, while the *sélam* was not exactly like the language of flowers as it developed in the West, it did give the idea of a language of love conveyed by objects rather than words.

The associations of romantic love, flowers, and the Orient were strong, not just when directly related to the concept of the *sélam*. The exotic flowers and enclosed gardens of the Near East excited the imaginations of romantically inclined readers in eighteenth-century Europe. The landscapes of the Oriental tales were flowery, although not so much so as in that later apotheosis of Eastern blossominess, Thomas Moore's *Lalla Rookh* (1817), which, for all its descriptions of flowers and associations between flowers and love, does not mention the language of flowers at all.

One interesting Oriental tale, Marianne de Fauques's *The Vizirs; or, The Enchanted Labyrinth* (1774) shows a connection between flowers and character, albeit not very clearly. This book, written by a French émigré with a romantic personal history of her own, was published by Riley, Wynne's publisher, and advertised in the back of his *Fables of Flowers for the Female Sex*.[1] The plot of the story, which is mainly the adventures of two princes, includes an enchanted labyrinth belonging to an old sage, Locman. Locman can "read" character from what flowers people bring back from their visits to the labyrinth. Upon entering the labyrinth, the person is given a basket and told to fill it with flowers in a special order. He must gather the required flowers to pass from one part of the enclosure to another. Then, on the way out, Locman opens the basket and gives each person a prediction based on the flowers he finds therein. At the end of the narrative the old man explains his powers; not surprisingly, they are not based on magic but on accurate observation. Over the years, he says, he has found "a most surprising analogy between the flowers and the passions of mankind," and as he reared a large number of young people in his castle and observed their tastes in flowers he developed a type of science based on flowers. He then gives a few examples of the meanings of flowers, which bear some resemblance to the later language of flower vocabularies:

rose	love
violet	soft sensibility
daisy	timidity and humility
amaranthus	constancy
white lily	purity
tuberose	ardent temper
jonquil	eager sensuality
jessamine	voluptuousness
carnation	moderation
myrtle	true love
tulip	vanity
narcissus	selfishness

Based on these observations Locman constructed his labyrinth, which enabled him to make predictions on the future character growth of individuals previously unknown to him. Needless to say, the details of just how this works "are too minute and tedious to be mentioned" (3:273).

The language of flowers, then, has its origins in Western notions of Oriental courtship. Europeans took the concept and Westernized it by choosing only flowers from the *sélam* objects and then by forming their meanings based on association of idea rather than sound. It is clear that by the beginning of the nineteenth century, flowers were associated with a language of love, their credentials strengthened by the Linnaean system and its popularization by writers like Erasmus Darwin. This language of flowers took flowers far beyond their previous general connotations of love, sex, and women as found in Renaissance poetry, for example. The language of flowers attempted to make flowers capable of expressing a wide range of ideas needed to conduct relationships between the sexes leading to romance and marriage and, what is truly different from previous associations of flowers and romance, they are as expressive of women's perspectives on romance as they are of men's.

But the idea of a language of flowers needs to be complemented by a study of its formation into actual vocabulary lists and ultimately into book form. For the origins of the language of flower *book* created as a genteel gift to a lady, we need to look at the development of the sentimental flower book, beginning in France.

The history of the flower book on the center table is fairly involved. We might begin with the story of a very famous flower book, *La guirlande de Julie*.[2] In 1641 the marquis de Montausier commissioned the calligrapher Nicolas Jarry and the painter Nicolas Robert to create a manuscript book of flower poems (many written by the marquis himself) and flower pictures as a birthday gift for his fiancée Julie-Lucine d'Angennes de Rambouillet. The idea was that, since her birthday fell in the winter, there were no flowers to give her, so a collection of flower poems and flower pictures was substituted. There were three copies of the manuscript by Jarry; then the collection was printed a number of times in the next century by various hands. In 1784 *La guirlande* was printed by Pierre-François Didot and again in 1818 by his son, Didot Jeune. Between these years it had become common to offer a woman a New Year's gift of a flower book, bound in pastel satin and contained in a small like-colored slipcase. *La guirlande,* the elegant, handmade gift of the aristocrat to his ladylove, thus became one of a number of similar gift volumes that were sold to the upper classes and then increasingly to the middle classes in France, as imitation of genteel society became popular again in the post-Napoleonic era. Many of these books were in the form of almanacs, especially suitable for New Year's gifts.

The almanac is an old genre, with a history of popularity in all classes. The type of almanac that evolved into the genteel New Year's flower gift book was the "literary almanac," which, toward the end of the eighteenth century, began to deal with nature and romance.[3] It was relatively easy for the publisher to make one of these little collections of verse and engravings into an almanac: the calendar, on one large sheet of paper, was pasted on the back page of the book. These almanacs were intended, in the words of one of their editors, Charles Malo, for "dames et gens du monde," or the fashionable world of genteel but not conservatively aristocratic, society. French publishers early in the century produced a quantity of such almanacs and other flower books that, without the calendars, would be suitable gifts at other seasons of the year. During the period 1810 to 1820, Charles Malo edited a number of flower-related almanacs for Louis Janet, among which are *Guirlande de Flore, Histoire des tulipes,* and *Histoire des roses.* The Hunt Institute Library owns a copy of *Histoire des roses,* bound in pink, with a calendar for 1819 pasted in the back. The library's two copies of *Guirlande de Flore* are different colors for different years—blue for 1815, pink for 1816. All these Malo almanacs are very small, but not really miniature, and they are illustrated with colored plates. His *Parterre de Flore,* a language of flowers book, appeared in the early 1820s. The language of flowers was an especially popular concept in this class of gift book, and indeed the most influential of all language of flower books, Charlotte de Latour's *Le langage des fleurs,* was first published in December 1819, no doubt intended for the New Year's trade.

While the flower book and the almanac are very closely related, another close relative is the literary annual. Most historians of the annuals trace their origin to the almanacs, feeling that the popularity of the "literary almanacs" as gifts led to the concept of gift annuals that would be available around the year. The historian R. Thompson traces the annuals back to the French *Almanach des muses* (from 1765) and the German *Musenalmanach* (from 1770). The annuals began to be really popular in the early 1820s, and they formed a very important class of center table books for about thirty or forty years (3). The annuals often had flower names—the first British title was *The Forget-Me-Not* (from 1823)—and flower material was often to be found in them.[4] While at first the editors of these volumes seem to have had some notion of literary worth, as Alaric Watts put it, soon "an element of taste in the externals rather than in the spirit" began to overtake the annuals, at which point the bindings became of more importance than the contents (2:48). Once they became fashionable and conventional, they became part of the furniture of the drawing room in a very real sense. Their popularity was phenomenal. S. G. Goodrich, the author of the Peter Parley books and the publisher of *The Token,* wrote in his autobiography that "The effect of the circulation of such works as these, in creating and extending a taste for the arts, and in their most exquisite forms, can only be appreciated by those who have examined and reflected upon the subject. Even in the United States alone, four thousand volumes of one of these works, at the price of twelve dollars each, have been sold in a single season! Not five hundred would have been sold in the same space of time, twenty years ago" (2:268).

On the drawing-room tables of genteel Frenchwomen early in the century would be found copies of *Le langage des fleurs,* the *Almanach de Flore,* or one of Charles Malo's almanacs, perhaps *Guirlande de Flore.* By later in the nineteenth century the taste for the language of flower book had reached the lower classes in France. Octave Uzanne, in his *The Book-Hunter in Paris* (1893), frequently mentions the cheapness and availability of language of flower books, and specifies their late-century audience: "*La Clef des Songes, Le Langage des Fleurs, Le Secretaire des Amants, L'Oracle des Dames,* in new and popular editions, in bindings glowing in gaudy colours, are sure to sell. Errand boys, gutter boys, bakers' boys, nurses, and soldiers, loiter before them, and unless the volume is already cut, and they can consult it easily on the spot, often feel in the bottom of their pocket for a few sous to buy it with" (113). The audience for sentimental flower material in France, then, was originally the upper classes, but the fashion spread to the lower classes as the century went on. (We should note that the type of flower book to appeal to Uzanne's *menu peuple* [little people] is the language of flowers in association with dream interpretation and horoscope books, not the type as a whole.) This history of descending to a lower class was not repeated, however, in England and America, for the sentimental flower book only became really exportable from France, when it sold well to the growing numbers of new readers. My estimation is that the vogue for the sentimental flower book among the upper classes in France peaked in the early 1820s, while it was only then that the influence of the language of flowers and other related notions reached other countries (Seaton, "French Flower Books"). There it combined with other factors to create specific kinds of flower books special to each country.

History shows us that the flower books found on the center table, along with the latest in fashionable gift annuals and albums, came by their gentility from their early association with French polite society. Their gentility was, however, only one selling point; another issue was equally important in England and America—respectability. This quality was assured by developments in flower books for women in England in the late eighteenth century, the moral fables, which were described in chapter three.

Development of the Language in France

The language of flowers is best defined as a list of flower names and their associated meanings, most relating to the conduct of a love affair. The list is often called a "dictionary" or a "vocabulary." These vocabularies, similar to the brief one in *The Vizirs,* apparently circulated in handwritten form in early nineteenth-century France, at least according to B. Dela-chénaye, the author of one of the earliest language of flower books, *Abécédaire de Flore ou langage des fleurs* (1810). Delachénaye, most of whose book is given over to explaining a very complex method of using flowers for different sounds in words, includes a vocabulary of what he calls "Emblems Drawn from the Vegetable Kingdom." In his introduction to this list, he argues that real *sélams* contained only flowers, citing as his evidence an obscure poem "translated from the Arabian," and quoting some vague passages that seem to identify the *sélam* as a bouquet of flowers. He takes his own vocabulary of flower emblems from three of the handwritten lists, but he is not happy with such lists (including, appar-ently, his own), for they cannot be authoritative. He has noticed that different lists give different meanings for flowers, and this is a problem. If only, he writes, Bernardin de Saint-Pierre had left us a complete list of such meanings, instead of a few suggestions (he quotes the passage in *Chaumière indienne* in which Bernardin has a character interpret the meanings of a few flowers): then we could be sure we had a truly authoritative language of flowers.

Since there is no such one true language of flowers, Delachénaye had invented a way of communicating in flowers, mainly through the decora-tive arts such as needlework. He cites the notion of the jeweler who invented the idea of communicating through jewels, using the first letter of the jewel's name as the alphabetic entry in an alphabet of precious stones. Thus, one can spell out messages in jewels—a fairly expensive method. He also mentions the idea, used in Stéphanie de Genlis's *Les fleurs; ou, les artistes* (1810), of using the initial letters of flowers to form an alphabet. Genlis's story shows the characters using enameled flowers in jewelry to spell out names, and she further suggests its application to real flowers in garlands and bouquets. Delachénaye's invention is a complex dictionary of flowers by sounds—*lilas* (lilac), for instance, stands for the long *a* sound in its second syllable; he lists all the possible sounds and connects them to a flower name and a picture which illustrates the sound. He suggests that artists use the flowers in combination to spell out words, and further suggests use of insects as accent marks and pansies in various states to represent marks of punctuation. Such a method is cumbersome and difficult to use, no doubt one of the reasons it had little influence. He envisioned the lady of the house, at home while her "hero" was abroad on deeds of glory (remember that these were the years of Napoleon's empire);

while he is gone she embroiders her feelings about him and their family in flowers, and upon his return he can "read" her feelings. Delachénaye is described on the title page of the book as "ex-militaire pensionné du Gouvernement," and he dedicated the book to Napoleon's new empress, Marie-Louise. This nonassociational method of floral communication was paralleled nearly 100 years later in *Phyllanthrography; A Method of Leaf and Flower Writing* (1909) by an American Egyptologist, Samuel Binion, who devised combinations of roses, rosebuds, and leaves to make a picture alphabet. Needless to say, the flower language using associations was far more successful as a concept than these rather complex systems, and far more interesting than simple first-letter flower alphabets.[5]

Of course, I have not been able to see any of the hand-written lists that Delachénaye mentions. In her *Nouveau manuel des fleurs emblématiques* (1837), Louise Leneveux attributes the introduction of the language of flowers to two individuals, one of whom was a well-known man of letters writing under a female pseudonym—obviously meant to be "Charlotte de Latour" in the person of Louis Aimé-Martin. The other I have not been able to identify—a person who made a language of flower list for Empress Josephine. I have speculated that this is Delachénaye, and his book's dedication to Napoleon's new Empress Marie-Louise is just an updating of his previous, probably unpublished, work. The publication of Latour's *Le langage des fleurs* in December 1819 is the beginning of the great proliferation of language of flower books, and while there were probably some other vocabularies in print during the period 1810–20, I have found only two other pre-1819 lists aside from that of Delachénaye: a very brief list attached to a floral fortune telling game in a book called *Oracles de Flore* by C. F. P. Del——— (1817), and a somewhat longer list printed in the notes to C. L. Mollevaut's collection of poems, *Les fleurs* (1818). A title published in 1816, *Les emblèmes des fleurs: pièce de vers, suivie d'un tableau emblématique des fleurs, et traité succinct de botanique, auquel sont joints deux tableaux contenant l'exposition du système de Linné et la méthode naturelle de Jussieu,* I have never seen. It appears in the *Bibliographie de la France* for January 1816. However, according to Jack Goody, the flower list in this work is repeated in Mollevaut's volume, so I am able to compare the meanings from this date with others by using Mollevaut (235). There was an ambitious language of flower book published just prior to Latour, however: Alexis Lucot's *Emblèmes de Flore* (January 1819). On the title page of this book, Lucot is identified as a law student, and on the opposite page he threatened to prosecute all "counterfeiters" of his material.

My attempts to identify Charlotte de Latour have had mixed results.

In J.-M. Quérard's *La France littéraire ou dictionnaire bibliographique,* the pseudonym is identified in volume 5 (1833) as that of Louis Aimé-Martin and in volume 11 (1854–57) as that of Louise Cortambert. One can only conclude that, between 1833 and 1857, Quérard discovered that he was wrong in the first instance. An explanation can be found in Quérard's *Les supercheries littéraires* (1869), where he writes, "This little work was falsely attributed to M. Aimé Martin, perhaps because he was asked by the author to deal with an editor" (2:674). In the same place, he further identifies Louise Cortambert as the mother of the geographer of the same name, in other words the well-known geographer Eugène Cortambert. There is no other confirmation of this identification, and my attempts to find out more have led to some problems. Eugène Cortambert's brother Louis was a prominent French-American journalist, editor of the *Messager Franco-Américain* from 1864 to his death, at Bloomfield, New Jersey, in 1881. My efforts to trace the American branch of the family led to John Francis McDermott, the historian, of St. Louis, who was Louis Cortambert's great-grandson. In a letter to me on August 14, 1979, he confirmed that his great-grandfather's mother had been named Louise; but he stated clearly that "she was not Charlotte de Latour, who wrote *Le langage des fleurs* and collaborated with a Comte de Bligny in a couple of romances." In an earlier letter to me, he said that his cousins in France were the source of his information. Since those letters, I have been unable to make contact with the Cortambert family. However, I do see an interesting problem: the romances that McDermott mentions I had long discounted as being from the same pen as *Le langage,* strictly by the time element, as they were published in 1864 and 1866, much later than *Le langage* (1819). Louise Cortambert's husband P.-L. Cortambert, a physician, was born in 1773, and their sons were born in 1805 and 1809, which would make these romances the product of Mme Cortambert very late in her life indeed. What is more likely is that the unknown Bligny used the very popular pseudonym as a draw for his own works, or else his collaborator did. At any rate, I now think that it is possible that Louise Cortambert did write the famous language of flowers book, but since it was not something a conservative and intellectual family would be proud of, it was buried in her past. But naturally I cannot be certain of any of this. I like to think that the author of *Le langage* had a son who became a prominent American citizen and a great-great-grandson who was an American historian of note. Given the lack of concern in French biographical dictionaries for the women of a family, my unsuccessful attempts to reach the family through letters, and the inability of my friends visiting France to find any information, I am unable to take this research any further. My best judgment, then, is that "Charlotte de Latour" could have been Louise Cortambert, but I cannot prove it.[6]

When we look at Louis-Eustache Audot (1783–1870), the publisher of *Le langage,* we find that he specialized in popular science and technology, often preparing the outline of the work himself. Among his popular titles were books on cooking and gardening, such as his own *La cuisiniere de la campagne et de la ville* (Werdet 159; and *Dictionnaire de biographie française*). From internal evidence we find that the author had a proficient knowledge of plants and also was well acquainted with contemporary polite literature about flowers, such as Aimé-Martin's *Lettres à Sophie.* My study of Aimé-Martin himself suggests that he would not have been capable of writing *Le langage*—it would be more likely that Audot wrote the book himself—but his connection with ephemeral literature made him a good guess for the author, and indeed many French books of the same sort published in Belgium during the height of the piracy period (1815–52) have his name on them (Dopp). A friend and pupil of Bernardin de Saint-Pierre, he was married to Saint-Pierre's widow, and she in turn left her entire estate to the French poet Alphonse de Lamartine, which gives Aimé-Martin some interesting literary connections. It is not unreasonable that Mme Cortambert could have known him and asked him to deal with Louis Audot on her behalf. So while we find relationships between *Le langage* and the world of polite letters of the time, they do not seem to be the usual ones of exploitation and imitation. Everything points to its author's membership in the upper middle class of professional and literary people.[7]

I will be examining Latour's work in greater detail in chapter six, but I need to say here that *Le langage* was a fresh departure for the language of flowers. Organized seasonally and continuing a good deal of nature description and other writing about flowers, the book went far beyond the simple lists of meanings that preceded it. In both organization and contents, it is put together cleverly. It struck just the right tone of nature sentiment and romantic drama for its readers, as is proven by its popularity and its history as a source for so many imitators. This does not mean, however, that its floral vocabulary is original.

I have studied all the vocabulary lists published before Latour in relationship to hers, in order to form an opinion on how much of her work was original. Her vocabulary contains 272 items, and I counted the plant-meaning pairs that were the same as hers in the previous works, as well as the plants and the meanings separately. Table 3 shows my results. I think

Table 3. Comparison of Latour's vocabulary to earlier works

	Pairs	Similar pairs	Similar plants	Similar meanings
Delachénaye	190	37	111	75
Oracles	36	7	27	26
Mollevaut	142	16	76	68
Lucot	291	53	155	114

these figures reveal a considerable similarity to the work of Lucot, but I doubt that Lucot sued either Latour or her publisher as he had threatened to do. Lest anyone think that all this similarity is due to communal agreement, however, I might add that the four lists share only two complete pairs in common: violet—modesty and narcissus—egoism. Certainly, we can hypothesize that both Lucot and Latour sat down to compile their vocabularies with other lists in hand, just as Delachénaye says he did. And that was just what later imitators of the popular concept did as well.

Latour took more than just meaning pairs from Lucot, however; she borrows many elements from his work. Some short entries she copies almost entirely, while in others she rewords the piece. Typical of this borrowing is the entry on *amandier* (almond). Her first three sentences echo parts of the first two in Lucot, which reads, "Symbol of heedlessness, the almond is the first to respond to the call of spring. Late frosts often punish it for its excess precocity" (8–9). Latour writes, "Emblem of heedlessness, the almond is the first to respond to the call of spring. Nothing is sweeter or more agreeable than this beautiful tree, when it appears in the first days of March, covered with flowers, in the middle of our leafless groves. Often the late frosts destroy the too precocious buds" (14). Most of her main entries—those in the first part of her text—are much longer than his and contain much more description and romantic content. A good example of this is his very brief, matter-of-fact piece on the violet, contrasted to Latour's long reminiscent item telling of her dreams of love at the age of fifteen, and how after one such dream she walked in the woods in late winter and found violets blooming. She makes only a weak connection between the narrative and the meaning—modesty—while Lucot is all business.

It is interesting to speculate on why the one book had such a success while the other is practically unknown. The times were ready for the language of flowers to become a fad, but Lucot's book did not seem to capture the imagination of the audience as did Latour's. There are some possible reasons for this external to the texts themselves: perhaps Lucot's *Emblèmes* appeared too late in January for the New Year's trade and was too old an item for the next year; perhaps his publishers did not push the book; or perhaps the lack of a handsome binding and illustrations kept it from being purchased as a genteel gift. Certainly one of his publishers, Louis Janet, knew the business of the gift book trade well and often produced illustrated volumes bound in pastel boards or satin. Perhaps publisher and author did not think of the book as belonging to the gift book type. The audience addressed on the title page of *Emblèmes* might prove this last point, for the title page reads: "Emblems of Flowers and Vegetables, Dedicated to Authors, as a Collection of allegories on Plants and Trees; to the Nobility, as a Treatise useful in heraldry; to Painters, as a Manual of vegetable attributes. AND TO WOMEN, AS A LANGUAGE OF FLOWERS." Whatever the facts, the book does not have the appearance of a gift book, lacking illustrations for one thing (I was not able to examine the binding, as I had to have the text microfilmed for my use). But there is a real difference in the treatment of the subject, too, which is very telling.

Lucot's book is simply an alphabetical listing of plants, describing the plant briefly and then giving its meaning, usually explaining the source of the meaning. At the end of this list there is a cross-index, called "Nomenclature," which lists the meanings alphabetically and refers to the plant. There is nothing very romantic about the whole business except that, of course, some of the meanings relate to love and romance. In contrast, the Latour text is organized around presenting flowers in the context of love, youth, and country life. A small amount of the Lucot material is worked into this and somewhat warps the concentration on its main topic, but other material is disregarded. She does not take "aerostation" (air navigation), "economy," or "navigation," for example, ignoring their emblematic plants as well. Interestingly, she also disregards "virginity." On the other hand, cabbage—"profit" and moss—"utility" are borrowings that are not particularly romantic, especially the cabbage itself.

The Latour text is much more complicated in organization than Lucot. The first part of the book is organized seasonally, and each season is divided into months, giving long pieces on flowers blooming that month and explaining their meaning. There are many more quotations of poetry and anecdotes in this material than in Lucot. This section is followed by a short account, titled "Langage allégorique," of a system of meaning related to which finger wears a ring or which hand proffers a flower, attributed to "many English towns" (155). Next there is a table showing how to indicate time with different bouquets of flowers, copied intact from Lucot, who, no doubt, copied it from somewhere else. Then, in later editions at least, comes a much more complete dictionary of the language, arranged alphabetically by meanings. There are many more entries here than in the main text, and each new entry has a brief explanation. The pieces in the main text are referred to here by page, so that a person can use this as a complete index of meanings. Finally, there is a dictionary of plants, giving a complete alphabetical list of flowers and their meanings. This indexing and cross-indexing gives an appearance of a practical, useful handbook.[8]

Probably the main difference between Lucot and Latour is one of tone; while Latour gives the appearance of a handbook, it is filled with love, romance, youthful memories, and description of country life and flowers. On the other hand, the Lucot text is a handbook pure and simple, which does not address an audience of women (as does Latour) and which does not romanticize youth and childhood. One of her entries is perhaps a commentary on this. He makes meadow-sweet the symbol of uselessness because, while it is an impressive plant, it has no medicinal uses: "This large plant appears to be no more than a jest of nature, and although we meet it everywhere, it is useless in medicine and has no known virtue. It is beautiful but useless" (156). On the same plant, to which she assigns the same meaning, Latour writes: "They accuse the meadowsweet, also called the Queen of the Meadow, of being beautiful but useless, because medicine finds no virtue in it and animals don't eat it. But is it then nothing to be beautiful?" (178).

I mentioned previously that the Lucot book does not appear to have been handsomely produced, but it was quite the opposite with Latour. According to the *Bibliographie de la France* for December 25, 1819, Latour's *Le langage des fleurs* could be purchased in several different formats: the smaller volume with fourteen plates and an engraved frontispiece sold for six francs, while the same volume with colored plates cost twelve francs. In larger format with colored plates the book cost twenty francs. The illustrations were by the famous miniaturist Pancrace Bessa. The publisher also produced—whether for sale, display, or presentation is not explained—two special volumes: a small one printed on rose paper with the pictures on satin and a large one printed on vellum. Perhaps the attractiveness of those first editions was such that the book's fortune was made by its appearance combined with the fashionableness of its topic.

The great popularity of *Le langage des fleurs* created a minor industry in France, England, America, and the rest of Europe. While I am sure that I have not been able to see all the French language of flower titles published after Latour, I have collected and studied six important works, ranging in date from 1825 to 1855.[9] The first of these, Charles-Joseph Chambet's *Emblème des fleurs* (*sic*) appeared in several editions, the first in 1825. Chambet claimed that he published a language of flower book prior to Latour, in 1816, and pointed to the previously mentioned 1816 *Les emblèmes des fleurs*. Nowhere is this book attributed to Chambet, and it is doubtful that he had anything to do with it. At any rate, his *Emblème des fleurs* is clearly dependent on Latour; mainly an alphabetical listing of plants and their meanings, with brief explanations, it copies Latour's plant to meaning vocabulary listing at the back of her book exactly. Chambet was the son of a Lyons publisher; born in 1791, he had a career as editor and writer of various ephemeral works. One contemporary said of him that he was a "Bookman who absolutely wished to pass for a man of letters."[10] I think we can consider Chambet an opportunistic individual whose word can hardly be trusted with claims of priority.

Louise Leneveux's *Nouveau manuel des fleurs emblématiques* (1837) is an ambitious attempt to systematize the language of flowers into a method of communication. Her other published works include a flower story for children, *Les fleurs parlants* (1848) and a number of other nature books for children, most of them published by Louis Janet's widow. The *Nouveau manuel* consists of an account of the meanings of flowers arranged alphabetically by the meaning, then a cross-index by flower name. Her contribution to the topic is a complicated system of grammar, which will be analyzed in chapter six.

Other works are quite derivative in a predictable way. J. Messire's *Le langage moral des fleurs* (1845) is a regional publication which follows no observable plan of organization, just talks about various flowers and their meanings, using some Latour material but not copying it blatantly. There are no vocabulary lists, and the hours and the colors are given in very shortened form. A listing of annual, biennial, and perennial plants follows the emblematic portion of the text. This work is typical of the casual use of the concept of a floral language in the nineteenth century. Messire was a professor (of what, his title page does not say); but on the page listing his other works—including a guide to weights and measures for persons of all classes and professions—there is advertised a course in handwriting and design, given every evening, 7–9 P.M., at what was no doubt his home, "Rue Saint-François-de Paule, 8," in Tours. He also illustrated the book, and several lithographs by him are advertised for sale, with subjects including a group of flowers, a young village girl, and Napoleon on a pedestal. At the end of the language of flowers part of his book is appended a short guide to the principal "curiosities" of Touraine.

Pierre Zaccone's *Nouveau langage des fleurs* (1855) has nothing "nouveau" about it, being a standard exposition of the subject introduced by a long, involved Oriental tale of romance featuring the *sélam*. The most ambitious of the books is Albert Jacquemart's *Flore des dames* (1841), which discusses the subject as presented by other writers, discourses on artificial flowers, gives examples of flower poetry written by women, and comments on flower painting. Jacquemart (1808–75) began his publishing career with this book; he was later known as an authority on ceramics and furniture. The *Flore des dames* contains more actual writing and discussion of the subject than is usual. In fact, in his preface—which begins with a letter from "Madame la Baronne Clémence D★★★ à D★★★," asking him to explain the language of flowers so she can understand it—he makes remarks on previous works. He commends Latour for her elegant and facile style, while Leneveux, despite all of her detailed illustrations, or perhaps because of them, he calls dry and laconic. He characterizes his work in preparing the book as quite difficult: "It is necessary, this time, to bring together a large number of books more or less rich in teachings, organize the scattered elements which they offer, co-ordinate them in a logical manner; it is necessary, in a word, to create from all these pieces a grammar of flowers" (3–4). The problem, as he puts it, is that some previous works are too learned, while others, those addressed to "a sex which, by taste as well as by nature, harmonizes intimately with flowers"—in other words, women—are too literary (whatever that means). He challenges his correspondent to compose a clear message in flowers using any other books; if she cannot, he will need to write a book to help her. The reader is not surprised that, as it turned out, the book was needed.

The last of these French-language titles is a Belgian production, *Nouveau langage des fleurs* (1839) attributed, as so many Belgian piracies were, to Louis Aimé-Martin. It was published by Lacrosse, one of the firms mentioned in Herman Dopp's book on the Belgian counterfeits as being active in the period (Dopp 39). It is a very slick pastiche, combining the Latour floral symbolism with the flower idylls of Constant Dubos. There is a dream-vision introduction, in which the flowers who brag are taught their place by a storm which leaves only the low-growing, humble flowers intact. This is an extreme example of an editing job, pure and simple, and probably the introduction was copied from somewhere although I don't know where.

When we look at the producers of the French language of flower books as a group, including Latour herself, we find that they are primarily middle-class literary folks, writing with an end to some profit, hoping to exploit the sentimental interest in flowers. The amount of actual writing they did differed, but their main task was to package the concept of a language of flowers in a consumable form. As I have already explained, the first French flower books were produced for the upper classes, but by the time it became really profitable to produce them, the middle and lower classes were interested. The publishers of these French works were the minor firms, specialists such as Audot, or juvenile and almanac publishers such as Janet. Sometime in the 1840s Latour's book began to be published by Garnier Frères. Many flower books attributed to Louis Aimé-Martin were published in Belgium during those years when Belgium, released from Napoleonic authority and eager to pay back some of the repression of its presses during Napoleon's reign, flooded the French market with pirated books selling at lower prices than French books (Dopp). This group of publishers could be expected to take advantage of a popular concept like the language of flowers, and they certainly did so, printing duplicates of Latour and attributing them to Aimé-Martin and doing the same with other flower books.

The history of the language of flower book in France after Latour shows very little introduction of new concepts, most books being mainly rearrangements of previous material with some little added anecdotes, quotations, or descriptions. So once again this subject became merely another sort of gift-book filler in many publications. Typical are two books from publisher Fleury Chavant: *Alphabet-Flore* (c. 1837), mainly a picture book with meanings printed under the pictures, and *La couronne de Flore* (1837), a "mélange de poésie et de prose," including a standard language of flower compilation, meant to accompany an illustrated book called *La naissance des fleurs,* with illustrations by Redouté, among others (which I have never seen). The language of flowers was apparently popular in other European countries, but I know very little about it. Latour's work was translated into German the year after its publication by Karl Muehler; his book, *Die Blumensprache oder Symbolik des Pflanzenreichs,* identifies itself on the title page as a translation from "Frau Charlotte de Latour." There are a few other German titles in my bibliography, and they seem to indicate that there was a German public for the language of flowers in the same sort of format acceptable in France and England. I have found no Italian examples, and the only Spanish-language texts I found were all published in the Americas, one in New York, one in San José (probably

Costa Rica), and one in Lima, Peru. There is a Portuguese text published in Rio de Janeiro. The catalog of the Bibliothèque Nationale lists a Spanish text published by Garnier in Paris. I think we are safe in assuming that there was an interest in the language of flowers among Spanish-language readers, although I have not been able to determine whether any of these were published in Spain itself.

V

Further Developments: England and America

An exquisite invention this,
Worthy of love's most honeyed kiss,
This art of writing billet doux
In buds and odors, and bright hues;
In saying all one feels and thinks
In clever daffodils and pinks,
Uttering (as well as silence may)
The sweetest words the sweetest way:
How fit, too, for the lady's bosom,
The place where billet doux *repose 'em.*

(Leigh
Hunt,
"Love
Letters
Made of
Flowers,"
355)

THE LANGUAGE of flowers reached England in the 1820s, but since the major publishing houses were not interested in such books, many were produced by firms with unfamiliar names like Bogue, Harrison, and Oliphant. The only well-known publishers whose imprint appeared on many books were Routledge, who turned out a number of similar little illustrated books edited by Anna Christian Burke from the 1840s through the 1880s, and Ward and Lock. Saunders and Otley were earliest in the field, with Henry Phillips's *Floral Emblems* (1825); Frederic Shoberl's adaptation of Latour, *The Language of Flowers; With Illustrative Poetry* (1834); and Frederick Marryat's parody, *The Floral Telegraph* (1836).

When the language of flowers was introduced to English readers, it had to be cleansed of unwholesome continental material, for there was not only the usual English distrust of French morality but also the general Francophobia generated by the French Revolution and the Napoleonic Wars. Henry Phillips, the author of the first English language of flower book I have located, *Floral Emblems* (1825), made this clear in his preface, right after acknowledging his indebtedness to "Madame la Comptesse de Genlis, to Madame de Latour and also to the author of 'Parterre de Flore' ":

In this symbolical assemblage the author has carefully avoided all indeli-
cate allusions or double-entendre *that could be offensive to modesty, his*
object has been to establish a settled collection of floral emblems, and to
render them as amusing as the decorative dress of the poet, and the
sparkling garb of the wit would allow. And although he presents a flower
(vii–viii)   *to fit every cap, none are personally intended, but the whole are offered for*
the selection of the wearer, and should weeds be discovered where flowers
are expected, he flatters himself they will be few, and that those few will
be found inoffensive, for although the work may be considered more
adapted for amusement than for utility, he would not willingly offer
entertainment through the assistance of immorality.

Phillips's book, which will be analyzed thoroughly in chapter six, is
handsomely produced with colored illustrations showing his ideas for
emblems of the days of the week and the months of the year. The major
part of the text is an alphabetical listing of meanings of flowers, with
explanations of the meaning, apt quotations, and such other filler material.
There is an index by flowers rather than the more usual dictionary list.
Significantly, the book is dedicated to "the Poets and Painters of Great
Britain," presumably the users of the book, although in his preface he
implies the book is more for amusement than utility. There is no indication
that the book is a language of flowers for the conduct of a love affair, and
thus, although the book is well illustrated, it was not especially popular,
although there was a second edition in 1831. The situation of this book
parallels that of Lucot's *Emblèmes de Flore,* in that it presumably did not
find success with the audience of genteel women readers. Another parallel
is this: the first really popular English language of flower book was
Frederic Shoberl's translation of Latour, first published in 1834, *The
Language of Flowers; With Illustrative Poetry.* Shoberl (1775–1853) was a
journalist who edited Rudolph Ackermann's popular annual *The Forget-
Me-Not* from 1822 to 1834. His own books included travel and historical
works intended for the average reader, as well as many translations from
the French.[1] The concept of flower emblems needed the packaging of
romance in order to sell to a mass audience in England as well as France.
    Shoberl's *Language of Flowers* is a slightly edited version of Latour. It is
arranged like her book but has substituted English plants in many situations in the main text. However, the dictionary portion is a direct translation from Latour. In his introduction Shoberl ridicules Phillips's *Floral
Emblems:* "In treating of so gay a subject, we will not make a parade of our

learning, to tell our fair readers what fine things Pliny has said upon it; or, in the spirit of prosing write a crabbed treatise upon the Egyptian hiero-glyphics. We will even spare them a dissertation upon the Floral Alphabet of the effeminate Chinese" (ix). This book remained in print through the 1840s, and was copied in America by Carey, Lea, and Blanchard soon after its publication.

The popularity of Shoberl's translation of Latour caught the attention of Robert Tyas, who, as we have already seen, was active in publishing a variety of types of flower books. With the language of flowers, he found his most profitable topic. Tyas's *The Sentiment of Flowers; or, Language of Flora* (1836) was in print through the 1840s and by 1839, one copy announces, it had reached its sixth thousand. Carey, Lea, and Blanchard also brought out American editions. In the 1860s Routledge published a revised version of this work, mainly a rearrangement of material. Like Shoberl, Tyas billed his work as being an English rendition of Latour, and the edition of 1839 carries this notice in its front papers:

> *We quote the following notice of "The Sentiment of Flowers," from the* Literary Gazette *of January 16, 1836, "A charming little book from Made de la Tour's Langage des Fleurs, in which all that was eligible for English readers in that popular time is preserved and translated, all that might be objectionable omitted, and much is added to the translator's original matter, which considerably enhances the attraction of the whole. With a dozen sweet floral coloured plates, it is precisely the thing for a fair lady's boudoir."*

From the 1830s on language of flower books appeared yearly in England, most of them destined for the gift book trade.[2] Popular volumes went through numerous editions just as Shoberl's and Tyas's work did. Thomas Miller's *The Poetical Language of Flowers; or, The Pilgrimage of Love* (1847) stayed in print through the 1870s and was issued in America under the title *The Romance of Nature; or, The Poetical Language of Flowers.* Miller (1807–74) was known as "the basket-maker," and he was one of those working-class writers championed by various patrons and the general class of gift annual readers. Henry Adams's *The Language and Poetry of Flowers* (1844) was especially popular in America, with many editions published in Philadelphia by a variety of publishers through 1876. Adams (1811/12–81) was a chemist and druggist who lived in Canterbury, and the author of a few other books, including some on song birds and cage birds. A book with the same title, *The Language and Poetry of Flowers* published by Marcus Ward, which perhaps first appeared in 1875, announced its thirty-ninth thousand in 1883. An interesting late title, *Flora Symbolica* (1869) by John Henry Ingram, looks forward to the flower folklores of later in the century. A very thorough compilation, *Flora Symbolica* is arranged by flowers, giving anecdotes and descriptions along with other sentimental material for each flower. There is a complete floral vocabulary, drawn from a number of sources, as well as a fortune-telling game, a Dial of Flowers, and saints' floral emblems. This was his first book. A great admirer of Edgar Allan Poe, Ingram (1842–1916) wrote a popular life of Poe and many other literary biographies, including those of Thomas Chatterton and Christopher Marlowe. His letters to Sarah Helen Whitman have recently been published. While there do not appear to be as many different language of flower books published in England as in America, the popular ones seem to have sold very well.[3]

It is not my intention to describe every language of flower book listed in my bibliography, nor would it be humanly possible to be sure that every edition of each title is exactly the same, even if that was important to know, which it is not in my view. There were a number of ways in which writers and editors organized the basic language of flower book, and many books show all of these permutations. To be categorized as a language of flower book, a volume needs to have at a minimum a list of flowers and their meanings. Most of these books have such lists alphabetized both by flower and by meaning, forming a cross-index. Many of the books have extensive annotated lists of flowers, basically communicating the flower name, its meaning, and then filling in with botanical and horticultural description of the flower, a few words about the meaning, any legends or folklore attached to the plant, and quotations of poetry either mentioning the flower or expressing the sentiment. Common features of the books are an explanation of the language of colors, the method of telling the time of day by the flowers (certain flowers open at certain times of day), floral weather prophecies, and floral games (which will be explained in more detail in a later section of this chapter). Many of the books, especially those with the word "poetry" in the title, have numerous pages of poems about flowers. Some books, those of Thomas Miller and Henry Adams for example, have prose pieces—short fiction or essays on sentimental aspects of flowers. Illustration and binding are, of course, important, as has already been discussed. These basic ingredients were combined in various ways to make the individual books marketable, and the whole process was probably motivated by a publisher needing such a title for his gift book list. This is true for the language of flower books in all three countries.

The language of flowers first flourished in France, and it was there that it first declined in popularity. The well-known parody of sentimental treatment of flowers, Taxile Delord's *Les fleurs animées* (1847), which will be discussed in chapter seven, marked the beginning of the end, and we notice very few late-century language of flower titles in France. The decline of its popularity was less swift in England, Kate Greenaway's often reprinted *Language of Flowers* (1884)—which merely uses the idea as a gimmick for some illustrations with little or no relationship to the genre— serving as a good landmark for the end of the era, although there were some things still appearing in the 1890s. In America the language of flowers seems to have reached popularity in the 1830s, judging from the publishing record, becoming a staple of the gift book trade in the 1840s, and thence gradually declining throughout the rest of the century. The genre was still around in the 1890s, of course, but by then it was a tired, old-fashioned notion, surviving into the early twentieth century in occasional amateur or commercial applications.

America

During its heyday in America, the language of flowers attracted the attention of many of the most popular women writers and editors, which gives the history of these books in America its main distinction from France and England—the association of the idea with upward mobility in the journalistic world almost exclusively for women. However, the first appearance of the language of flowers in print in America, as far as I can discover, was not the work of a woman writer, but of Constantine Samuel Rafinesque, the French-American naturalist.

Rafinesque (1783–1840) is famous for his eccentricity, both in his scientific work and his personal life. Born in Constantinople to a French father and a German mother, he had a business career in Sicily before coming to America for the second time in 1815. A self-educated botanist and ichthyologist, he claimed to have discovered many new plants and fishes, but scientists of the time discounted his claims. His reputation is not much better today, but the romance of his life and his work always commands interest. He taught for seven years at Transylvania University in Lexington, Kentucky, and during those years he roamed over the surrounding countryside botanizing enthusiastically. He made most journeys on foot, including several trips from Philadelphia to Kentucky, claiming that a naturalist should always walk. When he left Transylvania University, after a bitter dispute, he went to Philadelphia, where he added still more publications to the many titles he generated, most of them quite small and repetitive works (Rafinesque, *Travels*). Among his projects during those years was a series of lessons in popular botany published in two related periodicals, the *Saturday Evening Post,* which appeared weekly, and the monthly *Casket; or Flowers of Literature, Wit, and Sentiment.* Over the six years of its existence as a feature, "The School of Flora" did not appear regularly, but the first sixty-six entries have floral emblems attached to them. The rest of the "School" pieces are reprints from Rafinesque's newly published *Medical Flora* (1828). These pieces with flower meanings ran from 1827 to the end of 1828, and thus probably constitute the first language of flowers published (and created) in America (Seaton, "Rafinesque's Sentimental Botany"). Each of the "School" entries with floral emblems contains an interesting mixture of material, beginning with the botanic name, the English name, and the French name of the plant. The plant is described and perhaps the meanings of its Latin names are explained. In keeping with Rafinesque's interest in the medical uses of plants, properties and qualities of the plants often appear. Infrequently he gives bits of floral history, and more frequently he suggests garden uses for the plants. The emblematic meaning of the plant is given in a brief sentence, although sometimes he ventures on a slightly longer explanation of the meaning. The pieces are illustrated with woodcuts, some original, some copied loosely from such sources as Bigelow's *American Medical Botany* and Barton's *Vegetable Materia Medica* and *Flora of North America.* Both the kinds of plants chosen for the pieces—usually native American plants of botanical and medical interest—and the meanings themselves are distinctly different from the usual language of flowers. This will be discussed more fully in chapter six.

While it is pleasant to think that the introduction of the language of flowers to America was accomplished by a man born in Turkey (as the language itself was said to be) who was also a citizen of France, the country of its introduction to society, it fell to a "Lady" of Virginia to really popularize the concept for American consumers. Elizabeth Gamble Wirt (1784–1857) was the second wife of William Wirt, attorney general of the United States and author of *The Letters of a British Spy* and other popular works. Her *Flora's Dictionary* (1829), published under the pseudonym "A Lady," was a phenomenal success. According to her preface, she had put together her language of flower list from several "books and manuscripts" over the past few years, and she only allowed it to be published because she was not able to supply all the manuscript copies people asked for and because someone in Boston had, "last year," put her material in print. This Boston edition of *Flora's Dictionary* (if indeed it was called that) is unknown to me, and she remarks concerning it that "a few copies were struck, with great neatness and beauty of type and paper." Her purpose in mentioning this Boston printing is, she says, to let those who have copies know whose work it is and also understand that she had no "original purpose of publishing." A language of flower book which did appear in Boston in 1829 is Dorothea Dix's *The Garland of Flora,* a small and not very successful book. At that time the famous social reformer was a Boston schoolteacher. Her book is nothing but an alphabetical listing of flowers with their meanings explained briefly, along with other filler material of the usual sort. Some of the flowers do not have emblems assigned to them, and there is no other material except Mrs. Sigourney's poem "Flora's Party" at the end. It does not appear to be derived from Wirt's book and would seem to have appeared in print at about the same time. Wirt's remarks about copies of *Flora's Dictionary* extant in Boston prior to 1829 do perhaps explain one mystery, in that Dix mentions *Flora's Dictionary* in one of her entries, one that pairs up the same flower and meaning as Wirt does. I had wondered how this could have happened if the two books were produced about the same time; my guess is that Dix saw the manuscript or one of the copies. In contrast to Dix's book, *Flora's Dictionary* is a very complex production, which will be analyzed in detail in chapter six. It appeared in many editions throughout the 1830s and was also issued in a new illustrated format in 1855 from the same publishing firm, Lucas of Baltimore. It held the field until the appearance in the 1840s of many works edited by well-known women like Frances Osgood and Lucy Hooper. A striking feature of American flower language books is the fact that most of them were edited by a woman (a "lady"), often a poetess or a popular editor.[4]

Another important early volume is Sarah Josepha Hale's *Flora's Interpreter,* first appearing in 1832 and continuing in print through the 1860s. Hale was, of course, the editor of *Godey's Ladies' Book.* Unlike *Flora's Dictionary,* this work was an exploitative cut-and-paste job. Nevertheless, it was very popular, having added to it after 1848 a section on floral fortune-telling called *Fortuna Flora.* Another best-selling language of flower title was Catharine Waterman Esling's *Flora's Lexicon* (1839), which is on a par with *Flora's Interpreter,* mainly cut-and-paste.

One publisher, Riker of New York, issued two of the popular language of flower titles of the 1840s, Lucy Hooper's *The Lady's Book of Flowers and Poetry* (1841), which is mainly an anthology of flower poetry with a bit of the language of flowers, and Frances Osgood's *The Poetry of Flowers and Flowers of Poetry* (1841), which is a more standard exposition of the topic. In an interesting twist, Osgood writes that she had taken most of the prose portions of her work from Robert Tyas's *The Sentiment of*

Flowers, which she has undoubtedly done. We further notice, however, that just as he admitted that much of his material was taken from Latour with changes to suit the English audience, Osgood writes that she has adapted his material to American readers. Both of these books appeared throughout the next three or four decades. In addition to *The Poetry of Flowers,* Osgood edited a special gift book for Carey and Hart, *The Floral Offering* (1847), which is mostly illustrations and poems she has written about the bouquets pictured. A few years later, in 1851, Henrietta Dumont used the same title, *The Floral Offering,* for her standard language of flower work that was fairly popular through the 1850s and early 1860s. A final volume to mention is Laura Greenwood's *The Rural Wreath; or, Life Among the Flowers* (1853), which was in print in the 1850s and 1860s and had another edition in 1880.

From the illustrations, the titles, and the bindings of these American examples of the 1840s and 1850s we can see that these years were the high point of the popularity of the language of flowers for the mass audience, although the books had been very popular in the 1830s as well. They more or less follow the trail blazed by the gift annual, as has been discussed earlier. Just as in England, though, the publishers of language of flower books were the smaller firms, the bookseller-publishers who came and went with great frequency in pre–Civil War America. In New York this included Derby and Jackson, Claxton, Fenno, and Riker; in Boston Buffum, Cottrell, Mussey, Dayton and Wentworth, and Phillips and Sampson; in Philadelphia Peck and Bliss, Porter and Coates, and Claxton, Remsen and Heffelfinger. The only well-known firms to bring out such books were Lippincott and Carey, Lea and Blanchard. The latter firm published the first American annual, *The Atlantic Souvenir.* All the Carey, Lea and Blanchard titles were piracies of English books (or I assume they were—for they were direct copies of English works and I doubt that they paid for the rights). Lucas, Wirt's publisher, was a Catholic firm.

A related type of publication, the anthology of flower poetry, was published by the same type of publishers and put together by the same type of editors. Sometimes there is little difference between a language of flower book and an anthology of poetry or a collection of excerpts from poetry; for example, Sarah Mayo's *The Flower Vase* is little more than a collection of poems and excerpts from poems organized by flower meanings. Collections of poems about flowers are much less common, however; one of the most popular, Mrs. Kirtland's *Poetry of the Flowers* (n.d.) has a center section about the language of flowers, and Mary Griffin's *Dew-Drops from Flora's Cup* (1845) includes a language of flower vocabulary.

These anthologies look very much like language of flower books, with the same sort of illustrations and bindings.

Other Developments

Illustration of plants and flowers, always an important part of gift books, is featured especially in the language of flower books. Since so many of the flower books were bought as formal gifts, their bindings and illustrations were paramount considerations to buyers. John Grand-Carteret, in *Les almanachs français 1600–1895* (1896), quotes a journalist from 1816 who describes the crowd buying almanacs on New Year's morning as only interested in the bindings, not the contents. "O perfidious fine arts! You will ably sell the poetry, but I defy you to make them read it," he exclaims (li). The more plates, especially colored plates, the finer the gift.

These lovely floral illustrations have proved both a help and a hindrance to the preservation of the flower books. As the century wore on, flower books were plundered to make valentines, children's scrap books, and decorative objects of all sorts, such as screens and fans. The books, denuded of their plates, held very little value and were quickly discarded. On the other hand, those that retained their plates later attracted book collectors, such as Rachel McMasters Hunt (who was interested in bookbinding and botanical illustration), and so were preserved because of the illustrations. It is still possible to buy average nineteenth-century flower books with pleasant illustrations, but the finest ones are now very expensive. The books are also still being cut up, it appears, for one can find illustrations from them encased in plastic bags and filed under "Flowers" in antique shops, beside old car ads and Betsy McCall paper dolls.

The illustrations in the language of flower books have only a small role in the history of botanical art, for they emphasize sentiment and romance over accuracy. However, they are often very attractive and are particularly evocative of the period's perspectives on nature. In fact, there is a tendency today, in America certainly, to use flower illustrations as a cultural shorthand to represent the previous century, at least the years after 1840. Stylized roses—fat cabbage roses with a few ferns or drooping lily of the valley—are typically symbolic of the Victorian period. Such common images, while accurate, are not the whole story in sentimental flower book art, which went through a number of technical changes and which was sometimes associated with well-known artists.

I feel that the very best of the illustrations are those in the early French gift books, beautifully embellished New Year's gifts for ladies, most of which were almanacs. They were typically small, with pastel bindings and slipcases and gilt edges. The book covers were often decorated in gold, while the engravings in the book were colored by hand in clear, vibrant water colors. One well-known artist, Pancrace Bessa, did the designs for many of them (see Figure 3). Bessa (1772–1830), a pupil of Redouté, was specially known for his flowers and fruits. Among his works are the illustrations for Mollevaut's *Les fleurs* (1818), *Almanach de Flore* (1817), Latour's *Le langage des fleurs* (1819), and many of Malo's almanacs. His work is distinguished by its delicacy, which complements the size of the books, in contrast to other illustrators of the period who could either not command detail at such scale or who did not even try.

Illustrations in the earliest English flower books are not comparable to the art of Bessa, but the books themselves were not so small and delicate either. The hand-colored engravings in Henry Phillips's *Floral Emblems* (1825) are very much tied to the text, and they are often awkward and amateurish, whether showing groups of flowers or more complex emblems of the months (see Figure 4). While they are not so well produced as the French works, however, they do have the charm of the handmade, something lacking in the smoother products of mid-century flower books. Another interesting early set of illustrations are the woodcuts used by Constantine Rafinesque in his "School of Flora" essays in the *Saturday Evening Post* and the *Casket,* many of which were copied from other sources of botanical illustration, such as Barton's *Flora of North America* (1821–23), Bigelow's *American Medical Botany* (1817–20), or Barton's *Vegetable Materia Medica* (1817–18). Some of the illustrations are mirror images, suggesting that the engraver used a camera lucida to copy the picture. But apparently some of the woodcuts were original, made from drawings by Rafinesque himself.

Most typical of sentimental flower illustration are the plates in mid-century books, some hand-colored, others printed with new color-printing techniques. One of the finest of these illustrated books is *Le Bouquet des Souvenirs; A Wreath of Friendship* (1840), published by Robert Tyas, with botanical parts written by John Stevens Henslow, the Cambridge botanist. Some of these books showed bouquets, including those intended to convey a message. (The grammatical problems associated with the illustrated message will be discussed in chapter six.) Other times a grouping of flowers just illustrates the flowers themselves. Frances Osgood's *The Poetry of Flowers* (1841) shows a typically ornamental pairing of frontispiece and title page, the frontispiece featuring a rose and the title page picturing a vase draped with flowers (see Figure 5). Anna Peyre Dinnies's *The Floral Year* (1847) features a bouquet for each month (Figure 6

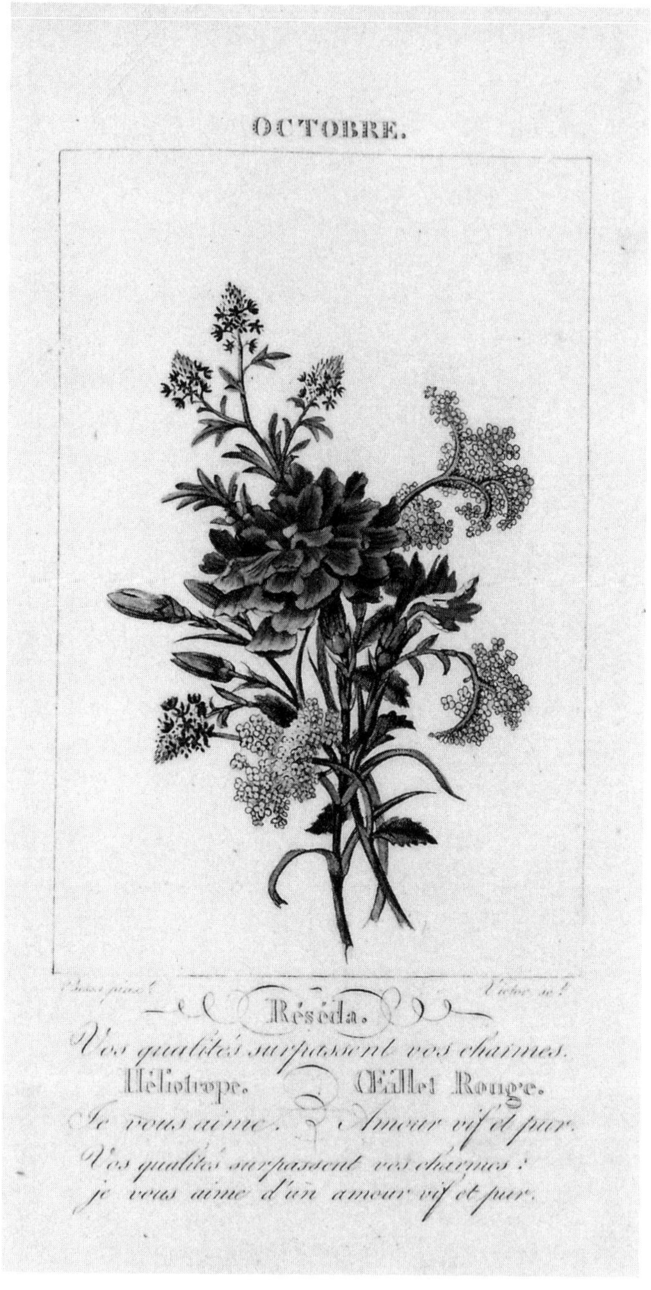

Réséda.

Vos qualités surpassent vos charmes.

Héliotrope.   Œillet Rouge.

Je vous aime.   Amour vif et pur.

Vos qualités surpassent vos charmes :
je vous aime d'un amour vif et pur.

Fig. 3. Pancrace Bessa engraving in Charlotte de Latour, *Le langage des fleurs*. Paris: Audot, [1840?]. (Courtesy of the Hunt Institute for Botanical Documentation, Carnegie Mellon University, Pittsburgh, PA.)

Floral Emblems

Danger accompanying Coquetry.

Publishd by Saunders & Otley 50 Conduit Stt

Fig. 4. Henry Phillips, *Floral Emblems*. (Courtesy of the Hunt Institute for Botanical Documentation, Carnegie Mellon University, Pittsburgh, PA.)

shows May). Many times the pages are decorated, either with ornamental capitals or page edgings showing stylized flowers. Catharine Esling's *Flora's Lexicon* (1841) has very neat pages, each giving a complete account of one flower, its botany, meaning, and snips of poetry, ornamented with a stylized capital letter; the page for Mignonette is typical (Figure 7).

Not all the illustrations showed flowers, of course. Romantic landscapes with figures, especially figures of women, were common. Frequently, the people were shown appreciating nature, either taking walks or actually contemplating something. The frontispiece for Laura Greenwood's *The Rural Wreath; or, Life Among the Flowers* (1853) shows this fashion, which was so prominent in the general gift annuals (Figure 8). The attractive woman associated in some way with nature was a staple image in gift book art. Figure 9 shows a typical family grouping.

While not found in language of flower books themselves, images of flowers personified as women are found in associated books, especially in the work of major artists such as Grandville and Walter Crane. In the narrative poetry about flowers for children (discussed in chapter three), the pictures often showed flowers and plants personified as people, frequently resembling people in flower costume. The illustrations for Crichton's *The Festival of Flora* (1818) are typical of this fashion, the rose appearing as a shapely woman with a large rose on her head (Figure 2), while the aloe is an old man with long white beard, a feather skirt, and a large aloe plant on his head.

The personified flowers in Delord's *Les fleurs animées* (1847) drawn by the famous artist J.-J. Grandville are well known today, having recently been published in an edition by Peter Wick (*The Court of Flora*, 1981). It is ironic that these images, meant to be satiric, are often taken today as typical of the flower sentiment they sought to ridicule. Grandville's personified flowers show silly, uncomfortable-looking damsels in very complete flower costumes; we need to see them in the context of the sort of illustration and sentiment they were satirizing. Figure 10, for example, shows Sensitive shrinking from the attentions of a pipe-smoking beetle and some type of slug, lifting her skirts in horror. Many of the other flower plates show insects as well, for Grandville loved doing insects, and the presence of the insects reduces the sentimentality of the personification, as do the fatuous expressions on some of the flower faces. The Rose, for instance, is shown with large beetles doing her homage while a caterpillar munches on the train of Carnation's dress. Honeysuckle is accompanied by a goat, and Thistle encounters a jackass dressed as a dandy.

Not satiric at all, but almost revisionistic in sentiment are the personified flowers of Walter Crane, which appear in books he both wrote and illustrated. His flowers are not referential, as are Grandville's, but rather are pictorial in motivation. His figures are both males and females dressed as flowers, with gorgeous colors and poses, while his poems, on traditional subjects such as the floral procession or a wedding among the flowers, belong to the convention of children's poems beginning early in the century; but somehow both pictures and text are lighter, less emotional, than earlier examples, perhaps owing to the pre-Raphaelite influence and the art for art's sake ideal. *Flowers from Shakespeare's Garden,* in which he illustrates flower passages from Shakespeare with personified flowers, is one of his more typically Victorian works; but it did not appear until 1906. Later children's illustrators such as Elizabeth Gordon and Cicely Barker drew on Crane's playfulness and interest in costume.

If Grandville's personified flowers satirize the sentimental tradition and Crane's ignore it, we can see the very end of sentimental flower illustration in the charming disregard of Kate Greenaway. Her *Language of Flowers* (1884) is well known today, and I regard it as the signal for the end of the language of flowers. It contains a vocabulary and some poems, but it is almost absentmindedly illustrated with whatever flowers she wanted, wherever she wanted them. There are wreaths, sprays, nosegays, vases of flowers, along with little vignettes showing women in nature and children at play. It is as if a child (talented, of course) found a language of flower book and drew in the margins and on blank pages. Here the illustrations and the text are almost totally separate, as if from two different worlds. Readers today seldom realize this, of course, naturally identifying the language of flowers and Greenaway as contemporaries, living in that quaint old world of yesterday. Greenaway's flowers are not only not sentimental in a meaningful way, they are sentimental in our twentieth-century way—conventional and superficial, with more than a touch of insincerity.

The early flower books of the century—the French almanacs ornamented by the designs of Pancrace Bessa—are the best of the illustrated books until late in the century, after the popularity of the language of flowers had diminished. The American Louis Prang, who had a lifelong interest in flowers, published gift books that show the perfection of color lithography between 1860 and 1897 (Golden). But, like Crane's personified figures, they are not integrated with a sentimental text and so stand outside the tradition of language of flower illustration.

While luxurious bindings, unusual size, and pretty illustrations all varied the product in appearance, such strategies were part of the gift book

Fig. 5. Frances S. Osgood, *The Po-etry of Flowers and Flowers of Poetry*

Fig. 6. Anna Peyre Dinnies, *The Floral Year*. (Courtesy of the A. and E. Rudolph Collection, Ohio State University Libraries.)

 IGNONETTE. *Reseda Odorata.* Class 11, DODECANDRIA. Order: TRIGYNIA. The odour exhaled by this little flower is thought by some to be too powerful for the house; but even those persons, we presume, must be delighted with the fragrance which it throws from the balconies into the streets of the city, giving something like a breath of garden air to the 'close-pent man,' whose avocations will not permit a ramble beyond the squares of the fashionable part of the town.

YOUR QUALITIES SURPASS YOUR CHARMS.

Now look ye on the plain and modest guise
Of yon unlovely flower — *unlovely?* — no —
Not *beautiful,* 't is true — not touch'd with hues
Like her's we late have gazed on; but so rich
In precious fragrance is that lovely one,
So loved for her sweet qualities, that I
Should woo her first amid a world of flowers;
For she is like some few beloved ones here,
Whom *eyes,* perchance, might slightingly pass o'er,
But whose true wisdom, gentleness, and worth,
Unchanging friendship, ever-faithful love,
And countless minor beauties of the mind,
Attach our *hearts* in deep affection still.

TWAMLEY.

No gorgeous flowers the meek reseda grace,
Yet sip with eager trunk yon busy race
Her simple cup, nor heed the dazzling gem
That beams in Fritillaria's diadem.

EVANS.

Fig. 7. Catharine Waterman Esling, *Flora's Lexicon.* (Courtesy of the Hunt Institute for Botanical Documentation, Carnegie Mellon University, Pittsburgh, PA.)

Fig. 8. Frontispiece, Laura Greenwood, *The Rural Wreath; or, Life Among the Flowers*

Fig. 9. Mrs. C. M. Kirtland, *Poetry of the Flowers*

SENSITIVE

Fig. 10. J.-J. Grandville, artist, in Taxile Delord, *Les fleurs animées*. (Courtesy of the Hunt Institute for Botanical Documentation, Carnegie Mellon University, Pittsburgh, PA.)

trade, selling for appearance alone. There were also a few ways of varying the arrangement of the text that also deserve to be considered. One of these is the application of the language of flowers to names and birthdays. In America, the Boston publishers who put out so many small books seem to have developed these notions profitably. Sarah H. Carter's *Lexicon of Ladies' Names with Their Floral Emblems; A Gift Book for All Seasons* (1852) appeared in several editions by Buffum and Cottrell until at least 1865. This work brought together names, flowers, and emblems: for example, Elizabeth, which means "God hath sworn," has as its emblem faithfulness; its emblem flower, the blue violet. I have seen several British examples of floral birthday books (see Figure 11), but none are so attractive as American John Wesley Hanson's *Flora's Dial; A Flower Dedicated to Each Day in the Year,* brought out in 1846 by Mussey and kept in print by these related Boston firms through 1875.[5] A very small volume, this book, like the English examples, gives a flower, a meaning, and a verse for each day in the year, presumably so that one can look up one's own birthday and those of friends. Hanson also created a similar book on gems: *The Ladies' Casket; Containing a Gem, Together with Its Sentiment, and a Poetical Description, for Each Day in the Week, and Each Month in the Year* (1846). The language of gems was never very popular as compared to the language of flowers, but Mussey also saw fit to publish a little companion volume to Hanson's *Ladies' Casket,* Hanna J. Woodman's *The Language of Gems, with Their Poetic Sentiments* (1848), which is an alphabetical listing of gems and their meanings with some brief scientific descriptions of the stones. These books all are presented for a kind of use, looking up birthdays and names.

Another way in which publishers packaged the language of flowers for use was the floral fortune-telling game. This idea goes back to the early days of the language of flowers; in 1817 Louis Janet published a tiny gift book, bound in pale blue, called *Oracles de Flore,* by C. F. P. Del———. Actually, this is a fairly complex floral game, using the meanings of flowers and a set of numbered fortunes. This game will be discussed in chapter six, when I consider the major cultural differences found in the language of flower books. Many language of flower books give a very short version of the game, using it amidst other filler material. For example, Shoberl, in his introduction to *The Language of Flowers; With Illustrative Poetry,* describes a divining game which matches flowers from a numbered list with a set of qualities which describe the character of one's lover. Thus, if a player draws a marigold from the bouquet, he learns that the character of his beloved is "jealous." A similar game is explained in Kirtland's *Poetry of the Flowers,* but this version gives lists for different

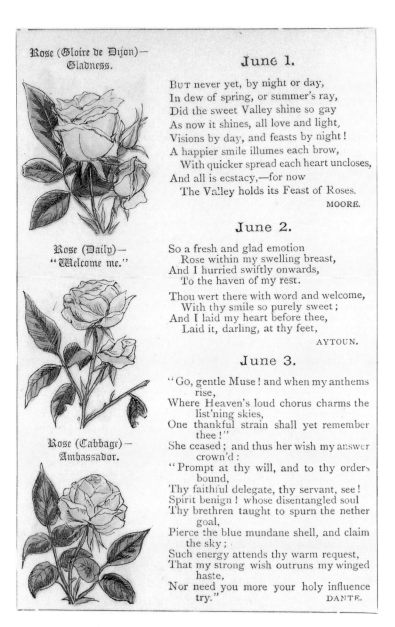

Rose (Gloire de Dijon)—Gladness.

June 1.

But never yet, by night or day,
In dew of spring, or summer's ray,
Did the sweet Valley shine so gay
As now it shines, all love and light,
Visions by day, and feasts by night!
A happier smile illumes each brow,
    With quicker spread each heart uncloses,
And all is ecstacy,—for now
    The Valley holds its Feast of Roses.

MOORE.

June 2.

So a fresh and glad emotion
    Rose within my swelling breast,
And I hurried swiftly onwards,
    To the haven of my rest.

Thou wert there with word and welcome,
    With thy smile so purely sweet;
And I laid my heart before thee,
    Laid it, darling, at thy feet,

AYTOUN.

Rose (Daily)—"Welcome me."

June 3.

"Go, gentle Muse! and when my anthems
        rise,
Where Heaven's loud chorus charms the
        list'ning skies,
One thankful strain shall yet remember
        thee!"
She ceased; and thus her wish my answer
        crown'd:
"Prompt at thy will, and to thy orders
        bound,
Thy faithful delegate, thy servant, see!
Spirit benign! whose disentangled soul
Thy brethren taught to spurn the nether
        goal,
Pierce the blue mundane shell, and claim
        the sky;
Such energy attends thy warm request,
That my strong wish outruns my winged
        haste,
Nor need you more your holy influence
        try."   DANTE.

Rose (Cabbage)—Ambassador.

Fig. 11. *The Floral Birthday Book: Flowers and Their Emblems with Appropriate Selections from the Poets.* (Courtesy of the A. and E. Rudolph Collection, Ohio State University Libraries)

seasons and includes some flowers to indicate professions as well. Playing by Kirtland's rules, the future consort of the person who draws the marigold will be rich (which does not seem to be a character designation, but there it is). And this meaning is further underlined by the fact that the profession matched with the marigold is "merchant."

One of the earliest complete American fortune-telling books comes from the Boston Universalist publishers, Sarah Mayo's *The Floral Fortune Teller,* which first appeared in 1846. The 1849 edition, published by Tomkins, is a tiny volume. The game combines poetry and flowers in seeking answers to five main questions, including the popular query, "What is the character of my future companion?" The answers to the questions are all bits of poetry. Different colored flowers answer different questions. For instance, white flowers describe the player's own character. So if a person draws a spray of white candytuft from a bouquet, the person with the book will read out a brief bit of verse, differing for male or female although partaking of the same general nature. If our player is a woman, we find that she is "Handsome, young, and hast all those requisites that folly and green minds look after." A male would find this: "You are one of those that will not serve God, if the devil bid you" (both of these quotations Mayo attributed to Shakespeare).

Probably the most famous of all the games is Sarah Hale's *Fortuna Flora,* bound with her *Flora's Interpreter* after 1848. This game has two aspects. In one, you find your fortune based on your birthday and your temperament (chosen from four—lymphatic, sanguine, bilious, and nervous). I worked this out for myself: my "flower of destiny" is the flower of the month of my birth, May; according to the game, this is the violet. My flower of temperament I determined by assigning myself a sanguine temperament (although I lack the curly hair that she makes a requisite); this led me to the grape, as the eighth flower listed for May. My "natal flower" is the one assigned to the exact date of my birth, May 1—the daisy. Thus, my fortune is this: Faithfulness (the violet), Mirth (the grape), and Beauty and Innocence (the daisy). Exactly how this applies to my life is up to me to decide, according to the book. I found it, as indeed befits my sanguine temperament, an occasion for Mirth. The other aspect of the game involves the use of numbered lists. If one receives a flower, one determines its meaning by adding up the day of the week, the day of the month, and one's temperament number. I can see that this could add considerably to confusion unless those using the system are in complete agreement. For example, a young man might send a girl a jonquil, which, according to the language of flowers explained in *Flora's Interpreter* means

"I desire a return of affection." But if the girl uses the other method of reading the flower, the one given in *Fortuna Flora,* and if she received the flower on Sunday, the first day of the week, on the nineteenth day of the month, and her temperament was lymphatic (1), she would add up 21, look up number 21 in the meaning list, and find this verse:

> The last link is broken,
>> That bound me to thee,
> The words thou hast spoken
>> Have rendered me free.

Such are the chances one takes in using the floral language.

Not all floral fortune-telling games appear in books, of course. An interesting floral game combining fortune-telling and art is *Pictures for Grouping; The Realm of the Queen of Flowers,* which describes itself as "Rational Entertainment." This game, explained in French, English, and German, includes a set of fifty numbered mottoes matched to a set of flowers to be cut out and inserted in vases that have slots for the insertion of the flowers. Players can choose flowers according to any rules, and make up bouquets or arrangements to suit themselves. Each flower has a number on its stem, which reveals its meaning. The motto of cornflower, for instance, is "As midst the corn those simple blue flowers spring, / Become, sweet love, the beauty of my life." The directions also suggest that one can make arrangements to serve as models for drawings, paintings, and embroidery.[6]

But there were also language of flower variations that were much less frivolous than the floral games. Many writers on flower topics complained that the "true" or "real" language of flowers was not the one found in the language of flower lists but a language which speaks only of God. Some writers, Henry Adams for one example, even made this point in books that contained the standard language of flowers. The cliché that flowers are God's messages was found in all kinds of flower writing, and naturally, then, one would expect that there would be attempts to create a language of flowers with specifically religious meanings. And such did occur, although not very thoroughly until almost the end of the century.

The Christian Sentiment of Flowers (1831) sought to associate flowers with passages of Scripture, so that "when any of these flowers are presented to the eye, they may speak a language, not of vanity and folly, as in many instances is the case; but one that will be conducive to the best interests of man,—a language at once gratifying and instructive to the mind of the Christian" (iii). The book is arranged by seasonal bloom, assigns a Bible verse to every flower, and also gives a snippet of poetry. The daffodil, for instance, is linked with "Behold, now is the acceptable time; behold, now is the day of salvation." In 1835 Seeley and Burnside brought out a similar little volume called *The Christian Florist,* which was published in several American editions by Carey and Lea (Kaser). This volume also did not attempt to imitate the form of the standard language of flowers, but instead found Bible verses to match some feature of the flower. For instance, the daisy, being a compound flower, "many florets in one flower," is matched to 1 Corinthians 10:17, "We being many . . . are one body" (11). The carnation, one variety of which is red and white, is matched to Solomon 5:10, "My beloved is white and ruddy" (57). Bits of appropriate poetry are quoted as well. The book lists suitable mottoes for flowers of different colors and forms, such as "Jesus Christ the same yesterday, and today, and for ever" (Hebrews 13:8), for "all Evergreens" (4). In the preface the publishers explain that all the profits for this book are dedicated to charitable purposes, especially an infant school.

The only examples of religion-oriented languages of flowers following the traditional form that I have found are the work of two late-century clergymen, an English churchman and an American Catholic priest. The American book, *The Floral Apostles; or, What the Flowers Say to Thinking Man* by Rev. Andrew Ambauen, professor in St. Thomas's Seminary, St. Paul, Minnesota, appeared first, in 1892. In a preface written by Rev. Edward Fitzpatrick, we find this justification for another book on flowers:

> *Still, in those evidently well-meant essays, with many things good and true and ingenious, with many critically acute and recondite observations, there will be found, unhappily, strong suspicions of sheer naturalism,*
(xviii) *gairish [sic] worldliness, exaggerated sentimentality, gushing emotionalism, and of a tendency, little disguised, to cater to the merely sensuous—if not precisely sensual—element in our being: defects that are unworthy of so high a theme and, by their equivocal consequences, most likely to cause failure of the object intended—and greatly desired.*

This work is arranged alphabetically by plants and contains an alphabetical listing at the back, but no cross-index from meaning to plant. The columbine, for example, symbolizes anxiety, although Ambauen does not explain why. The content of the little essay on the columbine is a sermon on not being anxious but on trusting to God (50). More obvious is the meaning of *Coronilla,* the phrase "May success crown your wishes," relating to the crown shape of the flowers and the allusion to the crown in its name. The sermon, however, concerns the nature of true success, that found by those "willing to tread the rugged road of *self-denial and toil*" (52). The list of meanings contains many not found in a traditional list, even a much-moralized one: "willingness ever to begin again, and early"; "remembrance of the dead"; "fidelity to divine grace"; and "the ever-blessed Virgin-Mother of Christ." Some of the meanings are obviously derivative of conventional lists, but the whole set of meanings had been worked over to produce proper meanings and a number of little sermon topics.

The Bible Language of Flowers, published in 1894 by Marcus Ward, is possibly the work of a person whom I have not been able to further identify, Rev. Canon Bramald, whose name is attached to the preface but does not appear on the title page. In that preface he writes, "And thus the old familiar language of flowers may be translated into a higher and more divine language, and may tell us the story of the love of God with all its kindred lessons" (n.p.). This list is much more related to the traditional lists than is Ambauen's work. The text of the book is arranged alphabetically by plants, and gives only the meaning and a Bible verse, with no sermons or explanations of any kind. Many of the meanings are the standard ones from the basic nineteenth-century continental lists, including cabbage (profit). The work is printed in a two column per page format and has illustrations around the pages as was common at that period. The illustrations appear to be photographs, although I really am not sure that they are. Naturally, the Bible verse relates to the meaning of the flower. Thus, amaryllis, symbolizing pride, is assigned Proverbs 16:18, "Pride goeth before destruction, and an haughty spirit before a fall" (2). I wonder if this effort was related to the work of the Bible Flower Missions; however, there is no mention of that in the preface.

It is interesting to consider that these attempts to create a religious language of flowers came so late in the century. My guess is that it was not attempted before because the traditional list was such a standard part of popular culture. Of course, another possible reason is that the concept of the language of flowers carried with it notions of love and romance and was thus unsuitable for religious teachings. Later in the century the language of flowers was a quaint, remote notion which perhaps could safely be remodeled along acceptable lines. Certainly, the middle years of the century saw many publications that brought together flowers and religion, but the language of flower format was not used, although writers commented on the term and criticized it.[7]

There is one unusual variety title in the language of flowers that calls for special mention, although it hardly had a mass appeal. The fact that it appeared at all, however, testifies to the popularity of the language of flowers in America in mid-century. Pliny Miles, an expert on memory improvement and author of *American Mnemotechny, or Art of Memory,* brought out a book on how to memorize the meanings of flowers: *The Sentiments of Flowers in Rhyme; or, The Poetry of Flowers Learned by Mnemotechnic Rules* (1848). In his introduction Miles explains that his work will be more useful than most language of flower books, because it not only lists flowers and their meanings but also explains how to remember the meanings (see Figure 12). He claims that the reason we find it so hard to remember flower meanings is the apparent lack of reason for the meaning. Thus, he has remedied the situation using the best mnemotechnic rules, mainly what he calls a "homophonic analogy," in which a "like sounding phrase" is associated with the flower name and also the meaning. (Ironically, this is very close to the *sélam* as explained by Hammer-Purgstall.) Most of the text of the book consists of these formulas. Some examples are shown in Table 4. This "practical" book also has the traditional pages of flower poetry and the cross-indexes of meanings.

The inclusion of the language of flowers in everyday life, at least in theory, led to its use in advertising. I have seen several advertising pamphlets, dating from later in the century, which mix advertisement with language of flower material. One, an ad for Woodward's Standard Preparations, is a very thin pamphlet titled *The Ladies' Floral Calendar* and contains a dial of flowers, a language of flower dictionary, and a few recipes along with ads. Another, from Walton, Hassell and Port Supply Stores, London, advertises Beecham's Pills with a floral vocabulary and a bit of verse. The language of flowers also found itself used, along with appropriate decoration, on various sorts of stationery goods such as postcards and paper fans.[8]

This mundane application of the "universal language of love" is underlined by its inclusion in general books on etiquette, domestic concerns, and the crafts. One French title, Auguste Debay's *Les parfums et les fleurs* (1861) sets exposition of the language of flowers in a work on perfumes and cosmetics. Another, *La fleuriste des salons* (n.d.) sandwiches the floral language between material on making artificial flowers and basic gardening for women. *The Emblematical Garden* (n.d.) by a Lady, published in Dublin, is a very small and brief exposition of the language "By the author of *The Indispensable Requisites for Dandies of Both Sexes.*" The American middle-class wife, rather than the dandy, of either sex, is the audience intended for *The American Lady's Everyday Handbook* (1847), a

Fig. 12. Pliny Miles, *The Sentiments of Flowers in Rhyme; or, The Poetry of Flowers Learned by Mnemotechnic Rules.* (Courtesy of the A. and E. Rudolph Collection, Ohio State University Libraries)

Table 4. Examples from Miles's *The Sentiments of Flowers in Rhyme*

Rosey cash,	enables one to dress with
Rose Acacia	Elegance
John Jacob Aster	is famed for his
China Aster	Love of Variety
A Sinking Fund	is about as good protection, as
Cinquefoil	Parental Love

work which includes sections on letter writing, the language of flowers, dream interpretation, and a cookbook featuring meat cookery. I have seen many other such inclusions of the language of flowers in similar general works, including, of course, the routine use in gift annuals.

The gift annuals published a lot of flower poetry, and poetry about flowers was a commonplace of the age. Naturally, there were some poems about the language of flowers. Leigh Hunt's "Love Letters Made of Flowers" is one of the most often quoted, as is Park Benjamin's sonnet, "Flowers Love's Truest Language," part of which appears as the epigraph to the next chapter. The first verse of James Gates Percival's "The Language of Flowers" is frequently quoted in language of flower books:

> In Eastern lands they talk in flowers,
> And they tell in a garland their loves and cares;
> Each blossom that blooms in their garden bowers,
> On its leaves a mystic language bears.

(Griffin 14)

The rest of the poem gives the meanings of some of the most popular flowers—the rose, myrtle, lily, bay, violet, evergreen, cypress, and forget-me-not. Elizabeth Barrett Browning mentions the language in a long poem, "A Flower in a Letter:"

> Love's language may be talked with these;
> To work out choicest sentences,
> No blossoms can me meeter;
> And, such being used in Eastern bowers,
> Young maids may wonder if the flowers
> Or meanings be the sweeter.

(166)

Catharine Esling, the American poet, wrote a long poem on the language as an introduction to her popular language of flower book, *Flora's Lexicon,* which orients the language more toward God's efforts to communicate with us than to Eastern customs:

(11)

> Yes—flowers have tones—God gave to each
>   A language of its own,
> And bade the simple blossom teach
>   Where'er its seeds are sown;

All of these poems treat the subject lightly yet favorably. However, Lydia Sigourney, the prolific Connecticut poet, who published an entire volume of flower poems, *The Voice of Flowers,* used the language in a somewhat sarcastic poem, "He Told His Love in Flowers." The young man of the title gave the girl various flowers that speak of love—the forget-me-not, the rose geranium, the hawthorn, and the moss rose—and she answered him with a white rosebud, meaning "Too young—too young to love." But he persisted with other flowers of love—the myrtle, the damask rose, the everlasting sweet pea, the laurel leaf, the primrose, and the amaranth, expressing his eternal love and devotion. She answered these with a French marigold—jealousy, "For over his vaunted love/ Suspicion's mood had power." (These meanings are from Wirt's *Flora's Dictionary.*) The young man left her, "sail'd o'er the faithless sea," ending the love affair: "So it faded away, that fickle love, / Like its alphabet of flowers" (9–11).

Despite these few poems, an anonymous verse which appeared in William Robinson's periodical *The Garden* for January 25, 1873, expresses what is probably the truth about the use of the language:

(72)

> "Teach thee their language? Sweet, I know no tongue,
>   No mystic art those gentle things declare;
> I ne'er could trace the schoolman's trick among
>   Created things so delicate and rare."

For all of this brings up a question which cannot be answered: how much did nineteenth-century people actually use the language of flowers. Some modern commentators on the topic, having seen a few books, assume that the books mean that people actually used flowers to communicate; and thus they write accordingly, with great authority, that "In Victorian times, when a gentleman wanted to send a lady a message, he frequently did so using the language of flowers." It seems to me that these commentators are as mistaken about the language of flowers as Mottraye and Lady Mary were about the *sélam,* for the language of flowers appears to be, just as was the *sélam,* merely an amusement for the genteel sex.

The fact is, I have not been able to document much actual use. One suspicious circumstance is the virtual absence of the idea from popular fiction, which would indicate that the language of flowers stayed in the pages of the presentation books. Lesley Gordon reproduces a painting, entitled *The Language of Flowers* (1885) in her book *Green Magic*. Painted by G. D. Leslie, it shows two young women with a basket of flowers, looking up the meanings, presumably, in a volume the size of a family Bible. I have found two references to the language in popular literature, one in an anonymous novel, *The Western Side; or Lights and Shadows of a Western Parish,* published in 1853 by the American Baptist Publication Society. In this book the minister's fiancée arranges some flowers to tell him her sentiments about leaving the East for a parish in "the wilds of Michigan." Her aunt advises that he won't get the message, but she is wrong, for "they had often exchanged epistles of this kind." Her arrangement of arborvitae, single China asters, and white chrysanthemums tells him that she is willing to brave the frontier with him.

In a different perspective on the floral language, William Fowle, a comic writer, ridicules it in his skit, "The School Committee." In the skit a candidate for a teaching post, an advocate of using older children or monitors to teach the younger children, is interviewed by one sensible woman, Mrs. Vestry, the minister's wife, and seven silly women. One of them, Miss Prim, asks Miss Fairman if she had ever studied botany:

> Miss Prim. *Did you study the philosophical part of the science, which treats of the loves and the language of plants?*
> Miss Fairman. *No, madam, I have only studied their structure and their uses.*
> Miss Prim. *I supposed you had neglected the only* ethereal *part of the science. This comes of your new-fangled* system, *I suppose.*
> Miss Fairman. *No, indeed, madam. Nonsense can be taught by the monitorial plan as well as by any other.*

(261)

These two examples, though, are hardly indicative of whether or not the language of flowers was much used.

Another source of evidence is autobiographical work, letters, and similar items. Again I have found little. Most of what contemporary documentation I have is from penciled notes in margins of books. One interesting example is the Penniman Herbarium, a collection of plants made by Fanny and Adelia Penniman, a mother and daughter pair. Fanny Penniman had previously been married to Ethan Allan. The herbarium, now housed at the University of Vermont, shows meanings of flowers written in beside the botanical descriptions. I have been unable to locate the exact source of these meanings, but they are very similar to Wirt's.[9] Of course, this does not tell us anything about the actual use of the language.

As I have examined many language of flower books, I have found a few which indicate some use. Several times I have seen names written in beside characteristics in vocabulary lists. In the copy of *Floral Poesy* (n.d.) owned by the Hunt Institute, someone penciled in "all beyond me" beside an explanation of the technicalities of the language. The Library of Congress copy of *The American Lady's Everyday Handbook* has further evidence of confusion; the owner has written, "Jan. 22nd, 1856, received a small bouquet of delicate flowers, pressed, Spruce, Daisy, Gilliflower & Aster." Then in the dictionary margin, she/he has marked the meanings: "hope in adversity," "innocence," "lasting beauty," and "variety." Perhaps the confusion is all mine, but I cannot decipher the message.

Throughout my presentation of the language of flowers, I have stressed its nature as a consumer phenomenon, something with only tenuous ties to real lives. Nineteenth-century people were very fond of flowers, but it does not appear that they tried to use the floral language very much. For one thing, there was no one standard of meaning; for another, its practicality was limited, at least with fresh flowers, as everything is not in bloom all the time. And, frankly, I suspect that most men were not especially attracted to the idea. Human nature does not change that much in 100 years.

The Twentieth Century

As the new century began, in the popular mind the nineteenth century joined all the rest of the past in that truly lost world where all the people were simple-minded yet safe enough, because it had been a golden age; the language of flowers became a feature of this wonderfully quaint past. Early in the century, references to the language survive in the reminiscences of older people, but some historical distance can be seen in Maurice Ravel's ballet, *Adélaide ou le langage des fleurs,* written and first performed in 1911. The narrative concerns a courtesan who communicates her feelings with flowers, and two lovers, a young man and a rich old nobleman, who also understand the art of the floral language. The ballet is a period piece, set in the period of 1820, and the story line obviously recalls *La dame aux camellias,* albeit with a happier ending (Goss 160–62).

In recent years there have been many reprints of language of flower books produced for the scholar and the general public as well. None of these have been as popular as Edith Holden's *The Country Diary of an Edwardian Lady,* although the Kate Greenaway volume is seen everywhere. Modern florists are interested in the idea of a floral language, and references to it can be seen in their advertisements. Of course, in these references the point of view is that there is one set of meanings for flowers, which everyone knew in the past. I have been interviewed on the radio several times about the language of flowers, and each time I have spent most of my time explaining that there was no one set of meanings for the flowers and the language of flowers was not a universally practiced method of communication in the good old quaint days of yore. The interviewer in each case was not only disappointed but certain that I did not really know what I was talking about after all.

VI

Love's Truest Language: Readings in the Language of Flowers

Flowers are love's truest language; they betray,
*   Like the divining rods of Magi old,*
Where priceless wealth lies buried, not of gold,
*   But love, strong love, that never can decay.*

(Park Benjamin, "Flowers Love's Truest Language": Griffin 129)

THE FACT THAT communicating in the language of flowers was not an everyday skill in the nineteenth century does not mean that it has nothing to tell us about the period. Since the language of flowers is an artistic construct, a fantasy game created as a romantic gift, it is perhaps more analyzable than otherwise, more open to interpretation uninfluenced by any real-life complications. One of my objectives in studying the language of flowers has been to discover what it communicates about the cultures that produced it. In fact, my task has been easier because there are different versions; this situation helps us to identify the central topic of the discourse. The changes that were made as the language of flowers migrated from France to England to America are instructive also of cultural differences that transcend the idea of a floral "alphabet of love."

My comparative analysis of the language of flowers in all three cultures, while based on studies of many books, is best presented by focusing on one major text from each country. Latour's *Le langage des fleurs* is the obvious choice from France, of course, and the American choice was equally easy—the early and influential work by Wirt, *Flora's Dictionary.* But the English choice was difficult, for the early book similar in popularity and precedence was Shoberl's *The Language of Flowers; With Illustrative Poetry,* but this is mainly a reworking of Latour. Since I wanted something more original for this study, I decided on Phillips's *Floral Emblems,* as comparable in date and completeness to Latour and Wirt. However, I have supplemented the Phillips material with study of Shoberl also, to give a reading of British material similar to the French and American in audience appeal.

While these three books have been mentioned many times already, before I begin my analysis I need to describe the structure of each one. The different structures immediately show different attitudes toward the audience: Latour is plainly first and foremost a handbook of the language of romance, but Phillips is addressing those who might use floral emblems in artistic work, while Wirt couches her Flora on a solid bedrock of botany. Latour (and for this reading I am using the fuller edition that perhaps did not appear until the 1830s) organizes the material this way:

> *Preface setting the tone;*
>
> *Flowers and their meanings explained, with added material such as poems and legends, organized not alphabetically but by months in which the flowers bloom;*
>
> *An alphabetical list of meanings and plants cross-indexed to the previous section, but adding many more meanings with brief explanations called "Dictionnaire du langage des fleurs avec l'origine de leurs significations pour écrire un billet ou composer un sélam" (Dictionary of the Language of Flowers with the Origins of Their Meanings in Order to Write a Letter or Compose a Sélam); and*
>
> *An alphabetical list by plant names, giving the meaning, called "Dictionnaire des plantes avec leurs emblèmes pour traduire un billet ou un sélam" (Dictionary of Plants with Their Emblems in Order to Translate a Letter or a Sélam).*

Phillips sets out his material as follows:

> *Preface on how he selected the material;*
>
> *Some French poems on the language of flowers;*
>
> *Introduction on the history of floral symbolism;*
>
> *Leaflet numbers (how to depict numbers with leaves);*
>
> *Emblematical leaves for each day of the week;*
>
> *Emblems for the calendar months;*
>
> *Floral emblems: an alphabetical list of meanings giving the emblematical flower and explanation; and*
>
> *Index, alphabetical by plant with page references rather than meanings.*

Wirt organizes her material in the following manner:

> *Preface on creating the texts;*
>
> *Botanical information in two sections, "Structure of Plants" and "Flowers," including a biography of Linnaeus;*

"Flora's Dictionary," an alphabetical list of flowers giving meanings and some verses relating to the meanings;

Notes presented alphabetically by flower, giving all sorts of information, sometimes including an explanation of meaning and a verse mentioning the flower;

Botanical information in two sections, "Explanation of Botanical Terms Used in Flora's Dictionary" and "Glossary";

Dedication of flowers—a flower for every day of the year with a few explanations (using Roman Catholic saints);

Botanical information and explanation of meanings of Latin terms such as lutea; *and*

Index: an alphabetical list of meanings for the flowers.

Both Latour and Phillips feature the explanation of the meaning in the main part of their text, but Wirt relegates it to the notes, along with all other material except snatches of verse. The Wirt arrangement is somewhat complicated, but manages a separation of the more romantic aspects of the language from the learned, whether scientific or historical. Thus, the arrangement of her text acknowledges the recognizably separate appeals of the material—the romantic, including the emblems themselves and poetry; the scientific, the botanical information; and the historic, including explanations of allusions that create the meaning pair. Phillips, however, unselfconsciously mingles appeal to artisans with the romantic material, as we have seen in the previous chapter. Many editions of Wirt also reinforce the genteel aspect of the book by interleaving blank sheets of pastel-colored paper similar to that in albums—pink, blue, and yellow—between the pages of "Flora's Dictionary," thus inviting the owner to write in it or press flowers. Some editions have fine illustrations (see Figure 13). The pages of Wirt are never numbered, at least in the editions I have examined, and the entries are often out of alphabetical order. The book, which is large in size, gives the appearance of an amateur effort in this lack of pagination and the interleaving, while in fact it is a sophisticated handling of the material.

Since the language of flowers is set up as a "language," with dictionaries and vocabularies, as well as a grammar, I turned to the language-based analytic techniques of semiotics for help in "reading" the texts; I designed a method of textual analysis using Latour, which has been published in *Semiotica,* and then used the same methods to analyze the other books. However, my results do not need to be presented along with

Fig. 13. Elizabeth Gamble Wirt, *Flora's Dictionary*. Baltimore: Fielding Lucas, Jr., 1835. (Courtesy of the Hunt Institute for Botanical Documentation, Carnegie Mellon University, Pittsburgh, PA.)

the critical apparatus used to reach them; I have torn away the framing structure of semiotics to broaden access to my material.[1]

The Alphabet of Love

One of the most common metaphors to indicate the symbolic value of flowers in love and romance is that flowers are "the alphabet of love." The notion is not rigorously carried out, each flower standing for one letter of our alphabet (except in some cumbersome and minor systems of floral communication mentioned briefly in previous chapters). Instead, individual flowers indicate words or even whole phrases. However, when speaking generally of the language of flowers, writers often liked to think of flowers as elemental bits of communication, as basic as letters of the alphabet. The historical background of this way of thinking can be discovered from reading some of the more pretentious introductions to language of flower books, as we have seen in chapter three. As I explained in the first part of that chapter, writers implied that the meanings were simply gathered from "nature," whereas, of course, they were created in various ways, all of which relate to other texts. But since they liked to show that nature provides the elements of the language, it might be interesting to discover what group of plants and flowers was chosen to form the vocabulary list of flowers.

The most common plants are annual and perennial flowers, native wildflowers, flowering shrubs, and trees, with significant numbers of vines and bulbs. Most plants are those grown in gardens or native to the country, the major exotic plants being those famous in legend such as the myrtle or the lotus. But, of course, the three lists are not identical. Phillips and Wirt both added and subtracted plant names at will, either because they wanted to include a plant or because they wanted a certain meaning and had to find a plant to correspond. Phillips's added plants do not reveal a pattern, at least to me, but Wirt's show a background of Southern gardens in the early years of the United States. Jasmine, camellia, azalea, and gardenia appear, along with many variations on the rose—daily rose, damask rose, deep red rose, red rosebud, and others. There are some native American wildflowers such as houstonia and goldenrod, along with several varieties of geraniums (pelargonium): apple, fish, ivy, nutmeg, oak, rose, and silver-leaved.

Another important point is that not all plant names are names of flowers. All three lists include trees, such as the oak, as well as more historically symbolic trees such as laurel. Vegetables, grains, and wild plants like the thistle and the burdock are very useful as carriers of meaning, and they also appear. Actually, the three lists are made up of plant names that would be familiar to persons in that culture, taking into account familiarity with both garden and wild plants. Although sometimes poets and commentators on the language of flowers write as if all the emblematic plants were growing in "Flora's parterre" or some such location, there is no sense of location or landscape in the plant list. Water lilies "grow" next to pumpkins, broom and marsh mallows are neighbors, and roses and lilies are jostled by turnips and wild grapes. I would find it difficult to comment on popular garden plants of the time based on such lists, for while there is obviously some relationship, the addition of plants from other lists and the necessity for finding suitable emblems dominate the list-making. Nor is the practicality of communicating in the language of flowers a concern in the choice of plant names, for there is no attempt to arrange for the differences in bloom time or the impracticality of using the emblematic plant. Thus, it seems that the plant names appearing in the lists were not chosen following any particular structural concept, but are a hodgepodge of plant names which can be made to appear emblematic. In contrast to the flowers popular in poetry, we find that the set of plant names chosen for the language of flowers is much less concerned with romantic overtones and pretty appearance and more concerned with some reason that the flower can be assigned a meaning.

Flora's Dictionary

We know from the history of floral symbolism presented in chapter three that the creators of the language of flowers in the nineteenth century, having only a few traditional meanings to work with, had to devise their own list of floral emblems, assigning meanings on some kind of basis. As we have seen, they freely copied from one another, yet at some point all of the early compilers had to originate new material. Since almost all the important early creators—Lucot, Latour, and Phillips—felt it necessary to explain the appropriateness of each emblem, it is easy for us to study their processes.

In his paper "Two Aspects of Language and Two Types of Aphasic Disturbances," Roman Jakobson commented that metaphor is more typical of the romantic period than metonymy, and I have indeed found that the majority of the dictionary pairs are made on the basis of metaphor rather than metonymy (92). But there are many metonymic pairings as well. Most of the meanings are based on some quality of the plant, finding a similarity between its emblem and some aspect of the plant itself, such as color, odor, shape, growth habits, or some other circumstance relating to

Table 5. Metaphoric and metonymic bases for floral symbols

Metaphor	
Qualities of the plant	Color, odor, shape, growth habit, natural habitat
Metonymy	
Tradition	Classical legends, major emblematic flowers (lily, rose, violet)
Use	Food, medicine, other
Allusion	Plant name, story or anecdote, quotation from literature

the plant. Many of the other meanings are assigned on the basis of tradition, use, or allusion, most of these metonymic in character. Table 5 illustrates this in more detail. While there are perhaps a few meaning pairs which do not fit one of these categories, most of them do so.

This group of fabricators was very creative in finding meaning in the qualities of plants, but they followed two very traditional guidelines with regard to color and odor. There was an established set of color meanings which these early creators acknowledged in their material, and which later editors incorporated directly as part of their books, under such headings as "The Symbolism of Colors." The sources of these color meanings are not easily traceable, of course, but relate to heraldry and religious symbolism of the Middle Ages. Table 6 summarizes the color symbolism used in the creation of flower emblems, drawn from a number of books. There is nothing startling to modern readers in these color meanings except perhaps the connotation of yellow, normally associated with a special case of infidelity, cowardice, in our day—but the meaning is still unfavorable. The author seeking emblematic meaning in a flower could count on the color carrying the above connotations, and indeed if he were seeking a flower to represent a meaning, as I strongly suspect was often done, color could help structure his search. The color symbolism is especially present in the assignment of meanings to different colored roses, as the strength of passion and love seems to diminish as one goes from red to pink to white. The yellow rose, of course, represents infidelity, aided by its lack of scent as well as its color (Latour 177).

A flower's scent—invisible yet real—has long been a standard emblem of the human soul. Thus, the presence or absence of scent in a flower usually determined whether or not it represented a favorable human

Table 6. Color symbolism used in the creation of flower emblems

Red	Love, Passion, Shame
Yellow	Infidelity and other unfavorable qualities
Green	Hope
Blue	Elevated spiritual qualities (color of heaven)
Purple	Power, Royalty
White	Purity, Innocence, Candor
Black	Death, Sadness, Mourning

quality. Flowers that are unusually beautiful but without scent, such as the dahlia and the camellia, seldom represent good aspects of human beings, while flowers of beautiful odor but insignificant appearance usually carry highly moralistic emblems. Thus, in the Latour vocabulary the mignonette means, "Your qualities surpass your charms." (Of course, it can be argued that a young person in love does not want to hear that.)

Most of the metaphoric significations, however, while they use the language of colors and the distinction of scent, are more complex. Usually, the meanings in Lucot/Latour relate to other aspects of plants—many times the plant's habit of growth—and the same is true of Phillips. For example, burdock is the emblem of importunity, because it is very difficult to eradicate from the land and because its seed capsules stick to one's clothing. The cinquefoil represents a cherished daughter, because when it rains, the leaves of the plant fold over the flowers to protect them from the drops of rain. The cherry tree represents a good education, because of the fine fruit created by plant selection and breeding. The orange tree is a fit emblem of generosity because it is in blossom and fruit at the same time. Significations like these indicate that at least some of these principal fabricators of the language were well acquainted with plant life.

Some of the metonymic pairings are based on traditional meanings—such as the rose with love and beauty—because it was always associated with Venus, or the hyacinth being made emblematic of a game because it was while playing a game that Hyacinthus met his death and was changed into the flower. Most of the classical metamorphic myths are utilized in these significations, the most obvious one being Narcissus, always made to represent egoism or self-love. Laurel of course means glory, because of the meaning of the laurel wreath in ancient times, and these writers found the association of meaning with wreaths and garlands in Greece and Rome a fruitful source of other meanings, such as parsley, "festivity." For some reason, perhaps the lack of a classical education, Phillips wondered why the linden tree was usually made the emblem of conjugal fidelity, when, of course, it is taken from the legend of Baucis and Philemon being changed into a linden tree and an oak. Latour even mentions the name of Baucis in her explanation of the meaning (which is conjugal love, rather than Phillips's conjugal fidelity, a typical change between the French and the English). At any rate, most of the creators of the language of flower dictionaries used the associations of flowers with classical mythology as a common source of meanings.

Such meanings are not always obvious, though, as can be seen in the case of the sunflower. The legend of Clytie, who was changed into a flower which follows the sun in his courses, specifies a purple flower, which some have thought was the heliotrope. But neither the heliotrope nor the sunflower actually turn with the sun much more than most plants do (Heiser). The sunflower, an American import, was so named because it looks like the sun. Thus, the makers of floral emblems were at a loss as to the exact plant (at least those who knew what the horticultural facts were). This confusion spills over into the area of meanings. Many writers assign a favorable meaning to the sunflower, based on its faithfulness to the sun god, while others give it an unfavorable meaning, as a flatterer. Latour was aware that the sunflower is not the flower mentioned in the Greek myth, and assigns to it an unfavorable meaning, "false riches," because it is a false form of gold. The heliotrope does not have a meaning assigned on the basis of the myth either, but is given the emblem "intoxication; I love you," on the basis of its powerful odor. However, Lucot, in an odd reading of the myth, makes the sunflower represent a courtesan and inconstancy, while his heliotrope simply symbolizes inclination. Phillips picks up the Latour meanings in their entirety; and Wirt, despite a learned discussion of the difference between the heliotrope and the sunflower in her notes, assigns both plants meanings related to the myth, making heliotrope represent devotion and the dwarf sunflower "your devout adorer." The tall sunflower, however, means pride or haughtiness in her vocabulary.

Historical figures as well as the principals in classical myths were used in the making of floral emblems based on associations. Thus Phillips makes broom the emblem of humility, rather than the more usual "neatness," because the earl of Anjou, founder of the Plantagenet family, wore a sprig of broom in his cap while on a penitential pilgrimage to the Holy Land. Here the association of the plant with this first Plantagenet creates the meaning rather than its everyday use. Modern historical figures are not as popular as ancient ones, however, and it is interesting that few figures from religious history appear.

Another way in which flowers were associated with human beings is by their use, which is also metonymical. Anchusa or bugloss represents falsehood because it is a principal ingredient in rouge. Achillea is the emblem of war because it was frequently used to heal wounds. Generally, plants of use to humanity are given good connotations, while those useless or even harmful are given bad connotations. Poisonous plants such as the datura (deceitful charms) are usually emblems of unpleasant, dangerous, or evil things. Phillips makes the purple rhododendron the emblem of danger because "these purple flowers abound in a poisonous honey, and have hence been made emblematical of the dangers that lurk about the imperial purple" (106), a meaning which brings together use and color symbolism.

Allusions are frequently used as a basis for the assignment of an emblem. One type is that based on the plant name itself. The French name for the calendula or marigold, *souci,* means care, and thus the emblem assigned that flower by Latour is chagrin or pain. Since the *Asclepias* (swallow-wort) was named for Aesculapius, god of medicine, this plant seems to be the proper emblem for medicine, according to Phillips. And since the *Rudbeckia* (coneflower) is named after botanist Olans Rudbeck, thus doing justice to his work, Phillips assigns it the meaning of justice.

Often the allusion is to a quotation from a literary source, the most famous example of which is the assignment of "happy memories" to the periwinkle, based on a passage in Rousseau. Sometimes the author tells a story or anecdote which involves the flower in some way, and thus the flower takes its meaning from such an association. An example of this is the emotional anecdote of childhood given by Latour in assigning happiness to, of all plants, artemisia, because during childhood her governess gave her a garland of the plant as a token of good luck. While she goes on in her explanation to give other information about the plant, she allows personal memory to dominate, as we see in her address to the plant: "I will ignore that the wisemen of antiquity and the doctors of our day occupy themselves with your healthy virtues; but that vain erudition has added nothing to my recognition. If sometimes, wandering in the countryside, I meet you, my heart beats, my eyes moisten with tears; I immediately dream of my happy childhood, of the bonfires of St. John's eve, of my poor nurse, of the chains of flowers on which she hung my youthful destinies" (58). One's faith in the sincerity of this story is somewhat shaken by the discovery that Lucot had also made artemisia the emblem of happiness, based on a common folk saying.

While I have taken space giving examples of the metonymic assignments of meanings, I should repeat that the metaphoric meanings predominate. The fact that metaphoric meanings were common helped create the notion that flowers practically wrote their own meanings. The color and scent of the rose, the stature of the lily, and the obviously unpleasant qualities of the thistle do seem to speak a universal language, but only until one actually sits down to compile such a language. Then invention has to take over, and the ingenuity of these pairings admirably betrays the hopeful notion that the meanings were just out there, waiting to be written down. One commentator, François Fertiault, went so far as to call this creation of a floral language a new mythology—"cette moderne mythologie des fleurs"—which underscores the motivation of so many similar remarks (185). For, as Barthes has shown, one of the features of myth is that it "transforms history into nature as if the signifier gave a foundation to the signified" (*Mythologies* 129–30). Thus, to think that the flower emblems are "natural" is to think that the social values outlined in the set of meanings are validated by nature.

Love Defined

We have seen that the language of flowers was controlled not so much by the flowers themselves—either their natures or past emblematic meanings—as by the vocabulary needed to conduct a love affair. Since the language of flowers is the language of love, the flower meanings chosen can sketch out some of the culture's ideas about love and romance. Thus, we can use the lists of meanings to identify some of these ideas. This cannot be a precise analysis, of course, given the nature of the material, but I have found the results very interesting.

In all three texts most of the meanings are nouns—sadness, impatience, belief, youth, refusal, love, or hatred—along with a number of modified nouns—humble and unhappy love, youthful love, or pensive beauty. There are no adjectives or adverbs in the Latour list, and only a few in Wirt and Phillips. Wirt has five verbs, while the other lists show none. One of the biggest differences in the vocabularies concerns the number of complete statements: thirty-one in Latour, nineteen in Phillips, and thirty-eight in Wirt. These are all, except one, either "I" (*je*) or "you" (*vous*) statements: "we will die together" (Latour) is the exception. In Phillips and Latour the "you" statements predominate, but in Wirt there are far more "I" statements. From this we can see that both Latour and Wirt were more concerned with the language of flowers being a medium of communication than was Phillips, for it is far easier to communicate with flowers if a single bloom signifies an entire statement.

Most of the meanings, whether nouns or complete statements, can be classified into three major groups: personal qualities, states of mind, and situations or aspects of life, most relating to romance. Of course, there are some meanings that do not fit these categories exactly and some meanings that could belong to two categories, but this classification system has proven reasonably suitable. The personal qualities include all the most obvious for the situations—beauty, charm, delicacy, pride, and infidelity, negatives as well as positives, with the emphasis on describing the typical female rather than the male. Most of the states of mind contained in these vocabularies relate to the love affair, such as bashful, shame, hope, suspicion, and gratitude. However, the situations are not only those related to the love affair, such as absence, widowhood, youth, but also some that probably only appear there because they are traditional emblems, such as poetry, the arts, and architecture.

Each separate set of meanings can be regarded as a model of the love affair; a dialogue without speakers, it sketches a generalized romance according to relevant cultural codes. To introduce this analysis, I would like to briefly discuss an interesting test case, the floral emblems in Rafinesque's "School of Flora." This is the only set of emblems that are almost certain to have been chosen by the creator of the list, Rafinesque himself, without a lot of journalistic consultation of other texts, indeed probably quite casually; and this is the only set of floral emblems in which I know something about the romantic life of its creator. There are only sixty-six emblem pairs in Rafinesque's work, making this a very compact language to work with.

In choosing his emblems, Rafinesque ignored popular meanings and included only two relatively ordinary ones, the moss rose (female beauty) and the ivy (friendship). He made an effort to explain the origins of some of his meanings, usually related to qualities of the plants, thus fitting the general picture of these in other texts. The division of the material into personal qualities, states of mind, and situations fits his work also. But there is one big difference between his list of meanings and those in the other texts: his meanings are overwhelmingly negative. Normally, positive-negative classification is just one that we make when we study a full floral vocabulary, but in Rafinesque it overwhelmed any other analysis. It is clear that, in Rafinesque's unselfconscious little vocabulary of the love affair, he clearly needed more negative emblems than are usual.

Out of sixty-six meanings, forty-two are negative, and of the remaining twenty-four positive meanings, many are not especially related to love: industry, gratefulness, strength, wealth, vernal delight, safety, practical philosophy, utility, thrifty and wary state, cordiality, good sense, and favorable opportunity. In fact, many of these seem quite commercial in meaning, a reflection of Rafinesque's strong commercial bent. There are only twelve positive romantic meanings, several related to female appearance, such as splendid and gorgeous beauty; an emblem for manly beauty; and several relating to good feelings, such as friendship, fidelity, and hope and remembrance. The many negative emblems give us a rather cloak-and-dagger image of the love affair. The words characterizing the relationship between the lovers tell us a story of betrayal and disappointment. These emblems, which I have arranged in a narrative form, tell a story: illusion and delusion; perplexity; caution; secrecy; vigilance; night beacons; nocturnal vigilance; difficulty; oddity and separation; deception and error; disgust (there are two plants with this meaning); ferocity; bitter reproof; war; and bitter regret. Characterizing the "innocent party" in this tragedy of love are a few emblems: ignorant simplicity, forbidding and prohibition, dejection, broken heart, and madness. Characterizing the "guilty party" we find a large vocabulary: mutability; folly; frigidity; pride; avarice; false ornament; presumption; slender merit united to importunity; hypocrisy and disguised bad temper; sour temper (two plants for this); inconstancy and variable temper; irritable temper; peevish and crabbed temper; flirting love; sordid deceit; concealment or swiftness; false or double heart; and hatred and mischief.

We do not know all the details of Rafinesque's affairs with women, of course, but it is known that, while he lived in Sicily, he lived with Josephine Vaccaro, whom he could not legally marry because he was a Protestant.[2] After he came to America in 1815 (landing penniless after a shipwreck off Long Island), she left him for an actor, taking their children with her. In his poetry and his drawings of Lexington friends (often these had comments written on them), he was frequently very courtly and respectful toward women, but there are indications of a bad experience through his own major love affair (Weiss). One is a passage in his long poem *The World* (1836), in which he is picturing those bad women who make unhappy homes:

> But there also, if wicked temper comes
> In mood perverse, to drive the happy scene;
(195)   There may arise a hell of doleful woes.
> If rare, it happens still, and men made sore,
> Reject the ties of love, to hatred changed.

Rafinesque was quite probably "made sore" himself, a conjecture made rather more certain by some of his pictures of unidentified women that carry mottoes and some floral emblems. One of these, labeled "Juliet," is inscribed,

(Weiss 60–61)

> I knew her in the prime of her beauty and youth:
> When she was the chaste emblem of candor and truth.
> But alas! what a change!

Juliet is surrounded by weeping willow and bittersweet, obviously emblematic plants for her character. Another portrait, of "Dorotea V.," carries the characterization of "falseness and stupidity." On the other hand, many of his other portraits of women, often identifiable Lexington friends, carry pleasant mottoes and show pretty flowers around them. His wisdom can be summed up in this most unromantic of mottoes, from his "Ethics, or Moral Philosophy": "Women are like flowers, do not judge of either by mere sight: the lily and the garlic look alike at a distance" (17).

Rafinesque did not make his romantic affairs public, and they became known only in his will. Perhaps he considered himself an unusual case, for while there are the above-mentioned indications of his feelings, there are many passages of praise for the wonders of womanhood, too, in a vague and courtly manner. However that may be, his choice of a plant to represent true love tells a tale. It is *Paris quadrifolia,* a European plant of the trillium family, and he explains its signification based on the strength of the European folk custom of lovers presenting it to their beloved. However, as he also explains, we know the herb paris of folklore for quite another association—it is the traditional symbol of good luck, in our culture known as the four-leaved clover.

This sample reading indicates that the vocabulary choices can tell us something about the love affair as seen by the creator of the list, especially when the creator knows that the language of flowers is supposed to be the language of the love affair. Rafinesque plainly did, as his vocabulary—negative as it is—reveals. Lucot and Phillips, however, while they knew that such was the general structure of the vocabulary, tried to also make the list work for artistic and literary purposes. Thus, they created somewhat unfocused texts, which probably had something to do with their lack of success.

Turning to Latour, we might begin by looking at the set of qualities. The first thing that struck me as I studied the qualities considered important in such a vocabulary was that it includes very few describing physical appearance: beauty, durable beauty, capricious beauty, deceitful charms, and ornament. Furthermore, these words are very general. Today, I think we pay a great deal more attention to the details of physical appearance in romantic issues. Perhaps this relates to the fact that we are a much more visually oriented society; I have observed this phenomenon in nineteenth-century popular fiction as well—a lack of specific details concerning the appearance of the characters. The heroine is either beautiful or not, while the hero is usually "manly." But there is another explanation; this language, while concocted for the amusement of women, is meant for a man to vocalize. But he is to speak as the woman would want a man to speak: not about her looks but about her personal qualities. This notion is borne out by the number of the qualities that picture delicate, gentle, feminine attributes, such as naivety, timidity, modesty, and sensitiveness. About the same number of meanings describe positive characteristics that are stronger, such as grandeur, inspiration, and promptitude; and then again about the same number describe negative characteristics such as weakness, folly, or disdain. Many of the last two groups of qualities can be applied to males in the context of nineteenth-century society, but the majority of qualities are those describing women rather than men. Of course, the qualities do not have to be describing human beings—one can, after all, speak of a "weak plan" or "modest finances"—yet given the kinds of things done with the language in the floral games and the general advice as to communication, it is obvious that these are meant to be mainly used to describe people.

The nouns used to describe states of mind are about 60 percent positive. Some of them can be classified as positive and passionate, such as ardor, flame, desire, or enchantment, but most of the positive words describe less passionate states such as platonic love, harmony, and sweet memories. The negative words could be used to describe one's state of mind concerning the conduct of either the affair or the lover him/herself, such as war, hatred, distrust, suspicion. Statements, of course, can belong to any of these categories, and an example which fits the negatives is "you are cold."

The situations or aspects of life range from "dear daughter" to "wealth," and most could be useful in a lover's dialogue in which the situations of the pair were being discussed. Other words in this category might be used to set up assignations, such as "night." But situations comprise the smallest category of meanings, which not unexpectedly gives an overwhelmingly psychological aspect to the vocabulary. According to this vocabulary, the things that interest the lovers are their own inward states and those of their loved ones. Appearances, situations in life, and other such things are all secondary to this. Practical issues are not stressed. For instance, there is no easy way to propose marriage, and we are aware that love and marriage were not necessarily related in early nineteenth-century France. In its concentration on the spiritual aspects of passion, this vocabulary recalls the poetry of the troubadours and those other *jeux floraux* (floral games).

This version of the love affair, a psycho-spiritual state of mind with little reference to society or marriage, is predictable for the reader of *Paul et Virginie* or *La nouvelle Héloïse*. But in the form of a language of flowers vocabulary it seems so innocent, so harmless, that it is interesting to discover the care that English and American editors took to purify the language for their audience. It seems that the French attitudes toward love were clearly identified by these writers, and just as clearly disapproved of. Thus, for the English and American readers, the romantic visions of the language of flowers had to be refined.

An example which clearly shows the differences between the French approach to love and romance and that of the English and Americans can be seen in the language of flower game, *Oracles de Flore* by C. F. P. Del——— (1816), published in almanac form by Louis Janet. This game is much more complicated than those described in the previous chapter, and the fortunes are much different. While some of the passages attached to the various flowers in Mayo's *The Floral Fortune Teller,* as quoted, are not all sweetness and light, they do not compare to the romantic intrigue envisioned in the fortunes in *Oracles*.

The approach to the reading is fairly complex. The player makes up a bouquet of flowers from two plates showing flower names, never naming the flowers. However, the controller of the game can tell what each flower is because the plates are arranged so as to reveal each flower choice. Then, when the controller has the names of all the player's "secret flowers," she reads off the meaning of each flower and also offers a "fortune" connected with each one. For example, if one of the flowers is the jonquil, the controller would explain that the meaning of the jonquil is infidelity, and then read this little story: "A young country girl, having lived some time in the capital, returned home less virtuous than when she left. As soon as she returned to the village, she betrayed Big Colas, her husband, in favor of a young lover; and to let him know when she was available, this crafty villager attached a bouquet of jonquils to Colas's hat when he left the house—this was the signal for her lover." After this is read, the player is required to choose among five numbers, which are numbered fortunes. If he chooses Fortune 142, he would hear: "Your efforts to inspire confidence in the person you love best lead you to discover infidelities on your lover's part; the letters which you find cause you to despair; but some time after these fatal discoveries you will have proof that you have been imagining things and that your lover has been faithful and loves you exclusively, but you will pay dearly for your lover's pardon." Of course, all the numbered fortunes connected with the jonquil concern infidelity. All of the fortunes, however, not just those connected with such a meaning as infidelity, picture a clandestine, dramatically eventful love affair conducted among scheming rivals, gossiping friends, and censorious social arbiters, approving of love affairs but savoring the troubles others have in their pursuit of love. Even favorable meanings, such as "sincerity," are attached to fortunes pointing out problems: the sincere person is sincere to the point of rudeness, or else is too trusting of others' sincerity and is betrayed. It is clear from such readings that the sensible person in such a situation regards love as a game and is careful not to be seen to lose. Such a view of love and romance was repudiated almost totally by the English and American writers and editors.

Love Refined

In the previous chapter I quoted a number of remarks by English editors about their work in purifying the language of flowers for their audience. Their concern is seen in the different meanings assigned to flowers; the vocabulary of love, the set of flower emblems, was the target of their reforms.

Before looking at the language of flowers specifically, however, we should examine the attitudes of English and American middle-class readers to the French. Of course, French-English relations had been strained by the French Revolution and the Napoleonic Wars, but even in a politically safer Bourbon France there was much dangerous opinion. While such affairs occupied the writers in important literary and political journals in England, popular editors had to contend with the notion that the French were immoral. In America, too, while there had been considerable political sympathy between America and France, the French were widely viewed as immoral and irreligious.

French habits of courtship and marriage differed greatly from the English, and it appears that the French regarded the English practices as immoral as well, especially divorce and the freedom of young single women. This point is made especially well in Frances Trollope's travel book *Paris and the Parisians in 1835,* in which she contrasts the freedom of

English girls before marriage with the repression of French girls, and the social dominance of young married women in France compared to the domestic confinement of young married English women. However, Mrs. Trollope only alluded delicately to the issue of marital infidelity, which was openly discussed by an American traveler of the same year, John Sanderson. He was not particularly censorious, picturing the great surplus of French women who could not find husbands as a good reason for the numbers of *grisettes*. He also indicated, however, that married women were apt to offer payment with their favors rather frequently (209). Something that obviously scandalized many commentators was not so much the keeping of mistresses by men of good society, but the situation of married women openly taking lovers themselves. Naturally, then, English (and American) editors had to be careful that impurities should not enter the meaning list in their floral vocabularies.

More pertinent to the issue, though, was what might be called the issue of refinement, or delicacy. The French habit of frankness in conversation, especially about sexual matters, was a constant source of English comment. Trollope allowed that English conversation in the eighteenth century was just as bad, but plainly feels that the English are ahead of the normally refined and graceful French on this issue. She was a sophisticated older woman, however, and perhaps the feelings of Mary Browne, a fourteen-year-old English girl who visited France in 1821 with her family, is closer to the average attitude. Her diary reveals dislike of all things foreign and strange, with a consequent judgment in favor of English practices in all things. She is shocked at the continental Sunday, and remarks of a priest they observed performing a marriage ceremony, "he reminded us of the Inquisition and everything horrible" (105). A second-hand sighting, by one of the maids, prompted a direct remark on French crudeness: "The French do not seem to have *any* idea what delicacy is," she wrote, after telling what the maid saw, the bread baker "standing at the street door talking to some women with *nothing* on him but a *small* apron" (123). The same kind of remark is quoted by John Sanderson the American traveler, the source being a fellow American whom he was taking around the Tuileries. The many nude statues (not even aprons here) occasioned this "modest Yankee" to leave the gardens, remarking that "I don't think this is a decent place" (109). Sanderson, however, says that this is not really a typical American reaction in that Americans are much more open to foreign habits than other visitors. These remarks are quite typical of English and American views of the French.

While the English or American reader was used to regarding the

French male looking for an English bride with suspicion—a good example appears in Rev. Henry Kett's *Emily, a Moral Tale, Including Letters from a Father to His Daughter* (1807), the scheming Count de Malmaison—and was equally suspicious of French novels—which Louisa May Alcott characterizes, in *Rose in Bloom* (1876) as "French bonbons with the poisonous color on them"—there was still widespread admiration for the femininity and elegance of French women. The best picture of French genteel society during the period of the creation of the language of flowers seen from the English point of view (albeit that of a somewhat liberated observer) is that of Lady Sydney Morgan, in her *France* (1817). Her picture of this society is positive, and she sees the French recovering from a shockingly immoral period in the late eighteenth century, which she describes as "gangrening every social and moral relation of life" (1:103). She speaks of the position of genteel French women as "delectable" and finds Parisian society superior in refinement and taste to any society on earth. She praises the strength of friendship she finds in these French women, and says that, to them, love is "almost a *jeu d'enfant*" (1:194). However, she also acknowledges the common habit of marital infidelity, and she uses this to try to explain the different attitudes toward morality in the two cultures. Outward propriety especially among the young is extremely important, and certainly one must not make a public scandal. But discretion is all that is asked, and to appear proper is the goal. This is a situation which can be referred to as "the morality of convention," and it was considered to be at least hypocritical if not sinful by English and American observers.[3]

Thus, when Letitia Landon wrote from Paris to William Jerdan, one of her literary associates, proposing the translation of some French literary works for an annual, she wrote that they would have to be translated with *judgment*. "I underline judgment," she explained, "for not a little would be required" (Jerdan 3:201). She did not need to explain what kind of judgment was needed. Or, as Alcott put it in *Rose in Bloom*, in a dialogue between Rose and her uncle over French novels:

> *"Some phrases are untranslatable, and it only spoils them to try. They are not amiss in French, but sound coarse and bad in our blunt English," she said a little pettishly; for she felt annoyed by her failure to*
>
> (179)   *prove the contested point.*
>
> *"Ah, my dear! if the fine phrases won't bear putting into honest English, the thoughts they express won't bear putting into your innocent mind."*

Henry Phillips was, as we have seen, quite concerned with not putting ideas into innocent minds, or, as he put it, "he would not willingly offer entertainment through the assistance of immorality" (vii). Of course, since his *Floral Emblems* was not a pure example of a floral language intended to be a language of love but an effort to combine such a vocabulary with emblems for artistic and heraldic purposes, one finds some differences between his meaning list and that of Latour related to the difference in focus. For example, he has emblems for all the arts: arts, architecture, sculpture, painting, music, poetry, and even restoration. But there are other differences between his set of meanings and those of Latour that show a different version of what words should be needed in a vocabulary of love. Since Phillips's work is not a translation of Latour but just a derivative work using numerous other sources, including Lucot, I am not treating this comparison fully, but will do so with the Shoberl text, which is a translation. However, a comparison between Phillips and Latour underscores the English preoccupation with morality when dealing with French sources.

Phillips's floral vocabulary has 311 pairs, to Latour's 272. He picks up many of her meanings and does not seem to avoid the more sexual ones quite as much as does Shoberl, but perhaps that is because he was a scientist of sorts. An example of this is the treatment of the meaning pair *ardeur—gouet* (Latour), which he translates properly as ardour—cuckow-pint or *Arum maculatum* (wild arum). Latour explains the meaning as being derived from the notion that the spadix of this plant is so hot that it burns the hand. Phillips picks up the same notion and expresses it by quoting a portion of French verse (from a source I have not yet identified) which gives the same idea. He reinforces the imagery, though, by writing, "The phenomenon which this plant displays at the period of impregnation, determined the poets to make it the emblem of ardour" (64). A more graphic illustration of a phallus than the spadix of the wild arum can hardly be found in the plant kingdom, and Phillips does not shrink from that observation. However, looking briefly ahead at Shoberl, we find an interesting situation: he uses the pair ardour—broom, possibly mistaking the French word *gouet* (wild arum) for *genet* (broom), but certainly avoiding the phallic image. His explanation is taken right from Latour, concerning the heat of the spadix.

The major thing noticeable about Phillips's meanings is that he adds categories of meaning, and these appear in all the classifications—qualities, states, and situations. These additions concern the arts (as we have seen), age, and moral issues. For example, he has emblems for old age, winter of age, and cheerfulness in age. Many of his qualities are those of a properly virtuous English maiden: charity, freshness, industry, talent, taste, temperance, virtue, and incorruptible. Some of her states of mind are pensiveness, thoughts, diffidence, and embarrassment. One of her possible thoughts is, "death said to be preferable to loss of innocence." There are numerous moral judgments among the meanings, including serious items like crime and more mundane sins like gossip; an upstart; or vulgar minds. He is concerned with religious issues and includes religious superstition; religious enthusiasm; and superstitious sanctity. Overall, his meanings are far more moralistic than Latour's, and include several more practical matters, such as a meaning perhaps considered immoral in France: paternal error.

This morality is underscored by the text of his explanations of the meanings. He frequently shifts the meaning from the love affair to moral issues by the context of the meaning he gives in his explanation. For example, he assigns the meaning "forsaken" to the lilac, which in Latour is given to the anemone; and while he explains that it is a suitable emblem for the meaning because "it is the flower lovers offer their mistresses when they abandon them," he further adds, "It may generally be observed, that those who forsake their family and friends, soon become anxious to run away from themselves" (152). He often makes remarks about marriage, such as this interesting one, on austerity (fuller's teasel): "Austerity in courtship is generally followed by brutality in wedlock" (70). He is rigorously Protestant, and his explanations of religious enthusiasm (lychnis) and religious superstition (passion flower) make this very clear. Chastity and chaste love are favored, of course, but not celibacy, about which he remarks, "Reason seems to tell us, that the most devout and strict celibacy cannot be so acceptable to the Almighty as the faithful observance of the duties of husband and wife, parent, child, and neighbour" (87). One of his most charming explanations relates to the issue of morality also: he makes *Cobaea scandens,* the cup-and-saucer flower (a vine) the emblem of gossip based on the habit of teatime gossiping, reminding the reader that all gossip is not "innocent chit-chat," that gossip is allied to "venomous scandal" (161). In fact, it often seems that he is trying to offset the very Frenchness of his sources. While he quotes French poetry about flowers in the beginning of his book, he does not like to see French polite society set up as the model of behavior, and French Catholicism and French politics are equally unsuitable. Added to the unfavorable remarks about Catholicism are several political points, including the assignment of the meaning "instability" to the dahlia, based on the fact that it was introduced to Europe in the first year of the French Revolution but was lost, only to be reintroduced during the first year of Napoleon's reign as emperor. He quotes Addison: "instability of temper ought to be checked, when it disposes men to wander from one scheme of government to another; such a fickleness cannot but be fatal to any country" (191).

Shoberl's work is a translation, and thus bears closer comparison. One of the most obvious differences is that there are many fewer meanings in Shoberl than Latour, 233 to 272. Shoberl has simply left out many of the pairs. As I studied the list of meanings left out, I found that most could be classified into three possible reasons for exclusion: sexual or immoral connotation, negative meaning, or linkage to an unfamiliar or unsuitable plant. The last of these is the most obvious; Shoberl, unlike Phillips, was not schooled in botany or horticulture, so he did not so easily add plants he thought more suitable or move plants around. Thus, meanings of unfamiliar or even unidentifiable plants might have been left off the list for that reason. A few examples of these pairs are *alisier* (service or sarvis tree, *Amelanchier ovalis*)—harmony; clandestine (unidentified)—hidden love; *foulsapatte* (an Indian plant taken from Bernardin de Saint-Pierre)—humble and unhappy love; and *Bon Henri* (Good King Henry, a vegetable)—benevolence. He also considered plants like pumpkin and lettuce unsuitable for a language of flowers. The negative meanings left out include shame, indifference, mistaken hopes, and hatred or gall. Some of these classifications overlap, as most of the negative meanings he left out are also assigned to unfamiliar or unusual plants. The most interesting category of omissions are those that might have been left out to protect innocent minds. There are not many of these, however, and a complete list from Latour is quite short (I am including here those that might also be assigned to other of my classifications):

voluptuous love	moss rose
scandal	bicolor rose
fecundity	hollyhock
heart on fire	white and red roses
frankness	water willow
shame	peony
I burn	prickly pear
naivety	argentine (silverweed)
rendezvous	chickweed
sleep of the heart	white poppy

Some meanings were changed a bit in translation: platonic love to friendship; intoxication, I love you to devoted attachment; bonds of love to generous and devoted affection; do not abuse to beware of excess; bashfulness to chastity; and voluptuousness to dangerous pleasures. Meanings added to the vocabulary are fleeting beauty, curiosity, girl, ingenuity, longevity, resolution, royalty, stratagem, temptation, and my bane, my antidote (from Wirt). Overall, the Shoberl version of the floral language shows an avoidance of the more passionate qualities and states of mind, and of situations possibly related to illicit love. On the other hand, he did not see fit to moralize it in the manner of Phillips, possibly because he knew his readers would not appreciate so much didacticism.

Robert Tyas also billed his language of flowers vocabulary as a translation of Latour, although his books are not organized along those lines. A brief comparison of his changes with those of Shoberl shows that Tyas was less afraid of the sexual material than was Shoberl: he includes fecundity; shame; assignation; sleep of the heart; voluptuous love; and voluptuousness. On the other hand, he changes "heart on fire" to "warmth of heart." His handling of the ardour issue is interesting: he makes the German iris (in Latour the emblem of flame), the emblem of both flame and ardor, reserving the wild arum for warmth, which allows him to mention the hot spadix in more proper surroundings.

These English versions of the vocabulary of love show a dependence on the French list coupled with an avoidance of certain concepts. Thus, these lists do not completely picture a proper English romance, for the spiritual and mature concepts considered proper in a French vocabulary follow the French notion that love is a matter of intrigue for the safely married. None of the English editors was able to dominate the vocabulary, and thus these lists look more like a compromise with French values than an avowal of English ones. This becomes very clear when we study what Elizabeth Wirt did with her American version.

First of all, *Flora's Dictionary* does not depend on Latour for much at all. Certainly, the work was known to Wirt—that can be determined from internal evidence. The list of plants is customized to America, however, and the meanings are very different. Wirt has 238 meaning pairs, which are divided into the usual qualities, states, and situations, but with far more complete statements than the other vocabularies have. There are many negatives, but not quite such a high percentage as in the Latour text. As we compare the content of the meaning list with that of Latour and the English imitations we see a clear distinction.

The first observation one makes in studying this list might well be that it names many varieties of love: estranged love; filial love; fraternal love; happy love; hopeless love; love at first sight; love in idleness; love positive; love returned; slighted love; decrease of love on better acquaintance; and consumed by love. It is obvious that these flowers could be made to speak of love directly. Special meanings are given for female qualities and situations: female ambition; domestic virtues; female fidelity; feminine modesty; and woman's love. There are some practical meanings that could be used in ordinary social life, such as good wishes; departure; serenade; time; ambassador of love; an appointed meeting; and an expected meeting. Some character types are indicated, including a boaster, a busy body, and a fop (foppery).

In fact, the overwhelming version of the love affair given by these emblems is that it is a social business, taking place openly and happily, concerning young people and their families. For example, there is an emblem for matrimony, which is missing in the Latour list. The qualities are more social ones than psychological or spiritual aspects of personality; I am thinking of such meanings as cheerfulness; chivalry; imagination; industry; scepticism; female ambition; beauty unknown to the possessor; cheerfulness in old age; sunbeam'd eyes; and ill-timed wit. The varieties of love already listed make it possible for the lover to characterize his/her exact feelings, which underscores his/her freedom in love. The complete statements are the most revealing, though, in their social nature, perhaps headed by "Your hand for the next quadrille?"

As is the case in Latour, many of the "I" statements in the Wirt vocabulary are more appropriately spoken by the woman than by the man, and the "you" statements by the man. The "I" statements communicate standard love messages such as "I love"; "I am your captive"; "I declare against you"; "I desire a return of affection"; "I am dazzled by your charms"; and "I live for thee," along with practical issues such as "I have a message for you"; "I will think of it"; "I would not answer hastily." More complex issues are addressed in such messages as "I fall into the Trap laid for me," and "If you do love me, you will find me out." The gallantry of the lover is depicted in such "you" statements as "You occupy my thoughts"; "You are young and beautiful"; "You are the Queen of Coquettes"; "Thou art all that is lovely"; "Your purity equals your loveliness"; and "Lady, deign to smile." The fact that the vocabulary includes so many complete statements emphasizes the social nature of the Wirt floral language.

In contrast to the French meanings, which depict the love affair as a profoundly spiritual experience not relating to marriage or social life, these American emblems reveal the love affair as seen in American culture, the business of young people seeking marriage partners in a highly visible, highly social milieu. Missing from the vocabulary are words for qualities such as weakness, audacity, reverie, or lamentation, or states of mind such as coldness or to live without love, and melancholy spirit, which illustrate Lady Sydney Morgan's remark that "A French woman has no hesitation in acknowledging, that the '*besoin de sentir*' is the first want of her existence" (1:200). Wirt was married herself at eighteen to a successful man, thirty years of age, and had numerous children. In one of her letters, the only one I have seen, she writes to one of her sons and mentions the affairs of her daughters in such a way as to communicate the cheerful, bustling, American home that she shared with her reportedly charming and musical husband.[4] Her version of the floral language fits very well the American notions of the business of romance as seen by such a woman. While a contrast between her vocabulary and that of Latour could not exactly function as a gloss on "Daisy Miller," the two lists do show the cultural notions of the proper conduct of love affairs in two contrasting cultures.

In looking at these lists of vocabularies to see how they portray each culture's notions of a love affair, we are able to see the conscious and unconscious shaping of material to meet popular ideas and tastes. From the beginning of the notion of a language of flowers, the vocabularies are shaped over and over again according to what plants are most suitable, what vocabulary is needed and proper, and what language the flowers would speak according to the culture's notions of the rapport between nature and human beings. The motivating factor in all this is the human desire (in *Mythologies* Barthes says it is a bourgeois desire) to find that our cultural conventions are endorsed by nature herself. If our love affairs can be communicated in flowers, they are "natural," "normal," "the way things should be." Thus, the language of flowers might be very well called a cultural myth, using nature to validate manners and morals. In fact, the creators of these vocabularies knew this, for otherwise why would there be such determined effort to shape the meanings to suit the culture?

There was also an element of pure nationalism in the different lists of floral emblems, often revealed in remarks about choosing poems, flowers, or emblems from one's own culture instead of France or the East. Such remarks as this one, from Edith Chamberlain's *The Gentlewoman's Book of Gardening* (1892), are echoed in many of the language of flower books: "The hyacinth is one of the few florist's flowers which has a perfume. But its smell is not an *English* one—it is too rich and heavy. Rather does it breathe reminiscences of its Eastern home" (44). Thomas Miller's *The*

Poetical Language of Flowers is one of the most nationalistic works. While acknowledging the preeminence of France in creating the language of flowers, he implies that the pairings of flower and emblem are carelessly done, by "a timid spirit and trembling hand," lacking the "old poetical spirit" of the great English poets. These poets—Chaucer, Spenser, Shakespeare, and Milton—are his sources, he explains (needless to say, he does not create anything complete from them). His language of flowers is basically that of Latour, with a few modifications to fit his own interpretations of flowers from the poets. But he brings in nationalistic points in his little essays on flowers, such as "Old Saxon Flowers," which describes the water lily, broom, bluebell, and rosemary, and attributes their emblems (purity, humility, constancy, and remembrance) to "the fair Saxon princess Rowena" as she watched her civilization being threatened by "the desolating Dane" (60–61).

American editors showed various nationalistic attitudes as well, although they tended to regard the old English poets as their own, by inheritance. In fact, the American preface to Miller's book, written by Mrs. E. Oakes Smith (Mrs. Seba Smith) for American editions, strikes directly at the subject of refinement. "Not the least pleasing inclination amongst us, is that far-spread and growing fondness for works of elegant taste and literature, which augures a tendency to the refined and elevating in our people, and will not fail to counteract much of that sordid, hardening character likely to be engendered by the money-getting spirit which is the reproach of the age, not a characteristic of our country, as has too often been insinuated, and might be most easily disproved" (iii). After discussing the virtues of this taste for poetry and refinements, she especially characterizes the Miller book as having "all the clearness and healthfulness of a thorough English mind" (vi). American editors did not locate virtues so much in the past as did English editors, inasmuch as there was no such American past to mine for floral material. The nationalism of Phillips and Miller can be paired with a self-conscious Americanness of the "lady editors" of American language of flower works: the contrast shows that the element of nostalgia is far greater in the English works, which pairs nostalgia with nationalism for maximum effect.

Miller's essay, "The Queen of May," evokes an old English May festival with the squire's daughter serving as queen, decorated with wild roses and hawthorn (emblem of hope). The entire essay is melancholy in tone, rather than festive. Along with other images of deserted maidens and separated lovers is this portrait of the May queen:

At the foot of the Maypole stood a rustic throne of trellis-work, covered with flowers and branches of Hawthorn blossoms, drooping in many a graceful form; and on it was seated the Queen of May, her beautiful brow crowned with a simple wreath of wild roses; while, hand in hand, young men and village maidens formed a circle around her, and, with smiling faces, timed their feet to the music of an old-fashioned country dance. At a distance stood the wealthy squire, surrounded by his family, his face beaming with smiles, as he gazed upon the merry group before him, and pointed proudly to his youngest daughter, who sat crowned the Queen of May. For ages past had some high-born daughter of the hall laid aside her dignity for the day, and condescended to preside over their May games. Many a proud beauty who now sleeps in the dark vault beneath the chancel pavement, had, in the rose-bloom of youth and loveliness, left her old ancestral hearth and mounted the flowery throne on the village green, to do reverence to May; but never before had there stepped out, from that long gallery of departed beauties, one lovelier than she who now sat the crowned queen of the month of flowers.

(136)

This rustic scene, itself recalling the past, is then shown to be in the past itself, Miller writing that "this innocent old English holiday has now all but passed away" (140). May festivals, he explains, "are but like flowers thrown into the sea of Time, and cast by the waves upon the long straggling shores, below the dim cliffs, whose heights are only overlooked by Memory" (140). This melancholic May queen, carefully shown to be the squire's daughter, is a very suitable figure of Flora for the English sentimental material. Miller naturally considers her a personification of Flora, but she is a Flora far from the abandoned spring queen of classical portraiture. The prominence of the hawthorn and its not particularly cheerful message of hope underscores the mood.

Actually, the figure of Flora can often be used to indicate important aspects of a period's attitude toward flowers and floral emblems. Beside Miller's May queen we can consider the American Flora of R. H. Stoddard's "Hymn to Flora," (which appears in a shortened form in Kirtland's *Poetry of the Flowers*). This Flora is a classical personification:

(11–12)

> O Flora! sweetest Flora, Goddess bright,
>   Impersonation of selectest things,
>   The soul and spirit of a thousand Springs,
> Bodied in all their loveliness and light,
> A delicate creation of the mind,
>   Fashioned in its divinest, daintiest mould,

> In the bright Age of God,
> Before the world was wholly lost and blind,
> But saw and entertained with thankful heart
>   The gods as guests—

While Stoddard's Flora is lauded as a goddess, she is called on to continue to bless the season—this goddess is not dead.

(17)

> O smile upon us, Goddess fair and true,
> And watch the flowers till summer's reign is o'er;
> Preserve the seeds we sow in winter-time
> From burrowing moles, and blight, and icy rime,
> And in their season cause the shoots to rise,
> And make the dainty buds unseal their eyes;

A figure from the classical past, Flora here is asked to participate in everyday domestic gardening life. While Miller's May queen personifies the nostalgic tendencies of the sentimental flower writers, Stoddard's Flora emphasizes the domestic, homely aspects of flower writing.

In contrast, the only detailed French Flora I can find is Taxile Delord's beleaguered goddess in *Les fleurs animées,* presiding over a masterful satire on floral emblems and their literature. The sweet, wholesome "impersonation of selectest things," melancholy or not, is far different from the dryly sarcastic Fée aux Fleurs (the Flower Fairy). But if we could generate a Flora from the French sentimental works, she would be much closer to the Roman prostitute Flora of Boccaccio's *Concerning Famous Women* than Ovid's Flora who refused to do her work until the Roman senate established the floralia in her honor (*Fasti*). Our French Flora is neither nostalgic nor domestic, but rather a very feminine, alluring person who embodies all the floral attributes of beautiful women. She is only a goddess insomuch as any beautiful woman is a goddess; and her associations with the country are calculated to make her more attractive. Painted by Watteau and Fragonard, she is a figure in the past only by virtue of her costume.

In his study of the differences between the French and the English, published in 1889, Philip Hamerton constantly points out that the supposed immorality or impurity of the French is only illusory, based on misunderstood manners. The "moral sense" is stronger in the English only because the French, being more worldly, are not so shocked at the evil in the world. This is different from being evil themselves, he explains, and he also comments that he has found the English to be no purer than the French, although they possess stronger principles. One of the reasons for some of the difficulties in understanding one another lies in the different ideas the two cultures have regarding the sexes; "the French have a very keen sense, perhaps an exaggerated sense, of what is feminine and what is unfeminine," he writes (377). This difference over the proper nature of woman, and her appropriate concerns, is at the heart of the differences in the language of flower books.

A Floral Grammar

The actual communication of ideas with flowers is very difficult, but such difficulty belies the interpretation given to the floral language by many commentators: that it was natural and obvious. So most writers simply ignored the problems of actual communication with flowers, while others presented partial "grammars" of the language. To use actual flowers as messages—to put them together in a sentence—requires far more grammar, however, than anyone ever proposed. The only really practical situation is when one flower represents an entire sentence itself. Analysis of the rules of floral communication set forth by several commentators will show the impracticality of the ideas as well as the cultural codes upon which they based the creation of their grammars.

I will begin with the ever practical Elizabeth Wirt, who, in her preface, mentions that some communications require answers, and in general the answer can be given by returning the same flower, for she lists both flower meanings and the answers to such communications in her text. The answers are given only in verse—she is not concerned with a simple yes or no. Not all her flowers have both first meanings and answers, but there are many that do, an example of which is the dogwood blossom, which means "I am perfectly indifferent to you." The verse answer, from Shakespeare, is, "She gladly shunn'd, who gladly fled from her." This usage is obviously tied to the use of the book and does not suggest that one can communicate complicated messages in bouquets. An equally pragmatic approach is found in the language of flowers portion of Kirtland's *Poetry of the Flowers;* she gives four pages of "flower dialogues," in which a flower or an action represents an entire message. For example, a red and a white rose together means "I love you silently," while the action of "breaking off and throwing away rose petals" means "I do not love you." While this seems practical, however, one message, "try to save me," requires chicory and narcissus, an unlikely combination of August and April blooms. Kirtland also lists bouquets with messages, some of which are much more interesting than most English or American material. For instance, a bouquet of abatina, almond blossom, cockscomb, and basil (another unlikely combination) means "You are fickle, indiscreet, and affected. Therefore you are hated."

Phillips presents several grammatical notions that were picked up in many of the later language of flower books, including those of Tyas, H. G. Adams, and Frances Osgood. He writes that there are two "principles" needed in such a grammar, a method of expressing pronouns and a way to express negatives. Only the first and second persons singular are needed, and the "I" or "me" is expressed "by inclining the flower to the left," while "thou" or "thee" is expressed "by sloping it to the right." This has to be reversed for drawings, he explains, as "the flower should lean to the heart of the person whom it is to signify." We will notice in all of these systems that the position of the heart in the human body is of great importance in structuring the grammar. Phillips explains that articles may be expressed by tendrils, but those remarks refer only to drawings.

Phillips's second principle is that a flower will express its negative aspect if presented upside down. Thus, one can use the same flower to express both an idea and its reverse; a pansy presented upright means "think of me" but when upside down the opposite, "forget me." In this discussion of negatives, however, Phillips is very confusing. He says that, presented upright, a rosebud with its thorns and leaves means "I fear, but I hope," and then can mean various other things if presented upside down, or without its thorns, or without its leaves. The first problem is this: nowhere in his floral vocabulary do we find the rosebud with thorns and leaves listed, so how would anyone know the basic meaning? The same is true in the work of those who pick up this paragraph from his introduction—their vocabularies do not include this emblem either, so they use an example which does not appear in the emblem list. In fact, this example of the rosebud shows the random nature of the idea of a floral grammar. Phillips explains, "if the thorns be stripped off, it expresses, 'there is every thing to hope'; deprived of its leaves, it signifies 'there is every thing to fear'" (25). Do the thorns represent fear, the leaves hope? And how did one arrange for the shift in persons?

Another aspect of Phillips's grammar is what he calls varying the expression of flowers by a change of position. Thus, a flower means one thing when placed on the head, another on the heart, and yet another on the bosom. I would find it difficult to know when the heart was not the bosom and vice versa, but perhaps he means left and right side of the body. At any rate, a marigold, the base meaning of which is despair, means trouble of spirits when placed on the head, trouble of love when on the heart, and weariness when on the bosom. The head–heart dichotomy thus appears in this grammar in its traditional symbolism.

A much more complex effort appears in Louise Leneveux's *Nouveau manuel des fleurs emblématiques* (1837), but it follows the same notions. Negatives are expressed by reversed order, and persons by the inclination of the flower. But she goes beyond Phillips to chart a complete set of persons, although she says that in a language of love *je* and *tu* are all that are really needed. She assigns the attribution of person to the hand in which the flower is held as well as the direction of the presentation.

Person	*Flower Leaning Toward*	*Hand*
je	right	right
tu	left	right
il	right	left

Plurals are indicated by using two flowers and following the same table as shown above. The tenses depend upon the height at which the flowers are held, presumably before being leaned in the direction of the addressee:

present	heart level
past	toward the ground
future	eye level

To use the flowers in "writing," some adjustments need to be made, so, she explains, to indicate the third person in picture form, the flower should be shown leaning horizontally, while the tenses can be shown by flowers in different stages of life. Thus, the past will be represented by a faded bloom, the present by one in full bloom, and the future by a bud.

When comparing this grammar to Phillips's, we immediately notice that the persons are completely the opposite, in that the flower leaning to the right indicates first person in Leneveux and second in Phillips, and vice versa. They are in agreement on the negatives but use the body positions for different purposes. Phillips uses the position of the heart on the left side of the body to signify persons but Leneveux does not bring the heart into her assignment of persons. Phillips does not indicate tenses at all, using the vertical body locations for other purposes.

These attempts to unify the flower and the human body presenting the flower are very sketchy but interesting in their use of traditional head–heart meanings and vertically organized concepts; and this is another example, in fact, of using nature to back up human concepts. However, ability to express persons, tenses, and negatives does not mean that

sentences are easily constructed. Phillips, in his last remark in the introduction, implies that such expressions are not the main task of the floral
language, but rather to serve as "floral mottoes," a much less gram-
matically taxing effort. Leneveux handles questions of syntax by specify-
ing that flowers be arranged in "the analytic order of thoughts or phrases"
(6). Of course, just how that is to be done is not clear. A bouquet is by
definition a grouping, a gathering, of flowers, defying syntax. The issue of
parts of speech is never brought up, and though, as we have seen, many of
the nouns in the vocabulary can easily be changed to verbs, how is one to
know which is meant in a floral communication? For example, some ferns
(sincerity) and jonquils (desire) might mean "I desire sincerity," or "you
possess desirable sincerity," or "I sincerely desire you," or "you are sincere
in your desire," and I cannot see how these distinctions can be made simply
by indicating persons. In examples given in some books of meanings of
bouquets, the meaning is not explained, and the syntax is far beyond what
can easily be seen.

   In fact, analysis of the famous and often-reproduced Bessa illustration
for Latour (Figure 14), a flower picture communicating a verse by Parny,
shows that even spread out in individual pictures rather than in a bouquet,
expression of ideas in flowers is not very easy. The frontispiece shows four
rows of flowers with four individual flowers in each row. The first thing
noticeable is that the flowers shown are not all represented in the language
proposed in the book, as in the Phillips rosebud example. The verse
illustrated is this, from Parny:

> Aimer est un plaisir charmant,
>   C'est un bonheur qui nous enivre.
> Et qui produit l'enchantement.
>   Avoir aimé, c'est ne plus vivre;
> Hélas! c'est avoir acheté
> Cette accablante vérité,
>   Que les sermens sont un mensonge,
> Que l'amour trompe tôt ou tard,
> Que l'innocence n'est qu'un art,
>   Et que le bonheur n'est qu'un songe.

(To love is a charming pleasure; it is a happiness which intoxicates us and
produces enchantment. To have loved, is to no longer live; alas! It is to
have achieved that grievous truth that promises are lies, that love deceives
sooner or later, that innocence is but an art, and that happiness is only a
dream.) The illustration changes this, as indicated in the writing below the

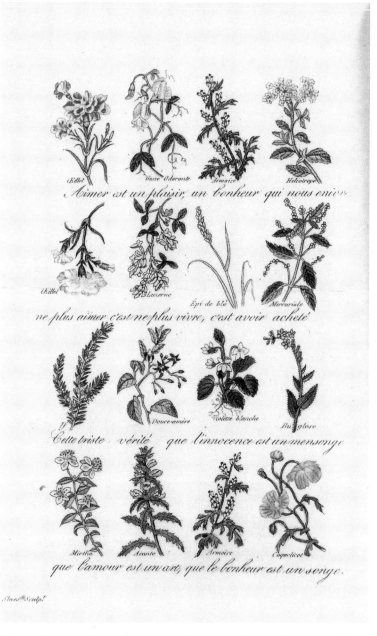

Fig. 14. Pancrace Bessa, frontispiece for many editions of Charlotte de Latour, *Le langage des fleurs*. Reproduced from Louis Aimé-Martin, attr., *Le langage des fleurs*. Brussels: Louis Hauman, 1830. (Courtesy of the Hunt Institute for Botanical Documentation, Carnegie Mellon University, Pittsburgh, PA.)

flowers, to "Aimer est un plaisir, un bonheur qui nous enivre; ne plus aimer c'est ne plus vivre, c'est avoir acheté cette triste vérité que l'innocence est un mensonge, que l'amour est un art, que le bonheur est un songe." (To love is a pleasure, a happiness which intoxicates us; to no longer love is to no longer live, it is to have achieved that sad truth that innocence is a lie, that love is an art, and that happiness is a dream.) The changes in meaning all simplify the grammar, although the switch between the attributes of love and innocence is not really so motivated. The flowers pictured, and their emblems, are shown in Table 7. The syntax is simply taken for granted, with the main meaning written under each picture and the verbs and other grammatical points simply wedged in. If we take the first two flowers, the carnation (love) and the sweet pea, presumably meaning pleasure, together, they could mean "to love is a pleasure," or "pleasurable love," or "the pleasure of love"; there is no way to indicate these differences. This kind of illustration was not repeated in other books. It does not make a pretty picture and could not have been easy to do, even if it does not really express what it says it does. Instead, the bouquet with or without explanations is typical.

To communicate ideas, then, a flower needs to either represent an entire statement or be presented individually in a clear context. A bouquet can communicate a cluster of feelings but not a syntactical statement. However, many language of flower books picture bouquets and "translate" them for us; for example, the frontispiece in Osgood's *The Floral Offering* (1847) shows columbine, white lily, and lupine, and is translated, "It was a dream of folly, from which I wake to weep." Thomas Miller's *The Romance of Nature* (n.d.) shows a grouping of crocus, scarlet pimpernel, Lancaster rose, and cowslips—an unlikely group, which is translated, "Your youthfulness causes me to fear that you may change; once united, I shall be no longer pensive." Sometimes the flower groups are not explained at all and yet messages are implied. In Robert Tyas's *The Language of Flowers; or, Floral Emblems* (1869), there is a handsome colored illustration of another unlikely bouquet—hepatica, hollyhock, and rest harrow—which is not translated for us (Figure 15). The meanings of the three given in the text are confidence, fruitfulness, and obstacle. I suppose one could read the bouquet to say, "Your fruitfulness is an obstacle to my confidence," although I suspect that such would not be thought a suitable sentiment for an English book. Another possibility, "Your confidence is an obstacle to my fruitfulness," is even less suitable. But it is an attractive illustration. Added to a lack of syntax is the fact that not all flowers bloom at the same time, and thus some floral communications might be as

Table 7. Flowers and their meanings from frontispiece
for Latour's *Le langage des fleurs*

oeillet	amour pur et vif
(carnation	pure and ardent love)
gesse odorante	no meaning listed [plaisir?]
(sweet pea	pleasure?)
armoise	bonheur
(artemisia	happiness)
heliotrope	enivrement; je vous aime
(heliotrope	intoxication; I love you)
oeillet reversed	amour pur et vif, negated
(carnation reversed	pure and ardent love, negated)
lucerne reversed	vie, negated
(lucern-grass reversed	life, negated)
blé	richesse
(wheat	wealth)
Bon Henri	Bonté
(garden mercury	benevolence)
if	douceur
(yew	sadness)
douce amère	vérité
(nightshade	truth)
violette blanche	innocence
(white violet	innocence)
buglose	mensonge
(bugloss	lie)
myrte	amour
(myrtle	love)
acanthe	art
(acanthus	art)
armoise	bonheur
(artemisia	happiness)
coquelicot	consolation [*songe* in picture]
(poppy	consolation [dream])

Hollyhock ___ Hepatica ___ Rest harrow.

Fig. 15. Robert Tyas, *The Language of Flowers; or, Floral Emblems of Thoughts, Feelings, and Sentiments*

unrealistic as those Dutch flower paintings that show tulips and roses or dahlias and daffodils in the same bouquet.

What we have, then, except perhaps in Wirt's *Flora's Dictionary*, is an imprecise set of emblems which only form a language in a book and which portray a concept of nature-human relationships through the guise of a language. The language of flowers devised by the hero of Honoré de Balzac's *Le lys dans la vallée* (1835) to communicate with his married mistress is close, in actuality, to what a true "language" of flowers really would have to be. He chose flowers to express his feelings of love under the circumstances, and there is no precision of meaning or grammatical structure, but rather a clustering of associations and impressions. His first bouquet makes an immediate impact:

(100)

> *Picture to yourself a fountain of flowers, gushing up, as it were, from the vase and falling in fringed waves, and from the heart of it my aspirations rose as silver-cupped lilies and white roses. Among this cool mass twinkled blue corn-flowers, forget-me-not, bugloss—every blue flower whose hues, borrowed from the sky, blend so well with white; for are they not two types of innocence—that which knows nothing and that which knows all—the mind of a child and the mind of a martyr? Love has its blazonry, and the Countess read my meaning.*

He does not rely on a dictionary of meanings but rather on color symbolism and the beauty of the flowers alone. In another passage he mentions creating a symbolism of grasses, but naturally does not bother to tell us what it is. Instead, when he describes a much larger flower arrangement (he calls them nosegays, but they must be very large), he again calls on impressions:

(102–4)

> *A small grass, the vernal anthoxanthum, is one of the chief elements in this mysterious combination. No one can wear it with impunity. If you put a few sprays of it in a nosegay, with its shining variegated blades like a finely striped green-and-white dress, unaccountable pulses will stir within you, opening the rosebuds in your heart that modesty keeps closed. Imagine, then round the wide edge of the china jar a border composed entirely of the white tufts peculiar to a sedum that grows in the vineyards of Touraine, a faint image of the wished-for forms, bowed like a submissive slave-girl. From this base rise the tendrils of bindweed with its white funnels, bunches of pink rest-harrow mingled with young shoots of oak gorgeously tinted and lustrous; these all stand forward, humbly drooping like weeping willow, timid and suppliant like prayers. Above, you see the slender blossoming sprays, for ever tremulous, of quaking grass and its*

stream of yellowish anthers; the snowy tufts of feathergrass from brook and meadow, the green hair of the barren brome, the frail agrostis—pale, purple hopes that crown our earliest dreams, and that stand out against the gray-green background in the light that plays on all these flowering grasses. Above these, again, there are a few China roses, mingling with the light tracery of carrot leaves with plumes of cottongrass, marabout tufts of meadow-sweet, umbels of wild parsley, the pale hair of travellers' joy, now in seed; the tiny crosslets of milky-white candytuft and milfoil, the loose sprays of rose-and-black fumitory, tendrils of the vine, twisted branches of the honeysuckle—in short, every form these artless creatures can show that is wildest and most ragged—flamboyant and trident; spear-shaped, dentate leaves, and stems as knotted as desire writhing in the depths of the soul. And from the heart of this overflowing torrent of love, a grand red double poppy stands up with bursting buds, flaunting its burning flame above starry jessamine and above the ceaseless shower of pollen, a cloud dancing in the air and reflecting the sunshine in its glittering motes. Would not any woman, who is alive to the seductive perfume that lurks in the anthoxanthum, understand this mass of abject ideas, this tender whiteness broken by uncontrollable impulses, and this red fire of love imploring joys denied it in the hundred struggles of an undying, unwearied, and eternal passion?

This passage indicates all that the language of flowers pretended to be, while tacitly showing what it cannot be. Such a torrent of feeling could not be expressed by a grouping of emblematic flowers tied to a vocabulary list and organized by a very feeble grammatical structure.

On the other hand, a Virginia belle could easily interpret a sprig of ivy geranium as a bid for the next quadrille, and surely "the rosebuds of her heart" would open at the gift of some ivy, symbolizing matrimony. The pragmatic Wirt took care that no one need ever miss a proposal because of the season, for the ivy is evergreen in Virginia. Flowers could express ideas in simple social matters not calling for complex syntax, provided that there is communal agreement on the meaning of the flowers. For instance, in most floral vocabularies the ivy means friendship. It seems, then, that the Virginia belle would have to be certain her suitor was using the right book. Thus we come around again to the dominance of the book, the list, the printed vocabulary—the true locus of the talking flowers. From this literary parterre the flowers speak to us today of nineteenth-century cultural codes that express relativistic ideas of the relationship between man and nature.

VII

Conclusions

*We are proud to be the first to pose
the following aphorism:
        Flowers are the expression of society.*

(Taxile
Delord, *Les
fleurs
animées*)

IN THE LAST years of the century, new sentimental flower books became scarce, especially the language of flower books. Changing social and cultural values contributed to this demise, some of which merit brief comment.

The sentimental flower book was intended for women, and as such presented a view of women which was seriously challenged by the end of the century. As America and England became more and more urbanized in reality, rather than in anticipation, women were no longer associated so much with the country and natural elements. New urban standards of femininity began to develop (for one example, the dedicated shopper). The country woman faded into the cultural background, and with her went the sentimentalization of her environment.

The popularity of botany as a hobby declined, along with the change in the science from the Linnaean system to the natural system of classification. In fact, in a fascinating study of seventeenth- and eighteenth-century attempts to model plant life, *Nature's Second Kingdom* (1982), François Delaporte has shown that, while these early attempts used a human model, by the late nineteenth century the tables were turned as botanical work on cellular structure was used to understand animal life. In general culture the differences between life forms became more important than the similarities.

Popular nature study changed greatly in emphasis. Before the public interest in studying flowers had run its course, the habit of serious consideration of natural history, coupled with concern over changes in lifestyle and landscape occasioned by industrialization, resulted in a social movement of considerable importance, especially in America. The hunting of animals, the gathering of specimens of all sorts, and the picking and selling of wildflowers in the large cities had, by the last quarter of the century, made considerable inroads in the natural scene. In *The Naturalist in Britain* David Allen states that the conservation or protection movement in England dates from about 1865 but did not get off to the start it did in America. While the issue of bird protection, brought to prominence by the fashion for feathered women's hats, was the central issue for many, the loss of wildflowers and places to find them was also important. By the turn of the century both England and America had the beginnings of a strong conservation movement, aiming to save the natural scene that some of the nineteenth-century fondness for nature had destroyed, especially in England and the environs of large Eastern American cities.

A sign of this movement is the appearance in great numbers of wildflower guides in both England and America. These books did not usually have much to say about botany, nor did they suggest gathering flowers and plants. Instead, they focused on the places to find plants and the romance of plant site. They encouraged walks in the woods and along lanes to spot flowers. Some of them were more scholarly than others, especially the English regional floras. While there had been wildflower guides since the early years of the century, the late-century guides are allied with the new attitude of experiencing nature rather than merely studying or collecting. Some of the books of F. G. Heath, a civil servant who wrote popular nature books and was an active crusader for open spaces in and near London, show this. His natural history was not very good—at least to judge from some of the unlikely subjects in his illustrations and descriptions—but *Sylvan Spring* (1880) and *Sylvan Winter* (1886), along with books on notable trees, represent a new type of nature sentiment. The American wildflower guides of the late century were usually the work of women writers, especially Frances Dana Parsons, who in 1893, under the name Mrs. William Starr Dana, published one of the most popular of all American wildflower handbooks, *How to Know the Wildflowers*. This book, along with its companion volumes, a collection of essays *According to Season* (1894) and *How to Know the Ferns* (1899), was intended for use by a person becoming knowledgeable about the outdoor environment.

The conservation movement is the final, perhaps culminating, expression of nineteenth-century nature sentiment. It was nourished by many sources that cannot be discussed here, but surely the love of flowers, fostered in so many ways in the century in both the physical and mental lives of the middle class, is among these sources.

One of the motivations of the sentimentalization of nature—the enlistment of nature on the side of conventional religion—early rivaled the language of flowers as a true interpretation of plants (see chapter two). But as religion diminished in influence in both England and America, this decline removed flowers from the value system more completely than any changes in flower fashions could do. In some of the later religious interpreters of flowers, including Ruskin and Hugh Macmillan, aesthetic values began to be attached to flowers, replacing moral and religious associations. This perhaps culminated in the flower essays of the Belgian writer Maurice Maeterlinck, whose great popularity in his own time led to a Nobel prize, but who is very much neglected today. These essays, in *Le double jardin* (1904) and *L'intelligence des fleurs* (1907), characterize flowers as mechanical marvels (using the discoveries of botanists like Darwin) and personify them as equivalents of happiness, joy, and femininity—this last on the basis of their beauty (Seaton, "Further Dialogue with a Nobel Laureate"). Maeterlinck, a symbolist without a theology to legitimize his symbolism, removed the power of the literary flower, keeping only the empty form.

While the decline of the romantic aesthetic, the finding of the self reflected in nature, was gradual throughout the century in the English and American flower books (with the self replaced by God in a natural evolution), in France the decline was sharp and violent. The sentimental flower book was really born in France and it died there, a casualty in the overthrow of French romanticism in the 1840s. When the English and American popular writers moved sentimental flowers toward religious and moral uses, French almanac writers, for example, who had introduced the language of flowers, found their audiences more interested in astrology, demonology, phrenology, and the prophecies of Nostradamus (Grand-Carteret lv). The downfall of the sentimental flower book was celebrated in Delord's monumental parody *Les fleurs animées* (1847). This serious, sustained parody can tell us many things about the demise of the romantic aesthetic, including specific details critical of the sentimental use of flowers.

The Tables Turned

Taxile Delord (1815–77), who played the Frost King in Flora's literary garden, was editor of *Le Charivari* (a sort of French *Punch*) for many years, author of a standard history of the Second Empire, and sometime legislator. He was a member of the corps of journalistic satirists of politics and society, which included among its members Alphonse Karr, Jules Janin, and Théophile Gautier.[1] The illustrator for *Les fleurs animées*, J.-J. Grandville (1803–47), is much more famous today than is its author, and recently a small reprint of the Grandville illustrations (edited by Peter Wick) was published under the title *The Court of Flora* (1981). *Les fleurs animées* is very large and occupies two volumes. It was translated into English almost immediately, under the title *The Flowers Personified*. Just as its author is no longer well known, the very fact that the book is a parody is practically unknown, mainly because modern readers are not familiar with the material being parodied.

In his essay on parody and satire in *Genre*, Joseph Dane creates a model of parody and satire which centers on the experience of the reader. Satire, having as its "target and referent" a "system of content (*res*)," and parody, having as its target and referent a "system of expression (*signa*)," are shown to be compatible within the same work but not the same reading. The reader can read the work for its parody or its satire; but not both at the same time. *Les fleurs animées,* while a parody of the flower texts, contains many elements of satire, whose referents (aside from general human nature) are related to the subject matter of the books being parodied. Among the subjects of Delord's satire are the popular writers who seek fame and fortune writing flower books, the cult of Napoleon, the self-importance of popular pedants, the fashionable life, and bluestockings—all of which relate in one way or another to the flower books. I am not sure that I agree with Dane's model, for only a reader who knows the sentimental flower book can understand the parody, and such a reader is also apt to appreciate the connections made between the texts being ridiculed and the social and cultural associates of those texts. However, it is true that modern readers of *Les fleurs animées* probably can appreciate the satire, exclusive of the parody. It seems that the relationship between the parody and the satire in *Les fleurs animées* increases the concentration of the discourse level with its message: the sentimental flower book is dead.

The text of *Les fleurs animées* written by Delord (there are other materials in the book that will be discussed later) consists of thirty-four long pieces and twenty-seven short pieces enclosed in a frame story which begins in the garden of the Flower Fairy. The flowers, led by Narcisse and Adonis, march on their goddess (she is reclining in a hammock) and present her with a petition demanding a chance to live on earth as women:

> *Madame,*
>
> (1:15)   *The flowers here present entreat you to kindly receive their homage and to hear their humble grievances. For thousands of years we have served as a subject of comparison to mortals; we diverted to ourselves all their metaphors; without us, poetry would not exist. Men attribute to us*

their virtues and their vices, their faults and their qualities; it is time for us to try out a few of these. The life of flowers bores us: we ask permission to assume the human form, and to judge for ourselves if what they say up there about our character conforms to the truth.

The revolt is successful, and the flowers turned women are set loose on society. The book, then, is described as a random history of their adventures. Thus, the frame story sets the subject for the work clearly before us: the uses that men have made of flowers in literature. At the end of the story the flowers return to the garden, having proved that there is very little truth in the fancies men have created about them. The narrative level is the story of the flowers turned women, and the discourse level reveals the falsehoods and silliness of literary flower personification in the sentimental flower books.

The short pieces in the book generally ridicule by exaggeration the themes and moods of flower poetry. Among these are many of the motifs to be found in both French- and English-language flower personification. Delord is especially hard on the themes of nostalgic memory of flowers, the association of flowers with lost youth, the choice of the lowly flower for one's own. For example, in "La fleur préferé," he states the idea simply:

(1:37)

> *We love flowers, but prefer one above all others.*
> *This is the flower of memory, the flower of love, the flower of youth; this is the one we gathered in the first days in the springtime of life.*
> *We associate the name and the traits of the beloved with the idea of a flower which brings her always to mind.*

The piece goes on to state the main idea over and over, exaggerating by repetition and occasionally by overreaction, as when he explains that a person who has never had tears in his eyes at the sight of a flower has never been a child or a young man, has never had a mother, a sister, or a lover. Most of these short pieces—others ridicule national and political flowers, flower legends, celebrations of the democracy of flowers, or adulation of the solitary flower—are like this one, flat overstatements of a theme which is made to appear ridiculous in ordinary prose. Some are humorous, as when the motif of the flowers debating their importance is shown in a meeting between coffee and tea, each one trying to outbrag the other. In a piece referring to the traditional daisy counting game, "he loves me, he loves me not," the speaking daisy gives the young Anna a piece of good advice: most men treat women like daisies, throw them away once they find the answer (whether or not you love them). So don't answer when asked.

The longer pieces carry the narrative along, giving little histories of the various flowers in their adventures as women. These also contain the major elements of parody. He chooses especially to ridicule the language of flowers, pastoral love stories, legendary plant histories or folklore, and the fragrance/soul connection. These narratives cover the sentimental flower literature very thoroughly, Delord no doubt owing his knowledge of the material to the attention that working journalists give to popular currents of thought and possible objects of income. His point of view throughout is that of an insider, one who knows that the subject has been exploited.

He presents the absurdity of the language of flowers in a complicated story in which Pansy, representing thought, is scorned when people recognize her—no one likes to *think*. Also involved is the story of how a man froze off the tip of his nose while waiting for his girlfriend on a cold night; she had communicated the time of their meeting in flowers and had picked the flower meaning 2 A.M. instead of 2 P.M. Then there is a pompous poet who hopes to get rich and famous from exploiting the language of flowers. In the course of this narrative Delord gives an entire language of flower vocabulary, which appears to be from Louise Leneveux. Far from giving the impression of being a natural and romantic way of expressing thoughts, the language of flowers is shown to be untrue and even dangerous.

The pastoral love story, the adventures of Coquelicot (Field Poppy) and Bluette (Cornflower), shows these two shepherdesses meeting defeat in love, albeit set in an exaggeratedly perfect pastoral setting in which foxes never catch hens and strawberries and grapes never are damaged by the weather. Also defeated in this story is Lily, who was wooed and won by the King of France, but lamented her lost innocence and purity (here Delord involves the two major connotations of the lily, the symbol of France and innocence/purity). The histories of Tulip (who enters a harem but proves so dull she is thrown into the sea in a sack) and of Camellia (so insensitive that her lover commits suicide) parody the assignment of soul and feeling to fragrance.

In the long narrative about the violet, Delord parodies the flower histories so common in the flower gift books, especially the origin stories (which we also find in the poetry). The violet, according to the Flower Fairy, was simply a country lass who wished to be a simple little flower, so the Fairy granted her wish. Thus the violet was seen to really be a daughter of the people, not of royal origin as the stories claim (daughter of Atlas). When the violet became a woman, she opted for the city life but was miserable there, whereupon the Flower Fairy reclaimed her for the woods and lanes. This short narrative is also about Napoleon, for the violet was his emblem; the association between this modest flower and the emperor was a grave mistake on the part of the flower. Unlike Mollevaut, however, who in *Les fleurs* (1818) severely criticizes the violet for her association with Napoleon, Delord did not punish the violet, but simply allowed her to be rescued.

The other material in the book is relevant to the book's message also. In the introduction Alphonse Karr, the noted flower grower, makes it clear that the book is not making fun of flowers but of people who don't love flowers for themselves. Karr also wrote the introductions to the standard botanical and horticultural sections, both of which were written by Louis-François Raban ("Le Comte Foelix"). In the introduction to the botanical portion, Karr criticizes botanical study as really inimical to flowers (he claims that one has to put such a section into a book, however); in the introduction to the horticultural advice, he points out that those who really love flowers learn how to grow them well. These features, along with Delord's constant emphasis on the stupidity of thinking that flowers are like human beings, make it clear that flowers need to be rescued from what sentimental literature has made of them.

Of course, Delord was not only parodying literary flower person-ification but also the emotions, especially nostalgia, which informed so much of this personification in the century. Throughout the book he keeps before us the point that we should face our past realistically, rather than through a veil of nostalgia. Flowers cannot speak for us; we must learn to speak for ourselves.

An interesting contrast is to look at Delord's dismantling of flower sentiment alongside the only other parody I have found, Captain Frederick Marryat's *The Floral Telegraph* (1836). In this book Marryat, English navy officer turned novelist and general literary hack, capitalized on the fame he had gained developing the system of flag signals used by the navy. Essentially a dream narrative, the story tells how the dreamer meets Floribel, the Guardian Spirit of the Garden Flowers. She dictates to him the system of flower language that Marryat details in the back of the book, a system not based on associations of the flowers but on their availability and seasonality. Marryat's text, while an amusing parody laced with standard satiric material (egotistical old men, faithless young women, and nephews waiting for their uncles to die), is by no means the tour de force we find in *Les fleurs animées*. For Marryat merely imitated the typical flower dream sequence and meeting with Flora, productive of the language of flowers, and ridiculed it with some exaggeration and a few reversals. Delord's text takes on the entire body of sentimental flower literature and addresses the major point, that the use of flowers as metaphors for human emotions is as absurd from the flower's point of view as from our own. This was done by destroying the ability of the literary flower to mediate between flower life and human life.

If one sign of changes to come can be found in parody like *Les fleurs animées,* an even more reliable indication that times are changing (or have already changed) comes when we see scholarly "histories" being written. Those plant histories and folklores of the late 1870s on, covered in chapter two, also signify the end of the sentimentalized flower. Thus, toward the end of the nineteenth century flower writers in England were writing the obituaries of the sentimental flower books and the language of flowers in historical works, while the French had already dispatched the form in parody. Just as many modern readers cannot see that *Les fleurs animées* is a parody, many also do not realize that these late-century flower histories and folklores occupy a region between the sentimentalization of flowers and a more modern view—they are both sentimental flower books and works that treat the sentimentalization of flowers as subject to scholarly analysis.

Even so, what is the importance of modern readers understanding the language of flowers and related developments?

Implications for Modern Scholarship

First of all, the history of our popular culture needs to be studied and written by trained scholars, not left to the casual hobbyist or amateur. The language of flowers has had its share of such shallow and inaccurate handling, leading to misunderstanding of Victorian life and literature. The way in which the language of flowers has been treated—as an integral part of ordinary life, as a common way of expressing oneself in society—helps create a picture of nineteenth-century life as both fantastic and simplistic, a golden age of charming and genteel folks and a fruitful source of decorative motifs. To know the social and cultural history of a people, including the popular culture, is to understand them better, to see them as completely as possible. While the language of flowers is not the most outstanding aspect of Victorian popular culture, its very popularity makes it important enough.

The study of the language of flowers also can be seen as a case study in cross-cultural intertextuality, as I endeavored to show in chapter six. To see how a popular form develops, and to trace its spread to other markets, models the dissemination of ideas and artistic concepts across cultural boundaries. As historians of cultures, we need to see examples of how this is accomplished. So I regard the accurate history of the language of flowers as important both in itself and as a model for other popular concepts.

Second, the language of flowers is an important part of the history of floral symbolism. There are not many sound studies of popular symbolic systems, but such works are needed for the proper study of the arts in particular. Too often, critical studies using symbolic readings are based on an inadequate or incomplete knowledge of the symbolic systems of the period.

At this point I would like to integrate the language of flower material into other sentimental flower material in order to present some conclusions about the floral symbolism of the century. For in the nineteenth century, flowers were made to represent human beings and their concerns in very specific ways. From materials in the sentimental flower books, including flower poetry, we can construct a correlation code or code of correspondences to illustrate the common correlations between flowers and people found in the period. This code was generated by the sentimental flower works themselves, beginning in the late eighteenth century. The generation of the code was the work of cultural forces that I have described in early chapters and their exploitation by writers for the popular audience. But the writers were aided in this by the example of some of the major Romantics, especially William Wordsworth. The Romantic tendency to look for correspondences between human emotions and nature is found throughout these sentimental flower works, in writers obviously influenced by Wordsworth such as Keble and in others with a more tenuous debt to the Romantic poets. Wordsworth did more than other major writers in that he singled out flowers for special attention. The generation of the code was a complex event, with elements from the social milieu interacting with literary texts; it was not a purely intertextual event. Yet, among other things, my studies of flower poetry—especially considering which flowers were the subject of poems—tell us that intertextuality was of more importance than "real life."[2] Added to this is the commercial element, the spread of popular literature to a newly enlarged audience, accomplished in this case by many new or small publishing firms and opportunistic journalists and editors.

From my study of the derivation of flower meanings in the language of flower texts, along with readings of popular flower poetry and other flower books, I can present a nineteenth-century code of correspondences which stands behind most sentimental flower writing. This is found in Table 8.

Table 8. Code of correspondence in sentimental flower writing

Flowers	Humans
Qualities	
fragrance	soul
no fragrance	no soul
size	social importance
tall	aristocratic
short	humble
climbing	dependent, parasitic
color	mixed colors/joy
red	love, passion
white	purity, innocence
blue	truth, spirituality
yellow	falsehood, riches
purple	power, royalty (sorrows)
green	hope
black	death, sadness
thorns	troubles
no thorns	no troubles
impermanence	death
rebirth in spring	immortal life
excessive fragility	sensibility
everlasting blooms	immortality
Situations	
difficult site	courage
blooming out of season	action beyond the call of duty
solitary site	individuality
commonness	democracy
high site	immortality

The color correspondences are especially interesting, for they clearly show the dominance of the three traditional flower colors, red (rose), white (lily), and blue (violet). This brings up the problem of what color is meant by the term "blue" in these contexts, and indeed it is a vexed horticultural as well as literary issue (Seaton, "Blue Roses and Other Horticultural Illusions"). The blue of the color charts and the spectrum is an uncommon color in flowers compared to various shades of violet, and so in flowers blue is spread out to include flowers of violet and purple shades in order to get across meanings (the color of heaven is the operative issue here). Flowers that really are blue in our normal sense of the word are used also, of course; but traditional use of the term "blue" for the violet, an extremely important flower, confuses the issue. The color meanings can be simplified by identifying the basis for the meanings:

red	blood
white	death, immaturity
blue	heaven

Purple shades (already included under blue in many situations) and yellow are thus saved for negative meanings. The unfavorable status of yellow is interesting; related to the sun, it should be favorable. (Perhaps, following along the interest of past cultures in body fluids, it relates to urine.) Although the liturgical colors do not parallel these color meanings and I am not referring to them as a whole, I place "sorrows" under purple as a most common borrowing from the liturgical tradition. Green and black are not commonly flower colors, but fit the scheme in parallel ways. Green is the color of spring growth; leaves turn black with frost. (One might speculate on the color meanings if the leaf changes of the North American autumn had been part of European experience.) A complex, somewhat contradictory nineteenth-century source on color symbolism is Fréderic Portal's *An Essay on Symbolic Colours* (1845). Portal identifies three "languages of colour": "divine" (the clergy—liturgical), "consecrated" (the nobility—heraldic), and "profane" (the people). The color symbolism in most of the sentimental flower books is like Portal's "profane" meanings, although there are many exceptions.

These correspondence codes are not lost in our day—nothing in literary tradition is ever "lost"—but in this century we regard flowers very differently. The sentimental flower was repudiated, along with all things Victorian, in favor of a more realistic look at flowers. What Delord did in a literary way, others did by direct criticism or by example. In the twentieth century, flowers still appear in the same contexts as in nineteenth-century life, but they do not carry so much meaning beyond the conventional gesture.

Today, references to the language of flowers often appear as newspaper fillers or even in television spots: just recently, a local television anchorwoman spoke very authoritatively, explaining the meanings of different roses as the rose names and meanings appeared on the screen. As one might expect, the roses chosen tell us that the source of the information is probably the modern florist who offers the roses for sale, while the charming and sweet meanings reveal a desire to have the flowers only say pleasant things.

But while the true nature of the nineteenth-century language of flowers is not of much importance to television journalists, scholars of the period need to know how to handle it when they see it. Art historians have a special interest in the sign-function of flowers in nineteenth-century painting, and I hope my work will be useful to art historians, while not encroaching on a field of study not my own. I might illustrate the application of my material to art history in the example of Penelope Fitzgerald, who raised the issue of flower meanings in the work of the pre-Raphaelite painters. In *Edward Burne-Jones: A Biography* (1975), she discusses the meanings of flowers in his paintings and casually attributes the creation of the language of flowers to an anonymous compiler of a derivative language of flower book published in Edinburgh in 1849 (97). After introducing the book, she refers to meanings from it as a matter of course, as if there were no other language of flower list available to Burne-Jones, and, since she nowhere explains that Burne-Jones owned the book or consulted it or whatever, I was left wondering about her conclusions.

My work would give the art historian the background to know that the language of flowers was not a product of the mid-nineteenth century, and would also make the art historian a more sophisticated interpreter of flower representation in nineteenth-century painting. For instance, I have often wondered if the carefully detailed ivy, fern, and wild rose in Arthur Hughes's *The Long Engagement* was meant to be significant, inasmuch as some common meanings for the three—friendship, sincerity, and simplicity—could reasonably be related to the picture's narrative. The flowers in three paintings of Ophelia—by Millais, Hughes, and Waterhouse—show differing treatments of her flowers. Is the forget-me-not along the stream in Millais's painting symbolic? Is the small blue flower surrounding the pool in Burne-Jones's *The Mirror of Venus* possibly forget-me-not as well? (It does not appear to be Venus's looking glass, a plant of the campanula family.) What might Rossetti mean by the daffodils and other yellow blooms (primroses?) in *Veronica Veronese*? What was the flower thinking behind Charles Collins's *Convent Thoughts,* in which the nun ponders a passion flower, and the garden shows all sorts of plants associated with the Virgin Mary and others simply beloved of Victorian flower writers? These are questions that, while I can ask them, I cannot answer, for the answers must come from those who know all about the artists involved, have read their letters, found out who they studied with, and learned where they lived and where they traveled. A representation of a flower in a painting is not necessarily symbolic, unless the symbolism is very obvious or very pointed (such as the passion flower in Millais's *Isabella*). Art historians must establish the validity of the symbolic interpretation, and then perhaps my work can help them with that interpretation. One very important issue is that the interpreter (whether art historian or literary critic) needs to establish that the artist was familiar with the language of flowers. Also, the particular source of the meanings needs to be established through biographical research—it is not enough to discover that a certain book was published before the art work and that the artist knew about the language of flowers. The special source needs to be identified, unless the symbolism is not complex.

Unlike a painting, the literary use of flowers usually carries with it a clue to its symbolic situation. However, I have no problem making a statement about the application of the language of flowers to literature, since that is my own field. Simply, there is little or no direct application to most nineteenth-century literature. Rather, the language of flowers is a popular, commercially successful development of the period's feelings about flowers. Poets and novelists who used flowers in their work drew from the same strong attachment to flowers and their importance as did the compilers of the language of flowers. The considerable body of poetry using flowers in major ways shares ideas and symbolic connections with the language of flower book's explanations of meanings—as I tried to express in the code of correspondences. There are a few writers whose flower work needs further study in line with the century's dominant floral symbolisms, the most important of whom is John Ruskin. Any writer using a significant amount of floral personification needs to be studied in relation to the popular sentimental flower books, as Ruskin's *Proserpina* needs to be related to his early reading in the popular annuals (and his attempts to write the kind of poetry he found in them). A better understanding of the situation of the symbolic flower in the period can help in the close reading of writers as diverse as Flaubert and Whitman.

Later, as the poets of the next century began to discard the Victorian period's habits of thought and expression, the literary flower came under attack—as early as 1857 in France, with Charles Baudelaire's association of flowers with evil in his title, *Les fleurs du mal*. As poets sought to "purify the language of the tribe," in Ezra Pound's phrase, they worked to rid words of their burdensome associations from the culture being repudiated. Probably the best known of these attempts is that of Gertrude Stein's famous line, "A rose is a rose is a rose is a rose," which relates specifically to the associations of the rose (see her remarks in *Lectures in America* and those quoted by Thornton Wilder in the introduction to *Four in America*). Nevertheless, in her defense of the famous line, she is unable to break completely with the past. Wilder quotes her: "Now listen! I'm no fool. I know that in daily life we don't go around saying 'is a . . . is a . . . is a . . .'. Yes, I'm no fool; but I think that in that line the rose is red for the first time in English poetry for a hundred years" (v–vi). Although real roses come in many colors, her literary rose is, of course, *red*.

But it is not my intention here to explore the literary uses of a thorough knowledge of the sentimentalization of flowers in nineteenth-century literature. Instead, I have merely tried to suggest that the language of flowers in itself has limits when used in scholarly interpretation, although with its associated material it needs to be considered as part of the background.

For itself, the language of flowers illustrates the dissemination of the romantic aesthetic, finding the self in nature. Further, its very prominence in the popular culture testifies to the success that the press had in spreading the gospel of gentility. The fact that, today, it is often misrepresented in such a way as to depict the Victorian period as one of excessive, impossible gentility, is ironic but probably inevitable. The current commercial exploitation of the language of flowers is part of the celebration of Victorian culture that has become fashionable. In truth, today's business ventures using the language of flowers, usually undertaken by women—needlework communications, bouquets, and gift books—are true to the entrepreneurial nature of the language itself. Even though the interpretation of the language is often mistaken, the applications that these interpreters are currently making of it are orthodox indeed.

A Combined Vocabulary

Notes

The Language of Flowers:
An Annotated Bibliography

Miscellaneous Flower Books:
A Bibliography

Works Cited

Index

A Combined Vocabulary

This appendix was made by creating a flower list from all the flowers included in the five chosen books: Latour, *Le langage des fleurs;* Delachénaye, *Abécédaire de Flore ou langage des fleurs;* Shoberl, *The Language of Flowers; With Illustrative Poetry;* Phillips, *Floral Emblems;* and Wirt, *Flora's Dictionary.* This shows an early list (Delachénaye), the most important list (Latour), a British list derivative of Latour (Shoberl), an original British list (Phillips), and a truly original American list (Wirt). It is not difficult to trace influences; for example, it is obvious that Wirt used Phillips. It is equally obvious that she used many flowers native to the South that do not appear in other lists. However, I do not mean to draw conclusions from the material, but simply to present it so that the reader can get a sense of the variety in the language.

I must add the caveat that there may be errors in plant classification in my combined list; certainly the compilers made them. However, I have tried to ascertain just which genus and species was meant by the plant name in the list and to group the same ones together, regardless of the name given to the plant by the individual author. For example, I determined hibiscus (Wirt) and mallow (Phillips) to be the same, inasmuch as Phillips had another meaning assigned to marsh mallow. Most troublesome were the convolvulus family, with so many and varied names for the different types. But these issues are not very important for artistic purposes. I also had to discard a few of the Latour items, the nonplants or unidentifiable plants "clandestine," "foulsapatte," "tremella nostoc," and generalized items not copied by many other writers such as "dead leaves" or "heap of flowers." I also discarded Phillips's "mushroom on grass turf."

It is impossible to give the botanical names in every case, as the writers used different names for what was obviously meant to be the same flower. Anyone familiar with Western garden flora should have no problem identifying most of the plants, and a good garden dictionary should do the rest. The plants are alphabetized under the most popular of their nineteenth-century names. Thus, some plants are listed under their botanical names at the time (many plants, such as "Aster Tradescanti," are no longer called by that name but it is not always possible to identify them as to exact species) while others are under their popular names (snapdragon). This follows the practice of the vocabulary makers themselves. For the sake of clarity I have used no italics for the Latin names, for most of them are no longer current scientific names for the plants. Since this vocabulary is only meant to give an idea of the different meanings and the varied plants used in the language of flowers, this lack of botanical rigor will have to be excused. The makers of the plant name lists were not botanists or even horticulturists, but producers of sentimental gift books.

I have translated the Latour and Delachénaye entries, but the entries from the English-language texts are in the exact words found there. This accounts for occasionally different wording and spelling.

Plant Name	Latour	Delachénaye
Absinthe	absence	absence
Acacia, garden	platonic love	mystery
" , rose	elegance	
" , yellow		
Acanthus	the arts	unbreakable bonds
Achillea	war	
millefleur		
Adonis (flos)	sorrowful remembrances	
Agrimony	recognition	
Almond	heedlessness	imprudence
Aloe	sorrow	botany
Althea		persuasion
Alyssum,	tranquillity	
rock-garden		
Amaranth	immortality	indifference
Amaryllis	pride	a coquette
Ambrosia		
Anemone	abandonment	abandonment
" , field	sickness	sickness
Angelica	inspiration	
Angrec		
Apple blossom	preference	
Arborvitae		old age
Argentine	naiveté	timidity
Artemisia	happiness	
Arum, wild	ardour	
Asclepias (Swallow-wort)		
Ash	grandeur	obedience
Ash, mountain	prudence	
Aspen	lamentation	
Asphodel	my regrets will follow you to the grave	
Aster, China	variety	
" , double		
Aster, large-flowered	mental reservations	
Aster Tradescanti		autumn
(Michaelmas daisy)		
Azalea		

Shoberl	Phillips	Wirt
absence	absence	
friendship	chaste love	elegance
elegance	elegance	friendship
		concealed love
the arts	art	
war	war	to cure
painful recollections	sorrowful remembrances	sorrowful remembrances
thankfulness		
indiscretion	heedlessness	hope
grief	acute sorrow, affliction	religious superstition
	persuasion	consumed by love
immortality	immortality	immortality
pride	pride	splendid beauty
		love returned
forsaken	expectation	
sickness	sickness	
inspiration	inspiration	
loyalty		
preference		
	old age	live for me
absence	absence	
	ardour	
	medicine	cure for the heartache
grandeur		
	prudence	
	lamentation	
my regrets will follow you to the grave	my regrets will follow you to the grave	
variety	variety	I will think of it
		I will partake your sentiments
afterthought	afterthought	
	cheerfulness in old age	cheerfulness in old age
	temperance	generous & devoted love

Plant Name	Latour	Delachénaye
Bachelor's button		
Balm, lemon	pleasantry, humor	
Balm of Judea (Gilead)		
Balsam	impatience	youth
" , red		
Balsam apple, pear	critique	
(Momordica)		
Barberry	sharpness	remorse
Basil	hatred	courage
" , bouquet of		I am offended
Bearbine	humility	
Beech	prosperity	treason
Bellflower		prairie
Belvedere	I declare war against you	
Betony		
Bilberry (whortleberry)	treason	
Bindweed, great		
" , small		
Bird's foot trefoil		
Bittersweet	truth	truth
Blackberry	envy	cares, jealousy
Blackthorn	difficulty	insouciance
Bladder nut	frivolous amusement	idleness
Borage	brusqueness	brusqueness
Box	stoicism	solidity, ancientness
Bramble		
Briony, black	be my support, my stay	
Broom	neatness	neatness
Buckbean	calm, repose	
Bugloss (anchusa)	falsehood	
Burdock	importunity	
Buttercup	ingratitude	benevolence
Cabbage	profit	
Cactus, creeping	horror	
" , Virginia		
Calla aethiopica		
Calycanthus floridus		

Shoberl	Phillips	Wirt
		I with the morning's love have oft made sport
	joking	sympathy
ıre	a cure	
ıpatience	impatience	impatience (yellow)
		impatient resolves
	a critic	
ourness of temper	sourness	
ıte	hatred	good wishes
osperity	grandeur	
	gratitude (white)	
eclare war against you		I declare against you
	surprise	
achery	treachery	
	dangerous insinuation	uncertainty
	obstinacy	
		revenge
ıth	truth	
vy	envy	
	difficulty	
volous amusement	frivolous amusement	
ıntness	bluntness, roughness of manners	
icism	stoicism	constancy
	remorse	
mility	humility, neatness	humility
m repose	calm repose	
ehood	falsehood	
ıch me not		
ratitude	childishness, ingratitude	riches
	profit	
	horror	
ror		
		feminine modesty
		benevolence

Plant Name	Latour	Delachénaye
Camellia		
Camomile		sorrow
Campanelle		elegance
Campion, rose		
Canary grass		
Canterbury bell	constancy	constancy
Cape jasmine		
Cardamine		
Carnation	strong and pure love	
" , Indian		painting
" , pink		
" , red		
" , white		young girl
" , yellow	disdain	
Catch-fly	trap or snare	
" , red		
" , white		
Cedar		majesty
Celandine		first sigh of love
Centaury	felicity	
(Sweet Sultan)		
Chaste tree	coldness, to live without love	
Cherry	good education	forget me not
Chervil		
Chestnut	render me justice	
Chickweed	rendezvous	
Chicory (endive)	frugality	
Chrysanthemum		difficulty
" , rose		
" , white		
" , yellow		
Cinnamon		chastity
Cinquefoil	beloved daughter	

Shoberl	Phillips	Wirt
	beauty is your only attraction	pity
	you are without pretension perseverance	only deserve my love
nstancy	constancy	gratitude transport, ecstacy
	paternal error	
		aversion
re love		woman's love
	lively and pure love	pure and ardent love
sdain	disdain	
are		
		youthful love I fall into the trap laid for me
	incorruptible, strength	
ppiness	felicity	
od education	good education sincerity	
der me justice	render me justice ingenuous simplicity	
gality	frugality cheerfulness under adversity	
		I love truth slighted love
oved daughter		

Plant Name	Latour	Delachénaye
Cistus (rock rose)	security, safety	
Citronella	sadness	
Clematis	artifice	
" , evergreen		
Clotbur (cleavers)	rudeness	
Clove	dignity	
Clover, purple		
Coboea scandens (cup- and-saucer vine)		
Cock'scomb (celosia)		
Colchicum (meadow saffron)	my best days are past	
Columbine	folly	hypocrisy
" , purple		
" , red		
Coreopsis, Arkansa		
Coriander	hidden merit	
Cornel, wild (Cornus mas)	duration	
Cornflower (bluet)	delicacy	delicacy
" , garden		education
Coronilla		
Cowslip (Primula vera)		
Crepis, bearded		
Cress		
Crocus		
Crown imperial	power	power
Currants (branch)		
Cyclamen		
Cypress	grief	death or grief
Daffodil		
Dahlia		
" , bouquet	my gratitude surpasses your cares	

Shoberl	Phillips	Wirt
	popular favor	
·tifice	artifice	filial love
	poverty	
·deness		
gnity		
	provident	industry
	gossip	
	singularity	foppery, affectation
·y best days are past	my best days are past	my best days are past
·lly	folly	
		resolved to win
		anxious & trembling
		love at first sight
·dden merit	concealed merit	
·rability	durability	
·licacy	delicacy	
	success crown your wishes	
	pensiveness	winning grace
	protection	
·solution		
	cheerfulness	
·wer	majesty & power	majesty & power
	you please all	
	diffidence	
·ourning	death and eternal sorrow	despair
·f love	deceitful hope	chivalry
	instability	forever thine

Plant Name	Latour	Delachénaye
Daisy (Bellis)	innocence	patience, sadness
″ , red		
Daisy, double	I share your sentiments	
Daisy, field	I will think of it	I will think of it
Dandelion	oracle	you are losing time
Daphne mezereum	coquetry, desire to please	
Datura	deceitful charms, disguise	
″ , violet		ecclesiastical
″ , white		science
Daylily, yellow		
Dew plant		
Dimorphoteca	foreknowledge	
Dittany of Crete	birth	
Dodder	baseness	
Dodecatheon	you are my divinity	
Dogwood (Cornus florida)		
Dragon plant (Arum dranunculus)		
Ebony	darkness	suppleness, grace
Eglantine	poetry	poetry
Elder	charity	
Elm	vigor	
Everlasting (Gnaphalium)		
Fennel		
Fern	sincerity	
″ , Maidenhair	discretion	
″ , Royal	reverie	
Fever root		
Fig		
Fir	elevation	fortune
Flag (water iris)		
Flax	I sense your qualities	simplicity
″ , dried		
Flax-leaved goldy-locks		
Forget-me-not	remember me, forget me not	remember me

Shoberl	Phillips	Wirt
nocence	innocence	innocence
		beauty unknown to the possessor
hare your sentiments	I partake your sentiments	
vill think of it		
e rustic oracle	oracle	coquetry
quetry, desire	desire to please	
ceitful charms	deceitful charms	deceitful charms
quetry	coquetry	
		a serenade
ldbirth	birth	
anness		
u are my divinity		
		I am perfectly indifferent to you
	snare	
ckness	blackness	
try	poetry	I wound to heal
	zealousness	compassion
	never-ceasing remembrance	never-ceasing remembrance
ength		
recy		
		delay
gevity	argument, prolific	
vation	elevation	time
	eloquence	
el your kindness	fate	
	utility	
	tardiness	
get me not	forget me not	

Plant Name	Latour	Delachénaye
Foxglove	salubrity	
Fraxinella	fire	
Frittilary, checkered		
Fuchsia		
Fumitory	gall, spleen	practice
Galega	reason	
Galium (rennet)		patience
Gentian, yellow		
Geranium		esteem
" , apple		
" , crane's bill		imbecility
" , fish		
" , ivy		
" , nutmeg		
" , oak		
" , pencilled-leaf		
" , rose	preference	
" , sad	melancholy spirit	
" , scarlet	folly	
" , silver-leaved		
Germander		the more I see you, the more I love you
Globe amaranth		
Goldenrod		
Good King Henry	benevolence	
Grass	utility	recompense for valor
" , scurvy		utility
Hawkweed		
Hawthorn	hope	prudence
Hazel	peace, reconciliation	
Heath	solitude	solitude
Helenium	tears	
Heliotrope	intoxication; I love you	violent attachment; to love more than oneself
Hellebore		folly
Hemlock		bad conduct
Henbane	defect	

Shoberl	Phillips	Wirt
	youth	a wish
·e		
	persecution	
	taste	th'ambition in my love thus plagues itself
	spleen	
	reason	
	ingratitude	
		present preference
:adfast piety		envy
		disappointed expectation
		your hand for the next quadrille
		an expected meeting
		lady, deign to smile
;enuity		
·ference		preference
elancholy spirit		
ipidity	preference	
		recall
		unchangeable
	precaution	encouragement
	goodness	
	utility	submission
	quick-sightedness	
·pe	hope	hope
ace, reconciliation	reconciliation	
itude	solitude	
rs	tears	
·voted attachment	intoxicated with pleasure	devotion
		calumny, scandal
	you will cause my death	
·sence	imperfection	

Plant Name	Latour	Delachénaye
Hepatica	confidence	apathy
Hibiscus		
Holly	foresight	
Hollyhock	fecundity	mother of family
" , white		
Honesty		
Honey flower (Melianthus)		
" , mourning bride		
Honeysuckle	chains of love	chains of love
" , coral		
" , French		
" , variegated leaf		
Hops	injustice	injustice
Hornbeam	ornament	
Horse chestnut	luxury	genius
Hortensia (Hydrangea macrophylla)	you are cold	courageous woman
Houseleek		spirit
Houstonia		
Hoya		
Hyacinth	game, benevolence	love, chagrin/you love me and give me death
Iberis	indifference	
Ice plant	your eyes freeze me	
Immortelle		endless love
Iris	message	message
Iris, flame	flame	
Ivy	friendship	reciprocal tenderness
Jasmine, of the Azores		envy
" , Spanish		sensuality
" , Virginia	separation	far country
" , white	amiability	candor
" , yellow		first languor of love
Jonquil	desire	desire, joys
Juniper	protection	ingratitude
Laburnum		

Shoberl	Phillips	Wirt
onfidence	confidence	
	sweet or mild disposition	delicate beauty
oresight	foresight	am I forgotten?
nbition	fecundity	
		female ambition
	honesty	sincerity
		speak low if you speak of love
		I have lost all
nerous, devoted affection	bond of love	I would not answer hastily
		the colour of my fate
	rustic beauty	
		fraternal love
justice	injustice	
nament	ornament	
xury	luxuriancy	
ou are cold	a boaster	a boaster
	vivacity	
		content
	sculpture	
me, play	play, or games	jealousy
	architecture, indifference	
our looks freeze me	idleness, you freeze me	rejected addresses
essage	message, messenger	I have a message for you
me	flame or passion of love	
endship	fidelity in friendship	matrimony
oaration		
iability	amiability	amiability
		grace & eloquence
sire	desire	I desire a return of affection
otection	asylum or succour	I live for thee
		pensive beauty

Plant Name	Latour	Delachénaye
Lady's slipper		
Lagerstraemia (crape myrtle)		
Lantana	rigor	
Larch	audacity	
Larkspur	lightness	lightness
" , pink		
Laurel	glory	glory, triumph
" , leaf		assured happiness
" , rose		beauty & goodness
" , thyme		purity
" , white		candor
Laurel, cherry	perfidy	
Laurel, Mountain (Kalmia)		
Laurustinus	I die if I am neglected	
Lavender	mistrust	
Lemon		
" , blossom		
" , tree		correspondence
Lettuce	coldheartedness	
Liana	knots or difficulties	
Lichen		
Lilac	first emotion of love	first emotion of love
" , white	youth	
Lily	majesty	
" , rose		rarity
" , white		candor, purity
" , yellow		inquietude
Lily of the valley	return of happiness	
Linden	conjugal love	
Lobelia cardinalis		
Locust leaves		
London Pride		
Lotus	eloquence	
" , leaf		
Love lies-a-bleeding		
Lucern	life	

Shoberl	Phillips	Wirt
		capricious beauty
		eloquence
	rigour	
oldness		
ghtness	lightness	lightness
		fickleness
lory	glory	the reward of merit
		I change but in dying
	perfidy	
		treachery
die if I am neglected	I die if I am neglected	a token
distrust	assiduity	distrust
	zest	
		discretion
	cold-hearted	
		solitude
rst emotion of love	forsaken	first emotion of love
outh		youth
majesty	purity, majesty	
		purity, sweetness
		falsehood
turn of happiness	return of happiness	delicacy
onjugal love	conjugal fidelity	
	distinction	distinction
		affection beyond the grave
ivolity	a love match	
oquence	silence	estranged love
		recantation
		hopeless, not heartless
fe	life	

Plant Name	Latour	Delachénaye
Lupine		
Lychnis (Jerusalem or Maltese Cross)		sorrows or voyages
Lythrum (loosestrife)	pretension	
Madder	calumny	
Magnolia grandiflora		
" , glauca		
Manchineel	falsehood	
Mandrake	rarity	
Maple	reserve	
Marigold (Calendula)	pain, chagrin	
" , African		
" , & cypress	despair	
" , French		
Marjoram		illusion or delusion
Marsh mallow	charity	humanity
Marvel of Peru	timidity	flee, dread love
Meadowsweet	uselessness	
Mignonette	your qualities surpass your charms	happiness of the moment
Milk-vetch		
Milkwort	hermitage	
Mint		
Mistletoe	I surmount all	
Monk's hood		
Moonflower	night	instability, inconstancy
Moonwort	forgetfulness	
Morning glory	coquetry	coquetry
" , red	I am attached to to you	
Moss	maternal love	
Moving plant (Hedysarum)		
Mulberry, black	I will not survive you	
" , white	wisdom	
Mullein		health

Shoberl	Phillips	Wirt
	voraciousness	imagination
	religious enthusiasm	sun-beam'd eyes
	pretension	
alumny	calumny	
	dignity	
		perseverance
alsehood		
arity	rarity, or extraordinary	
eserve	reserve	
rief	despair, jealousy or uneasiness	cruelty
	vulgar minds	
espair		
	jealousy	
	blushes	
eneficence	humanity	
midity	timidity	timidity
selessness	uselessness	
our qualities surpass your charms	your qualities surpass your charms	your qualities surpass your loveliness
	your presence softens my pains	
ermitage		
	virtue	
surmount all difficulties	obstacles, to overcome, or surmount	
	knight errantry	
ight		
orgetfulness		
	night, or extinguished hopes	busy body
attach myself to you	attachment	
aternal love	maternal love	recluse
	agitation	
will not survive you		
visdom		wisdom
	good nature	

Plant Name	Latour	Delachénaye
Mushroom	suspicion	rapid fortune
Musk plant	weakness	
Myrobalan plum	privation	
Myrtle	love	
Narcissus	egoism	egoism
" , field	false hopes	
Nasturtium		jest
" , scarlet		
Nettle	cruelty	sobriety
Nigella		
Nightshade, enchanter's	sorcery	
Oak	hospitality	love of country or strength & protection
Oats		
Oleander		
Olive	peace	peace
" tree		charity
Opuntia	I burn	
Orange blossom	chastity	generosity, magnificence
" tree	generosity	sweetness
Orchis, bee		
" , butterfly		
" , fly	error	
" , frog		
" , spider	cunning	
Oxalis	joy	
Ox-eye (Bupthalmum)		
Palm		dignity
Pansy		I share your sentiments
" , purple		
" , yellow & purple		
" , wild		
Parsley	a feast	
Pasqueflower	you have no claim	
Passion flower	belief	violent pain of love
Patience (Rumex)	patience	

Shoberl	Phillips	Wirt
uspicion	suspicion	
weakness	weakness	
privation		
ove	love	love positive
elf-love	egoism, self-love	egoism
		a warlike trophy
	splendour	
ruelty	cruelty	slander
	embarrassment	perplexity
pell	witchcraft	scepticism
ospitality	hospitality	bravery
		music
		beware!
eace	peace	peace
	I burn	
hastity	chastity	your purity equals your loveliness
enerosity	generosity	
rror	industry	
	gaiety	
	error	
	disgust	
ill	adroitness	
y		wit ill-timed
	obstacle	patience
	victory	
ink of me	thoughts/you occupy my thoughts	
		you occupy my thoughts
		forget me not
		love in idleness
stivity	feast or banquet	useful knowledge
ith	religious superstition	susceptibility
atience	patience	

Plant Name	Latour	Delachénaye
Peach blossom		constancy
Pennycress		inflexibility
Pennyroyal		
Peony	hardiness	heaviness
Peppermint	warmth of sentiment	warmth
Periwinkle	sweet memories	lifelong friendship
" , white		
Phlox		
Pimpernel, scarlet		
Pine	hardiness	light
" , black spruce		
" , Norway spruce		
" , pitch		
Pineapple	you are perfect	
Pink, garden	childishness	childishness
" , China		aversion
" , mountain (Cheddar)		
" , striped		refusal of love
" , white		
Plane tree	genius	umbrage
Plum	keep your promises	
" , wild	independence	
Polygonum		vigilance
Pomegranate	fatuity	perfect friendship
" , fruit		union
Poplar, black	courage	
" , white	time	youth
Poppy	consolation	repose
" , white	sleep of the heart	sleep
Potato	charity	
Pride of China (Chinaberry)		
Primrose	first youth	hope, first flower
" , auricula		
" , crimson-heart		
polyanthus		

Shoberl	Phillips	Wirt
		I am your captive
		flee away!
	bashful shame	anger, a frown
warmth of feeling		
tender recollections	pleasures of memory	pleasures of memory
		pleasing reminiscences
	unanimity	
	assignation	
	boldness	
		pity
		farewell!
		time & philosophy
you are perfect	you are perfect	
	aversion	
		aspiring
	refusal	refusal
	talent	ingenuousness
genius	genius	
keep your promises		
independence	independence	
	restoration	
	foolishness or mature &	
	finished simplicity	
elegance		
courage	courage	
time	time	
consolation & sleep	consolation to the sick	consolation
my bane, my antidote	sleep of the heart	my bane, my antidote
beneficence	beneficence	
		dissension
childhood	early youth	
	painting	
		the heart's mystery

Plant Name	Latour	Delachénaye
Primrose (*continued*)		
" , lilac polyanthus		
" , polyanthus		someone seeks to seduce you
" , rose color		
" , scarlet auricula		
Primrose, evening	inconstancy	
Privet	prohibition	prohibition
Pumpkin	grossness	
Quaking grass	frivolity	
Quince		
Ragged Robin (Lychnis)		
Ranunculus, aconitifolius		
" , asiaticus	you are radiant with charms	pride, impatience
Reeds	music	
" , feathery	indiscretion	
Rest-harrow	obstacle	
Rhododendron		
Rocket (Hesperis)		
" , Queen's		
Rose	beauty	ephemeral beauty
Austrian		
bicolor	scandal	study
bridal		
Burgundy		
cabbage		
cinnamon		
daily		
Damask		
deep red		
full blown, over two buds		
hundred-leaved	graces	
maiden's blush		
monthly	beauty always new	

Shoberl	Phillips	Wirt
		confidence
		unpatronized merit
		avarice
nconstancy	inconstancy	inconstancy
rohibition	defence	mildness
emptation		
		wit
	lustre	
ou are radiant with charms	you are rich in attractions	I am dazzled by your charms
usic	music	
discretion		
	danger	
		rivalry
		you are the queen of coquettes
ve	beauty	beauty
		thou art all that's lovely
		happy love
		unconscious beauty
		the ambassador of love
	precocity	
		that smile I would aspire to
	freshness, bloom of complexion	freshness
		bashful shame
	secrecy	
race	grace	pride
		if you do love me, you will find me out
eauty always new	beauty always new	

Plant Name	Latour	Delachénaye
Rose (*continued*)		
moss	love, voluptuousness	
multiflora		
musk	capricious beauty	caprice
pompon	prettiness	prettiness
red & white	sufferings of love/fires of the heart	
striped		summer
thornless		sincere friend
unique		
white	silence	innocence
white, dried		better to die than to lose innocence
wild	simplicity	simplicity
withered		
yellow	infidelity	infidelity
crown of roses	recompense for virtue	
rose leaf	I will never beg	
Rosebay willow-herb		
Rosebud	young girl	heart which ignores love
" , moss		
" , red		
" , white	heart which ignores love	
Rosemary	your presence refreshes me	good faith
Rudbeckia		
Rue		
" , wild	morality	
Rush	docility	navigation
Saffron	do not abuse me	
Sage	esteem	strength
Sainfoin	agitation	agitation
St. John's wort		originality
Sardony	irony	
Scabiosa		sensible & unhappy woman

Shoberl	Phillips	Wirt
	voluptuous love	superior merit
		grace
capricious beauty	capricious beauty	charming
	genteel, pretty	
		war, variety
		ingratitude
		call me not beautiful
silence		I am worthy of you
	death said to be preferable to loss of innocence	transient impressions
simplicity	simplicity	simplicity
fleeting beauty		
infidelity	infidelity	the decrease of love, on better acquaintance
	reward of virtue	
	celibacy	
young girl		
		confession
	you are young and beautiful	
heart unacquainted with love	heart ignorant of love	heart ignorant of love
your presence refreshes me	fidelity	remembrance
	justice	
	grace or purification	disdain
morality		
docility	docility	
beware of excess	do not abuse/mirth, laughter	
esteem	esteem	domestic virtues
agitation		
superstition	superstitious sanctity	superstition
irony		
	widow, widowhood	unfortunate attachment

Plant Name	Latour	Delachénaye
Sensitive plant	prudery	secret, profound sensibility
Service tree	agreement	
Snapdragon	presumption	coarseness, incivility
Sneezewort		freedom
Snowball (Guelder rose, Viburnum opulus)	good news	naiveté of childhood
Snowdrop	consolation	hope
Solomon's seal		secret
Spiderwort	the happiness of a moment	
Spindle tree	your charms are engraven on my heart	design
Star of Bethlehem	purity	harvest
Statice, sea	sympathy	
Stock	lasting beauty	
" , red		boredom
" , ten-week	promptness	
Stonecrop		
Straw	union	
" , broken	rupture	
Strawberry	perfect benevolence	perfume
Strawberry tree (arbutus)		
Sumach, Venice		
Sunflower	false riches	pride/my eyes see only you
" , dwarf		
Sweet pea		weakness
" , everlasting		
Sweet William	sensitivity	talent
Sycamore		hopes & cares
Syringa (Philadelphus)	fraternal love	
" , Carolina		
Tamarisk		
Tansy		
Tares	vice	vice
Teasel	misanthropy	
Thistle	austerity	criticism
Thorns, branch		
Throat-wort		

Shoberl	Phillips	Wirt
chastity	bashful modesty	sensitiveness
presumption	presumption	presumption
	winter of age	to bind
hope	consolation	refinement
	momentary happiness	I esteem, but do not love you
your charms are engraven on my heart		
purity		reconciliation
sympathy	dauntlessness	
lasting beauty	lasting beauty	bonds of affection
promptness	promptitude	
tranquillity		
union		
rupture of a contract		
perfection	perfect goodness	
		esteem & love
		splendour
false riches	false riches	pride, haughtiness
		your devout adorer
	delicate pleasure	departure
	lasting pleasure	an appointed meeting
finesse	craftiness	finesse
curiosity		
fraternal love	mercy	counterfeit
		disappointment
	crime	
	resistance	
	vice	
misanthropy	austerity, misanthropy	
surliness	importunity, intrusion	misanthropy
	severity, rigour	
	neglected beauty	

Plant Name	Latour	Delachénaye
Thyme	activity	cuisine
" , wild		thoughtlessness
Truffle	surprise	
Trumpet flower		
Tuberose	voluptuousness	sentiment
Tulip	declaration of love	honesty
" , red		
" , yellow		
Tulip tree flower		
Turnip		
Tussilago (colt's foot)	you will get justice	
Valerian, Greek	rupture	
" , red	accommodating disposition	
Venus's looking glass	flattery	ornament
Verbena (vervain)	enchantment	pleasantry
Veronica	fidelity	saintliness
" , spicata		
Vine	intoxication	intoxication
Violet	modesty	modesty, prudery
" , double		reciprocal friendship
" , white	candor	
" , yellow		perfect beauty
Wallflower	fidelity in misfortune	luxury
Walnut		
Watermelon		
Wheat	riches	
Willow, water	frankness	docility
" , weeping	melancholy	bitter sorrow
Winter cherry (Physalis)		
Wisteria	your friendship is sweet and agreeable to me	
Yew	sorrow	
Zinnia		

Shoberl	Phillips	Wirt
activity	activity	activity
surprise		
	separation	
dangerous pleasures	voluptuousness	le plus loin, le plus cher (the farther away, the dearer)
declaration of love	declaration of love	
		declaration of love
		hopeless love
		rural happiness
	charity	
justice shall be done to you	you shall have justice	
rupture	rupture	
accommodating disposition	accommodating disposition	
flattery	flattery	flattery
enchantment	superstition	sensibility
fidelity	fidelity	female fidelity
	resemblance	
intoxication	drunkenness	charity
modesty	modesty	love
innocence, candour	innocence, candour, purity of sentiment	modesty
fidelity in misfortune	fidelity in misfortune	fidelity in misfortune
stratagem		
	bulkiness	
riches	riches	prosperity
	frankness	
mourning	melancholy or forsaken lover	forsaken
	deception	
sorrow		
		absence

Notes

Introduction

1. Two recent books on flowers in the nineteenth century are Nicolette Scourse, *The Victorians and Their Flowers,* an introduction for the general reader, and Ella M. Foshay, *Reflections of Nature: Flowers in American Art,* the best book I have seen on flowers in the arts.

I. Flowers in the Nineteenth Century

1. My sources for the flower mission are various articles in periodicals: "Flower Services in Churches," *The Garden* 2 (June 1877): 463–64; Constance O'Brien, "History of a Flower Mission," *The Garden* 10 (March 1877): 199–203; F. S. Stowell, "Flower Missions and Their Work," *Demorest's Magazine* 18 (August 1892): 381–89; and brief articles in *The Garden,* ed. William Robinson, throughout the 1870s and 1880s.
2. For Henderson's remarks, see *The Gardener's Monthly* for May, June, and August 1880 (ed. Thomas Meehan). For early historical material on New York, see Grant Thorburn, *Forty Years' Residence in America;* Louis Menand, *Autobiography and Recollections of Incidents Connected with Horticultural Affairs, etc., from 1807 up to this Day, 1898;* and Michael Floy, Jr., *The Diary of Michael Floy, Jr.: Bowery Village, 1833–1837.*

II. The Sentimental Flower Book and Its Audience

1. See also F. E. Halliday, *The Cult of Shakespeare.*
2. There are a number of modern plant histories for the general reader, such as Alice M. Coats, *Flowers and Their Histories;* Peter Coats, *Flowers in History;* and John Fisher, *The Origins of Garden Plants.*
3. See Beverly Seaton, "Considering the Lilies: Ruskin's *Proserpina* and Other Victorian Flower Books."

III. Floral Symbolism

1. While I have based these remarks on the best material I can find, this topic requires much more knowledge of Oriental language and culture than I possess. Therefore, I trust that my comments will not be taken as authoritative, but rather in the context of my study of Western material.

2. I have published a semiotic analysis of Western flower personification which relates the shifts in floral symbolism along a biologic-social axis: Beverly Seaton, "Towards an Historical Semiotics of Literary Flower Personification."

3. There are many studies of allegory and symbolism in medieval literature. Several that are useful on flowers are Peter Dronke, *Medieval Latin and the Rise of the European Love-Lyric;* James J. Wilhelm, *The Cruelest Month—Spring, Nature, and Love in Classical and Medieval Lyrics;* and D. W. Robertson, "The Doctrine of Charity in Medieval Literary Gardens: A Topical Approach Through Symbolism and Allegory" *Speculum* 26 (1951): 24–49. For painting, see Elizabeth Haig, *The Floral Symbolism of the Great Masters.*

4. The *Partheneia Sacra* is explained in much greater detail in Rosemary Freeman, *English Emblem Books.* I consulted a copy of the *Partheneia Sacra* owned by the Folger Library. Franeau's *Jardin d'hiver* is owned by the Hunt Institute for Botanical Documentation.

5. See the lives of eighteenth-century American botanists written by Edmund and Dorothy Berkeley and studies of British botanists of the same time by R. Hingston Fox and Norman Brett-James. See also John Prest, *The Garden of Eden: The Botanic Garden and the Re-Creation of Paradise.*

6. Sources for the picturesque garden include studies by Dora Wiebenson, Christopher Hussey, and John Dixon Hunt.

7. G[eorge] F[isher] R[ussel] B[arker], "John Langhorne," *Dictionary of National Biography.*

8. John Nichols, *Literary Anecdotes of the Eighteenth Century,* 3:151–56; and Th[omas] S[eccombe], "John Huddleston Wynne," *Dictionary of National Biography.*

9. Samuel J. Pickering, Jr., in *John Locke and Children's Books in Eighteenth-Century England,* explains that animals were used to teach moral lessons and then later sentimentalized. This parallels the route of plants in children's literature.

IV. The Origins of the Language of Flowers: France

1. Biographical sources for Marianne de Fauques are *Nouvelle biographie generale,* vol. 13, and *Biographie universelle,* vol. 13. Born to a family who forced her into the religious life, after a long struggle she managed to renounce her vows. She lived in Paris and England, earning her living as a writer. Apparently, she came to England with a man who abandoned her.

2. This account of the book is found in François de Gaignières, "Notice sur *La guirlande de Julie,*" found in Didot Jeune's edition of the book.

3. Sources for the history of almanacs include John Grand-Carteret's massive volume, *Les almanachs français 1600–1895;* René Savigny de Moncorps, *Almanachs illustrés du XVIIIᵉ siècle;* and Bernard-Henri Gausseron, *Les keepsakes et les annuaires illustrés de l'époque romantique.*

4. See also Frederick Faxon, *Literary Annuals and Gift Books,* first published in 1912 but considerably revised in 1973.

5. A system similar to these was created by Capt. Frederick Marryat in his parody, *The Floral Telegraph,* which will be discussed in chapter 7.

6. Sources include an article in the *Dictionary of American Biography* on Louis

Cortambert and an article on the Cortambert family in the *Dictionnaire de biographie française*.

7. For Audot, see the *Dictionnaire de biographie française* and Edmund Werdet, *De la librairie française* 159. Biographical information on Louis Aimé-Martin can be found in *Nouvelle biographie générale,* vol. 34.

8. I have not been able to locate any first editions of this work, and my study uses an undated Audot edition—the second—from the Morton Arboretum Library; an 1840 Audot in the Hunt Institute; and a Garnier edition, c. 1854. However, I feel confident of the 1819 contents because I have access to a German translation of 1820 by Karl Muehler, owned by Harvard University, which establishes the text well enough for my purposes.

9. For other late French titles, see Jack Goody, *The Culture of Flowers* 241ff.

10. *Dictionnaire de biographie française* 8:247.

V. Further Developments: England and America

1. G]eorge] C[lement] B[oase], *Dictionary of National Biography* 18:147.

2. See the language of flowers bibliography for documentation of these titles.

3. Biographical information on Adams can be found in Frederic Boase, *Modern English Biography.* For Ingram, see John Carl Miller's edition of the letters that passed between Ingram and Helen Whitman.

4. See the language of flowers bibliography for documentation of these titles.

5. The Boston firms B. B. Mussey, Abel Tompkins, and others were associated with the Universalist Church and often published Universalist materials before the founding of the New England Universalist Publishing House in 1862 (Russell Miller 330). The Universalists were the most flower-oriented of the denominations, it seems, counting among their number Sarah Mayo, John Wesley Hanson, and Henry Bacon, all of whom published sentimental flower books under these Boston imprints or related ones in Lowell, MA.

6. This game, owned by James Moretz, director of the American Floral Art School in Chicago, who kindly sent me a xerox copy of the entire game, has no documentation whatsoever. My guess is that it is of German origin, as so many ephemeral paper items in colors were printed in Germany in the century.

7. Jack Goody, in *The Culture of Flowers,* describes several late-century French Christian language of flower works (243–44).

8. Some of these are pictured in Lesley Gordon's *Green Magic.* This well-illustrated book is riddled with factual errors that make it useless as history.

9. While the herbarium was made in 1814 and 1815, the meanings look like they were added later. There is no proof that the meanings were put on the pages at the time the flowers were pressed.

VI. Love's Truest Language: Readings in the Language of Flowers

1. In designing this reading I have used Roland Barthes, *Elements of Semiology* and *Mythologies;* and Louis Hjelmslev, *Prolegomena to a Theory of Language.* In preliminary form this reading was used in my article on Latour's book in

Semiotica. While I can now present my results without semiotics, I doubt very much if I could have learned much about the language of flowers without semiotic procedures.

2. Dr. Charles M. Boewe provided guidance for me in this analysis.

3. For a more general exposition of French-American differences, see Howard Mumford Jones, *America and French Culture 1750–1848;* and Henry Blumenthal, *American and French Culture, 1800–1900.* For the French-English see Philip G. Hamerton, *French and English: A Comparison.*

4. This letter, dated February 1, 1829, is in the Wirt Family Papers at the Wilson Library, University of North Carolina at Chapel Hill.

VII. Conclusions

1. Biographical information on Delord can be found in the *Nouvelle biographie générale* 13:490; and *Dictionnaire de biographie française* Fasc. 18:877–78. See also Charles Ledré, *La presse à l'assaut de la monarchie 1815–1848.*

2. In studying a large number of flower poems, from all three countries, I noted that the popular flowers in the poetry were the usual traditional flowers and that flowers prominent in gardens or home decoration appeared very seldom. See Beverly Seaton, "Extra-Coding in Nineteenth-Century Flower Personification."

The Language of Flowers:
An Annotated Bibliography

"Another flower book!" I think I hear some bright-eyed lassie exclaim.

(Mrs. J. Thayer, *Floral Gems*)

Most, but not all, of these books I have seen personally. A useful but unfortunately error-ridden bibliography of the language of flowers compiled by Morgan Riley appeared in the *American Rose Annual 1949* (Harrisburg, PA: American Rose Society, 1949). Riley made up his list from the collections in five major libraries. My own work is based on the collection of Rachel M. Hunt in the Hunt Institute for Botanical Documentation, Pittsburgh, and the collection of the Sterling Morton Library at the Morton Arboretum in Lisle, Illinois. I was also privileged to examine the collection of the late Emanuel Rudolph, professor of botany at Ohio State. Naturally, I visited the Library of Congress and several other libraries, as well as borrowing numerous volumes through Interlibrary Loan. This list is not meant to be a bibliographic description of editions as in a sales catalog, nor am I concerned with minor changes in editions, which usually took the form of different colored bindings, different illustrations, and sometimes rearrangements of text. Given the nature of the language of flower book, these changes are simply marketing strategies. The works are arranged alphabetically by author or title.

Adams, Henry Gardiner. *Flowers: Their Moral, Language, and Poetry.* London: Clarke, 1844. Under the title *The Language and Poetry of Flowers: The Floral Forget-Me-Not, a Gift for All Seasons,* this had numerous American editions from 1854. Publishers included Anners, Lippincott, and Claxton, Remsen & Hoffelfinger of Philadelphia; and Derby & Jackson of New York.

Adams, John Stowell. *Flora's Album, Containing the Language of Flowers Poetically Expressed.* Boston: Howe, 1847. Other editions were titled *The Language of Flowers Poetically Expressed, Being a Complete Flora's Album* (New York: Leavitt & Allen, 1847); and *The Floral Wreath: An Offering of Friendship* (Boston: Cottrell, 1851).

Aimé-Martin, Louis, attr. *Nouveau langage des fleurs ou parterre de Flore.* Brussels: Lacrosse, 1839.

Alphabet-Flore. Paris: Chavant, [c. 1837].

Ambauen, Rev. Andrew Joseph. *The Floral Apostles; or, What the Flowers Say to Thinking Man.* Milwaukee: Hoffmann, 1892.

The American Lady's Everyday Handbook of Modern Letter Writing. Language and Sentiment of Flowers. Dreams, Their Origin, Interpretation, and History. Domestic Cookery. Philadelphia: Anners, 1847.

Anna Elizabeth. *Vase of Flowers.* Boston: Cottrell, 1851.

Anonymous. No title, publisher, or place of publication. A very small book owned by the Morton Library. It has a crude color illustration on each page showing also the plant name and the meaning. English or American, late.

The Artistic Language of Flowers. London: Routledge, n.d. Late.

Attent, B., pseudo. Eugène Balland. *Les végétaux curieux ou les particularités les plus remarquables des plantes.* Paris: Blanchard, 1834. This is a revised version of an 1814 edition which I have not seen; I cannot be sure the early version contained the language of flowers, although it is listed as a source for the language of flower list in Almira Lincoln Phelps, *Familiar Lectures on Botany* (1831).

[Bacon, Mary Ann]. *Flowers and Their Kindred Thoughts.* [London]: Longman, 1848.

[Bertram, James Glass]. *The Language of Flowers: An Alphabet of Floral Emblems.* London: Nelson, 1853. This appeared in different editions through at least 1872.

The Bouquet; Containing the Language of Flowers and Their Poetic Sentiments. By a Lady. Boston: Perkins, 1844. This little book also appeared under the imprint of the Boston Universalist publisher Mussey, 1845–51.

[Bramald, Rev. Canon]. *The Bible Language of Flowers.* London: Marcus Ward, c. 1894.

Burke, Anna Christian (Mrs. L. Burke). *The Coloured Language of Flowers.* London: Routledge, [c. 1886].

———. *The Illustrated Language and Poetry of Flowers.* London: Routledge, 1881.

———. *The Illustrated Language of Flowers.* London: Routledge, 1856.

———. *The Miniature Language of Flowers.* London: Routledge, [c. 1848].

These titles are approximately the same text, packaged differently.

Burnett, Joseph. *Floral Handbook and Ladies' Calendar.* Boston: Burnett, 1869. An advertising booklet for Burnett's Standard Preparations for the Toilet and other products.

Campbell, Anna Maria. *The Floral Dictionary or Language of Flowers.* London: Rock, Brothers, & Payne, n.d. 10th ed.

[Carruthers, Miss]. *Flower Lore: The Teachings of Flowers Historical, Legendary, Poetical and Symbolical.* Belfast: McCaw, Stevenson, & Orr, Linenhall Works, [c. 1879].

Carter, Sarah H. *Lexicon of Ladies' Names with Their Floral Emblems: A Gift Book for All Seasons.* Boston: Buffum, 1852. This author is listed as Sarah C. Carter in the National Union Catalog. This book appeared in several editions through 1865.

Ch[ambet], Ch[arles]-Jos[eph]. *Emblème des fleurs ou parterre de Flore.* Paris: Audin, 1833. First published in Lyons 1825.

Chauncey, Mary. *The Floral Gift from Nature and the Heart.* Fitchburg, MA: S. & C. Shepley, 1846. Other editions were published in Worcester, MA, Philadelphia, and New York.

The Christian Sentiment of Flowers. Edinburgh: Oliphant, 1831.

La couronne de Flore, ou mélange de poésie et de prose. Paris: Chavant, 1837. An advertisement says that this work is meant to accompany *La naissance des fleurs* with illustrations by Redouté, Baget, and other artists, but I have not been able to trace such a volume.

Debay, Auguste. *Les parfums et les fleurs.* Paris: Dentu, 1861.

Del——, C. F. P. *Oracles de Flore.* Paris: Janet, [1816].

Delachénaye, B. *Abécédaire de Flore ou langage des fleurs.* Paris: Didot l'Aîné, 1811.

Delacroix, Mme. *Le langage des fleurs.* Paris: Delarue, n.d.

Delord, Taxile. *Les fleurs animées.* 2 vols. Paris: Garnier, 1847. Authors of other sections are mentioned in the text. Illustrations by J.-J. Grandville.

Diccionario do Bom Gosto ou genuina linguagem das flores em verso rimado. Rio de Janerio: Laemmert, n.d. 6th ed.

Dinnies, Anna Peyre. *The Floral Year.* Boston: Mussey, 1847.

[Dix, Dorothea L.] *The Garland of Flora.* Boston: Goodrich, Carter & Hendee, 1829.

Dumont, Henrietta. *The Floral Offering: A Token of Affection and Esteem; Comprising the Language and Poetry of Flowers.* Philadelphia: Peck & Bliss, 1851. Numerous editions through at least 1863.

The Emblematical Garden. By a Lady. Dublin: Jones, n.d. Late.

Embury, Emma C. *Love's Token Flowers.* New York: Riker, 1846.

Esling, Catharine H. Waterman. *Flora's Lexicon: An Interpretation of the Language and Sentiment of Flowers.* Philadelphia: Hooker & Claxton, 1839. Editions through at least 1863, probably later.

Fauçon, Emma. *Le langage des fleurs.* Paris: Lefèvre, n.d. Late.

Fertiault, François. "Le langage des fleurs." *La fleuriste des salons.* Brussels: Bruylant-Christophe, n.d.

The Floral Alphabet. London: Harrison, 1880. This little pamphlet sets forth a different concept of the language, arrangements of flowers to give words and numbers.

The Floral Birthday Book: Flowers and Their Emblems with Appropriate Selections from the Poets. London: Routledge, n.d.

Floral Poesy: A Book for All Seasons. London: F. Warne, n.d.

Floral Poetry and the Language of Flowers. London: Marcus Ward, 1877.

Flora's Pocket Dictionary: A Lexicon of the Language and Sentiment of Flowers. Philadelphia: Porter & Coates, n.d.

Flowers, Their Language, Poetry, and Sentiment. Philadelphia: Porter & Coates, 1870.

The Following of the Flowers; or, Musings in My Flower Garden. London: Marcus Ward, 1880.

Freeling, Arthur. *Flowers: Their Use and Beauty.* London: Darton, n.d.

Frisbie, Fannie. *Songs of the Flowers with Their Languages.* Boston: Cottrell, [c. 1855].

Genlis, Stéphanie de St. Aubin de. *Les fleurs; ou, les artistes.* Paris: Maradan, 1810. This is bound with *La botanique historique et littéraire.*

Greenaway, Kate. *Language of Flowers.* London: Warne, 1884. I suspect that Greenaway was responsible only for the illustrations, which do not have much to do with the text.

Greenwood, Laura. *The Rural Wreath; or, Life Among the Flowers.* Boston: Dayton & Wentworth, 1853. Editions through 1860. Published as *Life Among the Flowers* (New York: Worthington, 1880).

Griffin, Mary M. *Dew-Drops from Flora's Cup: or, The Poetry of Flowers.* Boston: Cottrell, 1845. A poetry anthology with a floral vocabulary attached.

Hale, Sara Josepha. *Flora's Interpreter; or, The American Book of Flowers and Sentiments.* Boston: Marsh, Capen & Lyon, 1832. This book had many editions, and after 1848 was titled *Flora's Interpreter and Fortuna Flora.* All editions I have seen or traced were published in Boston. According to Faxon (20) there was an English edition titled *Book of Flowers,* but I have not been able to confirm this at all.

Handbook of the Language and Sentiment of Flowers. Philadelphia: Anners, n.d.

[Hanson, John Wesley]. *Flora's Dial; A Flower Dedicated to Each Day in the Year.* Boston: Mussey, 1846. Editions appeared under the imprint of almost all of the Boston Universalist publishers as well as regional New England publishers such as Allen in Lowell, MA. A companion volume is Hanson's *The Ladies Casket* (Boston: Mussey, 1846), a language of gems.

[Henslow, John Stevens]. *Le Bouquet des Souvenirs; A Wreath of Friendship.* London: Tyas, 1840. Henslow is probably responsible for only the botanical parts, but his is the only name we can associate with the work. Perhaps Tyas himself did the flower language parts.

Hooper, Lucy. *The Lady's Book of Flowers and Poetry.* New York: Riker, 1841. Numerous editions by this publisher and others, including one titled *Floral Souvenir: A Perennial Gift; With a Complete Floral Dictionary* (Chambersburg, PA: Shryock, Reed, 1842). Her name does not appear on the title page of this last work, but it is identical to *The Lady's Book.*

Hoppe, O. B. J. *Die Neueste Blumensprache, nebst der Bisherigen Orientalischen.* Berlin: n.p., 1843.

Ildrewe, Miss. *The Language of Flowers.* Boston: De Vries & Ibarra, 1865.

Ingram, John Henry. *Flora Symbolica; or, The Language and Sentiment of Flowers.* London: Warne, 1869. An American edition was titled *The Language of Flowers; or, Flora Symbolica* (New York: Warne, 1887).

Jacquemart, Albert. *Flore des dames; nouveau langage des fleurs.* Paris: Neuhaus & Loss, [c. 1841].

Kirtland, Mrs. C. M. *Poetry of the Flowers.* New York: Crowell, [1845]. I think Kirtland may be a misprint for Kirkland, but I have no way of knowing for sure. Mostly poetry, this book includes a language of flower vocabulary as well as other language materials.

Le langage des fleurs. Paris: Delawe, n.d. Late.

The Language and Poetry of Flowers. Halifax, [England]: Milner & Sowerby, 1865. There is also a London edition of this work, probably later, published by Milner.

The Language and Poetry of Flowers. Boston: De Wolfe, Fiske, [1885].

The Language and Poetry of Flowers, and Poetic Handbook of Wedding Anniversary Pieces, Album Verse, and Valentines. New York: Hurst, n.d.

The Language and Poetry of Flowers with Beautiful Illustrations in Oil Colors. New York: Leavitt & Allen, n.d.

The Language and Poetry of Flowers with Floral Illuminations Printed in Colours and Gold. London: Marcus Ward, 1875.

The Language of Flowers: A Complete Alphabet of Floral Emblems. New York: Dick & Fitzgerald, 1875.

The Language of Flowers, and Alphabet of Floral Emblems. Cincinnati: J. A. & U. P. James, 1851.

The Language of Flowers and Boudoir Calendar for 1887. London: Walton, Hassell & Port, 1887. Advertising pamphlet for Beechams Pills.

The Language of Flowers—Being a Lexicon of the Sentiments Assigned to Flowers, Plants, Fruits and Roots. Edinburgh: 1849. I have not seen this book but am copying the citation from the Morgan Riley bibliography, largely because it is probably the book that Penelope Fitzgerald, in her biography of Burne-Jones, describes as the original language of flower book.

The Language of Flowers: Birthday Gems. London: Ward Lock, n.d. Late.

The Language of Flowers; With a Complete Vocabulary. London: Ward Lock, [c. 1875].

Latour, Charlotte de, pseudo. Louise Cortambert? *Le langage des fleurs.* Paris: Audot, 1819. See text for further publishing history. The citations in my text are from a late edition published by Garnier in 1854.

Leneveux, Louise P. *Nouveau manuel des fleurs emblématiques. Les fleurs emblématiques ou leur histoire, leur symbole, leur langage.* Paris: Roret, 1837. This is a volume in the series Manuels ou Encyclopédie Roret. In her introduction she says that the first edition of the book appeared in 1833, but I can find no record of this anywhere.

El lenguaje de las flores. Paris: Garnier, 1862. This is probably a translation of Latour.

El lenguaje de las flores y el de las frutas con algunos emlemas de las piedras y los colores. New York: Appleton, 1857.

Lenguaje de las flores, de las frutas, de los colores I de los piedros preciosas. San José, [Costa Rica?]: n.p., 1871.

Lucot, Alexis. *Emblèmes de Flore et des végétaux.* Paris: Janet, 1819.

[Malo, Charles]. *Parterre de Flore*. Paris: Janet, [1821].

Marryat, Frederick. *The Floral Telegraph*. London: Saunders & Otley, 1836.

Mayo, Sarah Carter Edgarton. *The Flower Vase*. Lowell, MA: Powers & Bagley, 1844. According to Russell E. Miller, in *The Larger Hope,* a history of the Universalist church, this book, which he says first appeared in 1843, went through 10 printings of 1,000 copies each "before the end of 1844" (562). A related publication by Sarah Mayo, not a standard language of flower book, is *The Floral Fortune Teller* (Boston: Tomkins, 1849).

Messire, J. *Le langage moral des fleurs suivi des principales curiosités de la Touraine*. Tours: Pornin, 1845.

Miles, Pliny. *The Sentiments of Flowers in Rhyme; or, The Poetry of Flowers Learned by Mnemotechnic Rules*. New York: Wiley & Putnam, 1848.

Miller, Thomas. *The Poetical Language of Flowers; or, The Pilgrimage of Love*. London: Bogue, 1847. Many editions. The American edition is *The Romance of Nature; or, The Poetical Language of Flowers,* ed. Mrs. E. Oakes Smith (New York: Riker, 184?).

Mollevaut, C.-L. *Les fleurs, poëme en quatre chants*. Paris: Bertrand, [1818].

Muehler, Karl. *Die Blumensprache oder Symbolik des Pflanzenreichs*. Nach dem Französischen der Frau Charlotte de Latour. (The Language of Flowers or Symbolism of the Vegetable Kingdom. From the French of Mme Charlotte de Latour.) Berlin: Karl August Stuhr, 1820.

Newman, John B. *Beauties of Flora, and Outlines of Botany, with a Language of Flowers, a Perennial Offering*. New York: Kearney, 1848.

————. *Illustrated Botany, Containing a Floral Dictionary and a Glossary of Scientific Terms*. New York: Fowler & Wells, 1850.

Nueva lenguaje de las flores y colores. Lima: Benito Gil, 1871.

Osgood, Frances S. *The Floral Offering; A Token of Friendship*. Philadelphia: Carey & Hart, 1847.

————. *The Poetry of Flowers and Flowers of Poetry*. New York: Riker, 1841. Many editions. This is an adaptation of Robert Tyas's *The Sentiment of Flowers*.

Le parfait langage des fleurs. Paris: Desloges, 1862.

[Partridge, Samuel W.] *Voices from the Garden; or, The Christian Language of Flowers*. London: Partridge & Oakey, 1851.

Phelps, Almira Lincoln. *Familiar Lectures on Botany*. Hartford, CT: Huntington, 1829. This work has a list of flower symbols appended to the scientific chapters.

Phillips, Henry. *Floral Emblems*. London: Saunders & Otley, 1825.

Raymond, Emmeline. *L'esprit des fleurs*. Paris: Rothschild, 1884.

Schmidlin, Eduard. *Die Blumensprache ausgedruckt durch in Deutschland wild wachsende Pflanzen*. Stuttgart: Metzler'schen, 1839.

Seelye, Charles W. ("Uncle Charlie"). *The Language of Flowers and Floral Conversation*. Rochester, N.Y.: Union & Advertiser, 1874.

Shoberl, Frederic. *The Language of Flowers; With Illustrative Poetry*. London: Saunders & Otley, 1834. Many editions. The American editions were published by Carey, Lea & Blanchard.

Stoeckler, J. R., pseudo. Johann Daniel Symanski. *Selam oder die Sprache der Blumen mit naturegetreuen, fein kolorirten Abbildungen.* Berlin: Christian, [1821]. Beautiful color plates, little content. Many other editions, published in both Würzburg and Vienna.

Strohm, Gertrude. *Flower Idyls.* Boston: Estes & Lauriat, 1887. Unusual development of the language of flowers, relating the flowers to various professions.

Thayer, Mrs. J. *Floral Gems or the Songs of the Flowers.* Boston: James French, 1847.

Turner, Cordelia Harris. *The Floral Kingdom: Its History, Sentiment, and Poetry.* Chicago: Moses Warren, 1876.

Tyas, Robert. *The Handbook of the Language and Sentiment of Flowers.* London: Houlston & Stoneman, 1845. There are also some American editions of this work, which probably was first published in 1844.

———. *The Language of Flowers; or, Floral Emblems of Thoughts, Feelings, and Sentiments.* London: Routledge, 1869. Several later editions.

———. *The Sentiment of Flowers; or, Language of Flora.* London: Tilt, 1836. Many editions, and some American ones. This is Tyas's most influential book.

Walser, George H. *The Bouquet.* Lincoln, NE: by the author, 1897. This is an amateur work, illustrated with photographs of the author and his wife.

Wirt, Elizabeth Washington Gamble. *Flora's Dictionary.* Baltimore: Fielding Lucas, Jr., 1829. For publishing history see the text. An 1833 edition is cited in the text.

Woodwards' Standard Preparations. *The Ladies' Floral Calendar.* Small pamphlet lacking title page. American, c. 1890.

Zaccone, Pierre. *Nouveau langage des fleurs avec la nomenclature des sentiments.* Paris: Victor Lecou, 1855.

Miscellaneous Flower Books:
A Bibliography

This list includes all sorts of sentimental flower books not in the language of flower bibliography, including the flower folklores, anthologies of flower poetry, some of the children's books that personify flowers, and moral and religious works. This list exists mainly to document some of the miscellaneous titles mentioned throughout the text and others like them, and does not pretend to be a list of all other sentimental flower books of the century. But it can be a good starting place for serious work. There are many more sentimental botanies and children's books, for example, and while I have named all the Bible plant books I have found, there are no doubt many more of these.

Alcott, Louisa May. *Flower Fables*. New York: Hurst, n.d. First published 1854.

Allen, Grant. *Flowers and Their Pedigrees*. New York: Appleton, 1884.

Almanach de Flore, ou description de douze plantes rares des jardins de Malmaison. Paris: Rosa, [1817]. Poems, essays, plates by Pancrace Bessa.

American Sunday School Union. *The Wonders of Vegetation*. Philadelphia: American Sunday School Union, 1845.

Bacon, Henry. *The Sacred Flora; or, Flowers from the Grave of a Child*. Boston: Tomkins & Mussey, 1856. First published 1845.

Badger, Mrs. C. M. *Floral Belles from the Green-House and Garden Painted from Nature*. New York: Scribners, 1867. Poems and illustrations.

Bailey, Alice Ward. *Flower Fancies*. Boston: Prang, 1889. Poems and gorgeously colored illustrations. Typical Prang.

Balfour, John Hutton. *Phyto-Theology; or, Botanical Sketches, Intended to Illustrate the Works of God*. London: Johnstone & Hunter, 1851.

————. *The Plants of the Bible*. London: T. Nelson, 1866.

Bible Flowers and Flower Lore. London: Hodder & Stoughton, 1885. These essays first appeared in *Jewish World*.

Blessington, Margaret. *Flowers of Loveliness*. London: Ackermann, 1836.

Buttercups and Daisies and Other Pretty Flowers. London: SPCK, [1866].

Callcott, Maria. *A Scripture Herbal*. London: Longman, Brown, Green, & Longman, 1842.

Chastenay-Lanty, Victorine de. *Calendrier de Flore, ou études de fleurs d'àpres nature*. 2 vols. Paris: Maradan, 1802.

The Christian Florist; Containing the English and Botanical Names of Different Plants. London: Seeley & Burnside, 1835. There was an American edition as well, published in Philadelphia by Carey, Lea & Blanchard in 1835.

The Christian Garland; or, A Companion for Leisure Hours. London: Religious Tract Society, n.d.

Church, Ella Rodman. *Flower-Talks at Elmridge.* Philadelphia: Presbyterian Board of Publications, 1885.

Clarkson, Lida. *Fly-Away Fairies and Blossom Babies.* London: Griffith & Farrar, 1892. Poetry and illustrations.

———. *Little Stay at Home and Her Friends.* Philadelphia: Robinson, 1879.

Cooke, Mordecai Cubitt. *Freaks and Marvels of Plant Life; or, Curiosities of Vegetation.* London: SPCK, 1882.

The Coronal; or, Prose, Poetry, and Art. London: Religious Tract Society, 1858.

The Cottage Garland; or, Poems on the Love of Flowers, Kindness to Animals, and the Domestic Affections. Williamsburg, [VA?]: John M. Stearns, 1847.

Coxe, Margaret. *Floral Emblems; or, Moral Sketches from Flowers.* Cincinnati: Henry W. Derby, 1845.

Crane, Walter. *The First of May: A Fairy Masque.* Boston: Osgood, 1881.

———. *A Floral Fantasy in an Old English Garden.* London: Harper, 1899.

———. *Flora's Feast.* London: Cassell, 1889.

———. *A Flower Wedding.* London: Cassell, 1905.

———. *Flowers from Shakespeare's Garden.* London: Cassell, 1906.

———. *Queen Summer or the Tourney of the Lily and the Rose.* London: Cassell, 1891.

Crichton, Rev. Arthur. *The Festival of Flora: A Poem.* London: N. Hailes, 1818. 2d ed.

Crommelin, May. *Poets in the Garden.* London: Fisher Unwin, 1886. This is an example of an anthology of flower poetry that does not give complete poems, but little bits on the flowers listed alphabetically.

Daubeny, C. *Essay of the Trees and Shrubs of the Ancients.* Oxford: Henry & Parker, 1865.

Deakin, Richard. *The Flora of the Colosseum of Rome.* London: Groombrdige, 1873.

Deas, Lizzie. *Flower Favorites: Their Legends, Symbolism and Significance.* London: George Allen, 1898.

Delitzsch, Franz. *Iris: Studies in Colour and Talks About Flowers.* Trans. Rev. A. Cusin. Edinburgh: T. & T. Clark, 1889.

De Vere, M. Schele. *Stray Leaves from the Book of Nature.* New York: Putnam, 1855.

Dierbach, Johan Heinrich. *Flora Mythologica oder Pflanzenkunde in Bezug auf Mytholgie und Symbolik der Griechen und Romer.* Frankfurt am Main: Sauerlander, 1833. This book was recently reprinted (Wiesbaden: Sandig, 1970).

Dowling, Alfred E. P. R. *The Flora of the Sacred Nativity.* London: Kegan Paul, Trench, Trubner, 1900.

Dubos, E. Constant. *Les fleurs: Idylles.* Paris: Janet, 1817. 2d ed. Probably first published 1808.

Du Molin, J.-B. *Flore poétique ancienne ou études sur les plants les plus difficiles à reconnaître des poètes anciens, grecs et latins.* Paris: J.-B. Ballière, 1856.

Elder, William. *Burns's Bouquet: The Flowers and Plants of Burns.* Paisley, Scotland: Paisley Herald Office, 1875.

Ellacombe, Henry N. *Plant-Lore and Garden-Craft of Shakespeare.* Exeter: for the author by William Pollard, [1878].

Embury, Emma S. *American Wild Flowers in their Native Haunts.* New York: Appleton, 1845. Poems, prose, fine illustrations.

Euchholz, J. B. *Flora Homerica.* Culm: Lohde, 1848.

Ewing, Juliana Horatia. *Dandelion Clocks and Other Tales.* London: SPCK, 1887.

———. *Mary's Meadow and Letters from a Little Garden.* London: SPCK, 1886.

Eytinge, Margaret. *The Ball of the Vegetables and Other Stories.* New York: Harper, 1883. Flower stories are included among these prose works. She also wrote a poem, *The Ball of the Fruits,* published as an advertisement "souvenir" by Baldwin the Clothier of New York in 1872.

Flora and Thalia; or, Gems of Flowers and Poetry Being an Alphabetical Arrangement of Flowers, with Appropriate Poetical Illustrations. By a Lady. London: Washbourne, 1835. Small volume with color plates; an edition was published in 1826 by Carey, Lea & Blanchard of Philadelphia.

Flora's Gala. Philadelphia: B. C. Buzby, 1809. Originally published by John Harris (Newbery) in 1808.

The Florist or Poetical Nosegay and Drawing Book. London: Hooper, 1775.

Flower Emblems; or, The Seasons of Life. New York: Appleton, 1871. An anthology of verse and prose about flowers.

Flower Stories and Their Lessons: A Book for the Young. London: Nelson & Sons, 1861.

Flowers from Many Lands: A Christian Companion for Hours of Recreation. London: Religious Tract Society, n.d.

Folkard, Richard. *Plant Lore, Legends, and Lyrics Embracing the Myths, Traditions, Superstitions, and Folk-Lore of the Plant Kingdom.* London: Sampson, Low, Marston, Searle, & Rivington, 1884.

Friend, Hilderic. *Flowers and Flower Lore.* 2 vols. London: Sonnenschein, 1884. First published 1883.

———. *The Flowers and Their Story.* London: Culley, n.d. Folklore for young readers.

Fuller, Jane Gay. *Uncle John's Flower-Gatherers: A Companion for the Woods and Fields.* New York: Dodd, 1869.

Garden Amusements for Improving the Minds of Little Children. London: Darton & Harvey, 1803. American edition (New York: S. Wood, 1814).

Gatty, Margaret (Mrs. Alfred). *Parables from Nature.* 2 vols. New York: Putnam, 1893. First published 1855–71.

Genlis, Stéphanie de St. Aubin de. *La botanique historique et littéraire.* Paris: Maradan, 1810.

[Gilbert, Ann Taylor]. *The Wedding Among the Flowers.* London: Darton & Harvey, 1808.

[Giraud, Jane E.] *The Flowers of Shakespeare.* [London: Ackerman, c. 1850?]

Grindon, Leo H. *Echoes in Plant and Flower Life.* London: Pitman, 1869.

———. *Life: Its Nature, Varieties, and Phenomena.* London: Whittaker, 1856.

———. *Phenomena of Plant Life.* Boston: Nichols & Noyes, 1866.

———. *The Shakspere Flora.* Manchester, England: Palmer & Howe, 1883.

———. "The Tennyson Flora." *Manchester Field-Naturalists and Archeologists Society Report and Proceedings.* Manchester, England: n.p., 1887.

Gubernatis, Angelo de. *La mythologie des plantes ou les légendes du règne végétal.* 2 vols. Paris: Reinwald, 1878.

Hey, Rebecca. *The Moral of the Flowers.* London: Longman, Rees, Orme, Brown, Green, & Longman, 1833. There were several later editions.

Hibberd, Shirley. *Brambles and Bay Leaves: Essays on Things Homely and Beautiful.* London: Groombridge, 1872. 3d ed.

———. *The Golden Gate, and Silver Steps.* London: Allen, 1886.

Hommage rendu à la rose par les poètes anciens et modernes. Paris: Didot, [1818].

Hulme, Frederick E. *Bards and Blossoms; or, The Poetry, History, and Associations of Flowers.* London: Marcus Ward, 1877.

———. *Natural History Lore and Legend.* London: B. Quaritch, 1895.

Jerome, Irene. *Nature's Hallelujah.* Boston: Lee & Sheperd, 1887. A typical late-century large illustrated gift book with flower poetry.

K., J. L. *The Voice of Flowers.* London: Broom, 1871.

Keese, John, ed. *The Floral Keepsake, with Thirty Engravings Elegantly Colored from Nature.* New York: Leavitt & Allen, 1845.

Kirkland, Mrs. C. M. (Caroline M.) *Garden Walks with the Poets.* New York: Putnam, 1852. See C. M. Kirtland in the Language of Flower Bibliography. The introduction to this work is a simple reworking of the introduction in *Poetry of the Flowers.*

Kitto, John. *Thoughts Among Flowers.* New York: Leavitt & Allen, 1864. First published in England by the Religious Tract Society, 1843.

Langhorne, John. *The Fables of Flora.* London: Harding, 1791.

Leneveux, Louise P. *Les fleurs parlants.* Paris: Mme Ve Louis Janet, [1848].

Lorimer, Mary, pseud. M. O. B. Dunning. *Among the Trees: A Journal of Walks in the Woods, and Flower-Hunting Through Field and by Brook.* New York: Hurd & Houghton, 1869.

Macmillan, Hugh. *Bible Teachings in Nature.* New York: Appleton, 1867.

———. *The Deeper Teachings of Plant Life.* New York: Whitaker, 1903.

———. *The Ministry of Nature.* London: Macmillan, 1872.

———. *The Sabbath of the Fields.* London: Macmillan, 1889.

Malo, Charles. *La corbeille de fruits*. Paris: Janet, [1819].

———. *Guirlande de Flore*. Paris: Janet, 1815.

———. *Histoire des roses*. Paris: Janet, 1818.

———. *Histoire des tulipes*. Paris: Janet. n.d.

Mant, Richard. *The British Months*. 2 vols. London: Parker, 1835.

[Mason, Mary]. *A Wreath from the Woods of Carolina*. New York: General Protestant Episcopal Sunday School Union & Church Book Society, 1858.

Mathews, F. Schuyler, ed. *The Golden Flower: Chrysanthemum*. Boston: Prang, n.d. Another late-century illustrated work.

Mayo, Sarah Carter Edgarton. *Fables of Flora*. Boston: Mussey, c. 1844.

Meredith, Louisa Anne Twamley. *The Romance of Nature; or, The Flower-Seasons Illustrated*. London: Tilt, 1836.

Miller, Thomas. *Common Wayside Flowers*. London: Routledge, Warne, & Routledge, 1860.

Montausier, Charles de St.-Maure (Marquis de). *La guirlande de Julie*. Paris: Didot Jeune, 1818.

[Montgomery, James]. *Prose by a Poet*. 2 vols. London: Longman, Hurst, Reese, Orme, Brown, & Green, 1824.

Montolieu, Maria Henrietta. *The Enchanted Plants*. Cincinnati: J. A. & U. P. James, 1850.

My Flower Pot: Child's Picture Book. Concord, NH: Rufus Merrill, c. 1840.

Newman, John B. *Boudoir Botany; or, The Parlor Book of Flowers*. New York: Harper, 1847.

Osborn, Henry S. *Plants of the Holy Land*. Philadelphia: J. B. Lippincott, 1861.

Osgood, Frances S. *The Flower Alphabet, in Gold and Colors*. Boston: S. Colman, 1845.

Parsons, S. B. *The Rose: Its History, Poetry, Culture, and Classification*. New York: Wiley & Putnam, 1847.

The Pastime of Learning with Sketches of Rural Scenes. Boston: Cottons & Barnard, 1831.

[Perkins, Elizabeth Steele]. *The Botanical and Horticultural Meeting; or, Flora's and Pomona's Fete*. By a Lady. Birmingham, England: Beilby, Knott, & Beilby, 1834.

———. *Flora's Fancy Fete; or Floral Characteristics: A Poem Illustrative of the Language and Sentiment of Flowers*. Brighton, England: n.p., 1839.

Phillips, Henry. *Flora Historica; or, The Three Seasons of the British Parterre*. London: E. Lloyd & Son, 1824.

Pindar, Susan. *Legends of the Flowers*. New York: Appleton, 1851.

Porter, Rose. *Flower Songs for Flower Lovers*. New York: Anson Randolph, 1880. An anthology of flower poems and excerpts from poems mentioning flowers.

———. *The Story of a Flower and Other Fragments Twice Gathered*. New York: Anson Randolph, 1883.

Pratt, Anna M. *Flower Folk*. New York: Stokes, 1890.

Pratt, Anne. *Flowering Plants and Ferns of Great Britain*. 5 vols. London: SPCK, [1855].

————. *Flowers and Their Associations*. London: Charles Knight, 1840.

The Queen of Flowers: or, Memoirs of the Rose. Philadelphia: Lea & Blanchard, 1841. Illustrations, prose, poetry.

Rambossom, J. *Histoire et légendes des plantes utiles et curieuses*. Paris: Firmin Didot, 1868.

Roberts, Mary. *Flowers of the Matin and Even Song; or, Thoughts for Those Who Rise Early*. London: Grant & Griffith, 1845.

————. *The Wonders of the Vegetable Kingdom Displayed in a Series of Letters*. London: G. & W. B. Whittaker, 1822.

Rolland, Eugène. *Flore populaire ou histoire naturelle des plantes dans leurs rapports avec la linguistique et le folklore*. 9 vols. Paris: L. Rolland, 1896.

The Rose's Breakfast. Philadelphia: B. C. Buzby, 1809. A prose relative of the personified flower poems for children.

Ruskin, John. *Proserpina*. Vol. 25 of *Works*. Ed. E. T. Cook and Alexander Wedderburn. London: Allen, 1906.

The Scripture Garden Walk; Comprising the Botanical Exposition and Natural History of Every Plant Occurring in the Sacred Scriptures. London: Hatchard, 1832.

Set of Flowers, Alphabetically Arranged, for Little Children. New York: Wood, 1819.

Sigourney, Lydia H. *The Voice of Flowers*. Hartford, CT: Parsons, 1846.

Skelding, Susie Barstow. *Flowers from Glade and Garden*. New York: White, Stokes, & Allen, 1884.

————. *Flowers from Hill and Dale*. New York: White, Stokes, & Allen, 1883.

Smiley, Sarah Frances. *Garden Graith; or, Talks Among My Flowers*. New York: Anson Randolph, 1880.

The Songs of the Seasons and Wild Flowers of the Months. Halifax, [England]: Milner, 1850.

Strickland, Agnes. *Floral Sketches, Fables, and Other Poems*. London: Hamilton, Adams, n.d.

Taylor, John Ellor. *Flowers: Their Origin, Shapes, Perfumes and Colours*. London: David Bogue, [1878].

————. *The Sagacity and Morality of Plants*. London: Chatto & Windus, 1884.

Thiselton-Dyer, T. F. *The Folklore of Plants*. London: Chatto & Windus, 1889.

Thomas, Carrie N., ed. *Trailing Arbutus: Poems Selected*. Brockport, NY: C. N. Thomas, 1879. Gift book on theme of arbutus.

Thornton, Robert. *The Temple of Flora*. Part 3 of his *New Illustration of the Sexual System of Linnaeus*. London: Bensley, 1807. This large volume, combining magnificent plates, poetry, and bits of romantic prose, was meant to be the popular portion of the scientific work to which it belongs. Thornton lost his fortune publishing it.

Tonna, Charlotte Elizabeth Browne ("Charlotte Elizabeth"). *Chapters on Flowers*. London: Seeley, 1848. 7th ed.

———. *The Flower Garden*. New York: Dodd, 1840. There are many different collections of her pieces. These are two that I have used.

Tyas, Robert. *Favourite Field Flowers; or, Wild Flowers of England Popularly Described*. London: Houlston & Stoneman, 1848–50.

———. *Flowers and Heraldry*. London: Houlston & Stoneman, 1851.

———. *Flowers from Foreign Lands*. London: Houlston & Stoneman, 1853.

———. *Flowers from the Holy Land*. London: Houlston & Stoneman, 1851.

———. *Popular Flowers*. London: Houlston & Stoneman, 1843–54.

[Waring, Miss S.] *The Wild Garland*. London: Harvey & Barton, 1827. This author wrote other works on botany and natural history, including a popular life of Linnaeus.

[Warner, Anna]. *Pond Lily Stories*. Philadelphia: American Sunday School Union, 1857.

Watson, Forbes. *Flowers and Gardens*. London: John Lane, 1901. First published 1872.

Wild Flowers of the Year. London: Religious Tract Society, [1846].

Wynne, John Huddleston. *Fables of Flowers for the Female Sex*. London: Riley, 1773.

Yonge, Charlotte M. *The Herb of the Field*. London: Macmillan, 1887. First published serially 1853.

[———]. *The Instructive Picture Book or Lessons From the Vegetable World*. Edinburgh: Edmonston & Douglas, [1877].

The Young Botanists; In Thirteen Dialogues. London: Phillips, 1810.

Works Cited

This list includes all secondary sources and a number of primary sources (sentimental flower books of all kinds, which will also be found in the two other bibliographies). The flower books are listed here if they were quoted from or discussed extensively. Listings given in the bibliographies are abbreviated here to just author and title.

Aimé-Martin, Louis. *Lettres à Sophie*. 2 vols. Paris: Gide, 1814. First published 1810.

Alcott, Louisa May. *Flower Fables*.

———. *Rose in Bloom*. New York: Grosset & Dunlap, 1927.

Allen, B. Sprague. *Tides in English Taste 1619–1800: A Background for the Study of Literature*. 2 vols. Cambridge, MA: Harvard Univ. Press, 1937.

Allen, David Elliston. *The Naturalist in Britain*. London: Allen Lane, 1976.

Altick, Richard D. *The Cowden Clarkes*. London: Oxford Univ. Press, 1948.

American Florist. Chicago and New York: 1885–1931.

Anna Elizabeth. *Vase of Flowers*.

Balzac, Honoré de. *The Lily of the Valley*. Trans. James Waring. Philadelphia: Gebbie, 1899.

Barrett, W. A. *Flowers and Festivals or Directions for the Floral Decoration of Churches*. London: Rivington, 1868.

Barthes, Roland. *Elements of Semiology*. Trans. Annette Lavers and Colin Smith. New York: Hill & Wang, 1979.

———. *Mythologies*. Trans. Annette Lavers. New York: Hill & Wang, 1979.

Beecher, Henry Ward. *Norwood: or, Village Life in New England*. New York: Scribners, 1868.

Beecher, Mrs. Henry Ward. *From Dawn to Daylight: By a Minister's Wife*. New York: Hurst, n.d. First published 1859.

Berkeley, Edmund, and Dorothy Berkeley. *Dr. Alexander Garden of Charles Town*. Chapel Hill: Univ. of North Carolina Press, 1969.

———. *Dr. John Mitchell—The Man Who Made the Map of North America*. Chapel Hill: Univ. of North Carolina Press, 1974.

———. *John Clayton: Pioneer of American Botany*. Chapel Hill: Univ. of North Carolina Press, 1963.

———. *The Life and Travels of John Bartram: From Lake Ontario to the River St. John*. Tallahassee: Florida State Univ. Press, 1982.

Bibliographie de la France. Paris: Pillet Ainé, 1812–present.

Binion, Samuel A. *Phyllanthography: A Method of Leaf and Flower Writing*. New York: R. F. Fenno, 1909.

Biographie universelle: ancienne et moderne. 2d ed. 45 vols. Paris: Delagrave, n.d. ("Michaud").

Blumenthal, Henry. *American and French Culture, 1800–1900*. Baton Rouge: Louisiana State Univ. Press, 1975.

Boase, Frederic. *Modern English Biography*. 6 vols. Truro, England: Netherton & Worth, 1892–1921.

Brett-James, Norman G. *The Life of Peter Collinson*. London: privately printed, [c. 1927].

Browne, Mary. *The Diary of a Girl in France in 1821*. Ed. H. N. Shore. New York: Dutton, 1905.

Browning, Elizabeth Barrett. *Complete Poetical Works*. Boston: Houghton Mifflin, 1900.

Bungay, George W. "Thoughts in My Garden," quoted in Mary D. Wellcome, *Talks About Flowers*. Yarmouth, ME: I. C. Wellcome, 1881.

Cabral, Fernand, and Henri Leclerq. *Dictionnaire d'archéologie chrétienne*. 15 vols. Paris: Letouzey et Ané, 1924–53.

Cannon, Susan F. *Science in Culture: The Early Victorian Period*. New York: Dawson & Science History, 1978.

Carew, Thomas. *Poems*. Ed. Rhodes Dunlap. Oxford: Oxford Univ. Press, 1949.

Chamberlain, Edith L. *The Gentlewoman's Book of Gardening*. London: Henry, 1892.

Chastenay-Lanty, Victorine de. *Mémoires*. 2 vols. Paris: Plon, 1896.

Clement, Ernest W. *The Japanese Floral Calendar*. Chicago: Open Court, 1911.

Coats, Alice. *Flowers and Their Histories*. London: Adam and Charles Black, 1968.

———. *Garden Shrubs and Their Histories*. New York: Dutton, 1964.

Coats, Peter. *Flowers in History*. New York: Viking, 1970.

Cooke, Mordecai Cubbitt. *Freaks and Marvels of Plant Life; or, Curiosities of Vegetation*.

Cowley, Abraham. *The Second and Third Parts of the Works of Abraham Cowley*. Trans. Nahum Tate. London: Harper, 1689.

Coxe, Margaret. *Floral Emblems; or, Moral Sketches from Flowers*.

Dana, Olive E. *Under the Eaves*. Augusta, ME: Burleigh & Flynt, 1894.

Dane, Joseph A. "Parody and Satire: A Theoretical Model." *Genre* 13 (1980): 145–59.

Daniel, Stephen H. "Political and Philosophical Uses of Fables in Eighteenth-Century England." *Eighteenth Century* 23 (1982): 151–71.

Darwin, Erasmus. *The Botanic Garden*. London: Jones, 1824.

Del———, C. F. P. *Oracles de Flore*.

Delachénaye, B. *Abécédaire de Flore ou langage des fleurs*.

Delaporte, François. *Nature's Second Kingdom: Explorations of Vegetality in the Eighteenth Century.* Trans. Arthur Goldhammer. Cambridge, MA: MIT, 1982.

Delille, Jacques. *Les jardins, Poëme en quatre chants. Oeuvres.* Paris: Michaud, 1824. Vol. 7.

Delord, Taxile. *Les fleurs animées.*

"Demetrius de la Croix." *Le mariage des fleurs.* Trans. P. Trante. Paris: Drost aîné, 1798.

Dictionary of American Biography. 20 vols. New York: Scribners, 1946.

Dictionary of National Biography. 21 vols. London: Oxford Univ. Press, 1950.

Dictionnaire de biographie française. Paris: Letouzey et Ané, 1933–present.

Dinnies, Anna Peyre. *The Floral Year.*

Dopp, Herman. *La contrefaçon des livres français en Belgique 1815–1852.* Louvain: Librairie Universitaire, 1932.

Dronke, Peter. *Medieval Latin and the Rise of the European Love-Lyric.* Oxford: Oxford Univ. Press, 1968.

Earle, Maria Theresa. *Potpourri from a Surrey Garden.* London: Thomas Nelson, [c. 1896].

Elder, William. *Burns's Bouquet: The Flowers and Plants of Burns.*

Fauques, Marianne de. *The Vizirs; or, The Enchanted Labyrinth.* 3 vols. London: Riley, 1774.

Faxon, Frederick. *Literary Annuals and Gift Books: A Bibliography 1823–1903.* Ravelston, Middlesex, England: Private Libraries, 1973.

Fisher, John. *The Origins of Garden Plants.* London: Constable, 1982.

Fitzgerald, Penelope. *Edward Burne-Jones: A Biography.* London: Michael Joseph, 1975.

Fitzpatrick, T. J. *Rafinesque: A Sketch of His Life with Bibliography.* Ed. and revised by Charles M. Boewe. Weston, MA: M & S, 1982.

La fleuriste des salons. Brussels: Bruylant-Christophe, [c. 1850].

The Florist or Poetical Nosegay and Drawing Book.

Floy, Michael, Jr. *The Diary of Michael Floy, Jr.: Bowery Village, 1833–1837.* Ed. Richard Brooks. New Haven, CT: Yale Univ. Press, 1941.

Foshay, Ella M. *Reflections of Nature: Flowers in American Art.* New York: Alfred A. Knopf, 1984.

Fowle, William B. "The School Committee." *American Life in the 1840s.* Ed. Carl Bode. Garden City, NY: Doubleday, 1967. 254–62.

Fox, R. Hingston. *Dr. John Fothergill and His Friends.* London: Macmillan, 1919.

Franeau, Jean. *Jardin d'hiver.* Douay: Borremans, 1616.

Freeman, Rosemary. *English Emblem Books.* New York: Octagon, 1966.

Friend, Hilderic. *Flowers and Flower Lore.*

Gaigniéres, François de. "Notice sur *La guirlande de Julie.*" In C. S. Montausier, *La guirlande de Julie.* Paris: Didot Jeune, 1818.

Gausseron, Bernard-Henri. *Les keepsakes et les annuaires illustrés de l'époque romantique*. Paris: Auguste Fontaine, 1896.

Gélis, François de. *Historie critique des jeux floraux*. Toulouse: Privat, 1912. (Bibliothèque méridionale, 2d series, vol. 15.)

Genlis, Stéphanie de St. Aubin de. *La botanique historique et littéraire*.

―――. *Les fleurs; ou, les artistes*.

[Gilbert, Ann Taylor]. *The Wedding Among the Flowers*.

Golden, Jack. "Louis Prang." *Publishers for Mass Entertainment in Nineteenth-Century America*. Ed. Madeleine B. Stern. Boston: G. K. Hall, 1980. 251–60.

Goodrich, Samuel G. *Recollections of a Lifetime*. 2 vols. New York: Miller, Orton, & Mulligan, 1867.

Goody, Jack. *The Culture of Flowers*. Cambridge: Cambridge Univ. Press, 1993.

Gordon, Jean. *Pageant of the Rose*. Woodstock, VT: Red Rose, 1961.

Gordon, Lesley. *Green Magic*. New York: Viking, 1977.

Gorer, Richard. *The Flower Garden in England*. London: Batsford, 1975.

Goss, Madeleine. *Bolero: The Life of Maurice Ravel*. New York: Holt, 1940.

Grand-Carteret, John. *Les almanachs français 1600–1895*. Paris: Alisié et Cie, 1896.

Greenwood, Laura. *The Rural Wreath; or, Life Among the Flowers*.

Griffin, Mary M. *Dew-Drops from Flora's Cup; or, The Poetry of the Flowers*.

Grindon, Leo. *The Shakspere Flora*.

Haig, Elizabeth. *The Floral Symbolism of the Great Masters*. London: Kegan Paul, 1913.

Halliday, F. E. *The Cult of Shakespeare*. London: Duckworth, 1957.

Hamerton, Philip G. *French and English: A Comparison*. Boston: Roberts, 1889.

Hammer-Purgstall, Joseph. *Fundgruben des Orients*. 2 vols. Vienna: A. Schmid, 1809–11.

Hassard, Annie. *Floral Decorations for Dwelling Houses*. London: Macmillan, 1876.

Hawkins, Henry. *Partheneia sacra*. Rouen: Cousturier, 1633.

Hayden, Ruth. *Mrs. Delany: Her Life and Her Flowers*. London: Colonnade, 1980.

Hazard, Paul. *Books, Children, and Men*. Trans. Marguerite Mitchell. Boston: Horn Book, 1944.

Heath, Francis George. *Sylvan Spring*. London: S. Low, Marston, Searle & Rivington, 1880.

―――. *Sylvan Winter*. London: K. Paul, Trench, 1886.

Heiser, Charles B., Jr. *The Sunflower*. Norman: Univ. of Oklahoma Press, 1976.

Hervey, James. "Reflections on a Flower Garden," in *Meditations and Contemplations*. New York: Robert Carter & Brothers, 1856. First published 1745–46.

Hjelmslev, Louis. *Prolegomena to a Theory of Language*. Trans. Francis J. Whitfield. Madison: Univ. of Wisconsin Press, 1969.

Hunt, John Dixon. *The Figure in the Landscape: Poetry, Painting, and Gardening During the Eighteenth Century*. Baltimore: Johns Hopkins Univ. Press, 1976.

Hunt, Leigh. *The Poetical Works of Leigh Hunt.* Ed. H. S. Milford. London: Oxford Univ. Press, 1923.

Hussey, Christopher. *The Picturesque: Studies in a Point of View.* London: Putnam, 1927.

Jakobson, Roman. "Two Aspects of Language and Two Types of Aphasic Disturbances." *Fundamentals of Language.* With Morris Halle. The Hague: Mouton, 1961. 69–96.

Jerdan, William. *Autobiography.* 3 vols. London: Hall, 1852.

Johnson, Sophia Orne. "Daisy Eyebright's Journal." *Country Gentleman,* Sept. 23, 1869–Feb. 2, 1871.

Jones, Howard Mumford. *America and French Culture 1750–1848.* Chapel Hill: Univ. of North Carolina Press, 1927.

Karr, Alphonse. *A Tour Round My Garden.* Trans. Rev. J. G. Wood. London: Warne, [c. 1845].

Kaser, David. *The Cost Book of Carey and Lea 1825–1838.* Philadelphia: Univ. of Pennsylvania Press, 1963.

[Kent, Elizabeth]. *Flora Domestica; or, The Portable Flower-Garden.* London: Taylor & Hessey, 1823.

Kett, Rev. Henry. *Emily, a Moral Tale, Including Letters from a Father to His Daughter.* 2 vols. London: Rivington, 1809. First published 1807.

Kingsley, Charles. *Miscellanies.* 2 vols. London: Parker, 1859. Vol. 2.

Koehn, Alfred. *Chinese Flower Symbolism.* Tokyo: Lotus Court, 1954.

———. *Japanese Flower Symbolism.* Peking: Lotus Court, 1940.

Kresken, H. Acosta. *Wonders of Flora: The Preservation of Flowers in Their Natural State and Colors.* Dayton, OH: Philip A. Kemper, 1879.

Ladies' Floral Cabinet. New York: 1871–86.

Lambert, Agnes. "The Ceremonial Use of Flowers." *Nineteenth Century* 4 (1878): 457–77.

———. "The Ceremonial Use of Flowers, A Sequel." *Nineteenth Century* 7 (1880): 808–27.

Langhorne, John. *The Fables of Flora.*

Latour, Charlotte de, pseudo. Louise Cortambert? *Le langage des fleurs.*

Ledré, Charles. *La presse à l'assaut de la monarchie 1815–1848.* Paris: Armand Colin, 1960.

Leneveux, Louise P. *Nouveau manuel des fleurs emblématiques. Les fleurs emblématiques ou leur histoire, leur symbole, leur langage.*

Loudon, John Claudius, ed. *Gardener's Magazine.* London: Longman, 1826–34.

———. *Gardener's Magazine, and Register of Rural and Domestic Improvement.* London: Longman, 1835–43.

Lucot, Alexis. *Emblèmes de Flore and des végétaux.*

McLean, Teresa. *Medieval English Gardens.* New York: Viking, 1980.

Maeterlinck, Maurice. *Le double jardin*. Paris: Charpentier, 1913. First published 1904.

———. *L'intelligence des fleurs*. Paris: Charpentier, 1912. First published 1907.

Malo, Charles. *Guirlande de Flore*.

Marryat, Frederick. *The Floral Telegraph*.

Meehan, Thomas, ed. *The Gardener's Monthly*. Philadelphia: 1859–87.

Menand, Louis. *Autobiography and Recollections of Incidents Connected with Horticultural Affairs, etc., from 1807 up to this Day, 1898*. Cohoes, NY: L'Independent, 1898.

Meyer, Gerald D. *The Scientific Lady in England 1650–1760*. Berkeley: Univ. of California Press, 1955.

Miller, John Carl, ed. *Poe's Helen Remembers*. Charlottesville: Univ. Press of Virginia, 1979.

Miller, Russell E. *The Larger Hope: The First Century of the Universalist Church in America*. Boston: Unitarian Universalist Association, 1979.

Miller, Thomas. *The Poetical Language of Flowers; or, The Pilgrimage of Love*.

Montagu, Mary Wortley. *The Complete Letters*. Ed. Robert Halsband. Oxford: Oxford Univ. Press, 1965. Vol. 1.

Montausier, Charles de St. Maure (Marquis de). *La guirlande de Julie*.

Montolieu, Maria Henrietta. *The Enchanted Plants*.

Moretz, James. *Posey Bouquet Holders*. Chicago: Flowerian, 1984.

Morgan, Sydney. *France*. 2 vols. New York: Eastburn, 1817.

———. *France in 1829–30*. 2 vols. New York: Harper, 1830.

Morley, John. *Death, Heaven, and the Victorians*. London: Studio Vista, 1971.

Mottraye, Aubry de la. *Voyages du Sr. A. de la Mottraye en Europe, en Asie et en Afrique*. 2 vols. The Hague: T. Johnson & J. Van Duren, 1727.

Müller, Max. *Natural Religion*. Vol. 9 of *Works of Max Müller*. New York: Longmans Green, 1898.

Nichols, John. *Literary Anecdotes of the Eighteenth Century*. London: n.p., 1812. Vol. 3.

Nouvelle biographie générale. Ed. M. Le Dr. Hoefer. 46 volumes. Paris: Firmin Didot, 1852–77.

Ovid, *Fasti*. Trans. James G. Frazer. London: Macmillan, 1929.

———. *Metamorphoses*. Trans. Mary M. Innes. New York: Penguin, 1978.

Parny, Evariste Désiré-Desforges, Chevalier de. *Oeuvres choisies*. Paris: Roux-Dufort, 1826.

Parsons, Frances Theodora Smith Dana. *According to Season*. New York: Scribners, 1894.

———. *How to Know the Ferns*. New York: Scribners, 1899.

———. *How to Know the Wildflowers*. New York: Scribners, 1893.

Perkins, Elizabeth Steele. *Flora's Fancy Fete; or Floral Characteristics*.

Phillips, Henry. *Flora Historica; or, The Three Seasons of the British Parterre*.

————. *Floral Emblems.*

Pickering, Samuel F., Jr. *John Locke and Children's Books in Eighteenth Century England.* Knoxville: Univ. of Tennessee Press, 1981.

Pliny. *Natural History.* 19 vols. Cambridge, MA: Harvard Univ. Press, 1964. Vols. 6, 7.

Portal, Fréderic. *An Essay on Symbolic Colours.* Trans. W. S. Inman. London: n.p., 1845.

Pratt, Anne. *Flowers and Their Associations.*

Prest, John. *The Garden of Eden: The Botanic Garden and the Re-Creation of Paradise.* New Haven, CT: Yale Univ. Press, 1981.

Quérard, Joseph Marie. *La France littéraire ou dictionnaire bibliographique.* 12 vols. Paris: Firmin Didot, 1827–64.

————. *Les superchéries littéraires.* 3 vols. Paris: Daffis, 1869.

Rafinesque, Constantine S. "Ethics, or Moral Philosophy." *Western Minerva* 1 (1821): 11–18.

————. *A Life of Travels. Chronica Botanica* 8:2. Waltham, MA: Chronica Botanica, 1944. First published 1836.

————. *The World.* Ed. Charles Boewe. Gainesville, FL: Scholars' Facsimiles, 1956. First published 1836.

Rapin, René. *Of Gardens.* Trans. Gardiner. London: Boyer, [1706].

Robinson, William, ed. *The Garden.* London, 1871–1927.

Ronsard, Pierre de. *Sonnets pour Helene.* Trans. Humbert Wolfe. New York: Macmillan, 1934.

Rousseau, Jean-Jacques. *Lettres sur la botanique.* Paris: Club des Libraires de France, 1962. First published 1781.

Rudolph, Emanuel D. "How It Developed that Botany Was the Science Thought Most Suitable for Victorian Young Ladies." *Children's Literature: The Great Excluded* 2 (1973): 92–97.

————. "Learning Botany by Rote, the Way of the Nineteenth-Century Catechisms." *Plant Science Bulletin* 24 (1978): 39–40.

————. "Women in Nineteenth-Century American Botany: A Generally Unrecognized Constituency." *American Journal of Botany* 69 (1982): 1346–55.

Ryder, Annie H. *Hold up Your Heads, Girls! Helps for Girls, in School and Out.* Boston: Lothrop, 1886.

Sanderson, John. *The American in Paris.* 2 vols. Philadelphia: Carey & Hart, 1839.

Savigny de Moncorps, René Jean. *Almanachs illustrés du XVIIIᵉ siècle.* Paris: Leclerc, 1909.

Scott, John, of Amwell. *Amoebaean Ecloques,* in Chambers, *The Works of the English Poets.* London: n.p., 1810. Vol. 17.

Scourse, Nicolette. *The Victorians and Their Flowers.* London: Croom Helm, 1983.

Seaton, Beverly. "An Annotated List of Victorian Garden Autobiographies." *Journal of Garden History* 4 (1984): 386–98.

————. "Blue Roses and Other Horticultural Illusions." *Semiotics 1985*. Ed. John Deely. Lanham, MD: Univ. Press of America, 1986. 203–15.

————. "Considering the Lilies: Ruskin's *Proserpina* and Other Victorian Flower Books." *Victorian Studies* 28 (1985): 255–82.

————. "Extra-Coding in Nineteenth-Century Flower Personification." *Semiotics 1992*. Ed. John Deely. Lanham, MD: Univ. Press of America, 1993. 17–24.

————. "French Flower Books of the Early Nineteenth Century." *Nineteenth-Century French Studies* 11 (1982–83): 60–72.

————. "Further Dialogue with a Nobel Laureate." *Semiotics 1984*. Ed. John Deely. Lanham, MD: Univ. Press of America, 1985. 51–61.

————. "The Garden Autobiography." *Garden History* 7 (Spring 1979): 101–20.

————. "A Nineteenth-Century Metalanguage: *Le langage des fleurs*." *Semiotica* 57 (1985): 73–86.

————. "Rafinesque's Sentimental Botany: 'The School of Flora.'" *Bartonia* 54 (1988): 98–106.

————. "Towards an Historical Semiotics of Literary Flower Personification," *Poetics Today* 10 (Winter 1989): 679–701.

Shoberl, Frederic. *The Language of Flowers; With Illustrative Poetry*.

Shteir, Ann B. "Linnaeus's Daughters: Women and British Botany." *Women and the Structure of Society*. Ed. Barbara J. Harris and Jo Ann K. McNamara. Durham, NC: Duke Univ. Press, 1984. 67–73.

Sigourney, Lydia H. *The Voice of Flowers*.

Smart, Christopher. *Jubilate Agno*. Ed. W. H. Bond. London: Rupert Hart-Davis, 1954.

Stein, Gertrude. *Four in America*. New York: Random House, 1935.

————. *Lectures in America*. New Haven, CT: Yale Univ. Press, 1947.

Tertullian. *De corona*, in *The Anti-Nicene Fathers*. Ed. Alexander Roberts and James Donaldson. Buffalo: Christian Literature, 1885. Vol. 23.

Thacker, Christopher. *The History of Gardens*. Berkeley: Univ. of California Press, 1979.

Thompson, R. *American Annuals and Literary Gift Books 1826–1865*. New York: H. W. Wilson, 1936.

Thorburn, Grant. *Forty Years' Residence in America*. Boston: Russell, Ordiorne & Metcalf, 1934.

Trollope, Frances. *Paris and the Parisians in 1835*. New York: Harper, 1836.

Tyas, Robert. *The Sentiment of Flowers; or, Language of Flora*.

Uzanne, Octave. *The Book-Hunter in Paris*. London: Elliot Stock, 1893.

Watts, Alaric Alfred. *Alaric Watts: A Narrative of His Life*. 2 vols. London: Richard Bentley, 1884.

Weiss, Harry B. *Rafinesque's Kentucky Friends*. Heartman's Historical Series 49. Highland Park, NJ: privately printed, 1936.

Werdet, Edmond. *De la librairie française: son passé—son présent—son avenir.* Paris: E. Dentu, 1860.

The Western Side; or Lights and Shadows of a Western Parish, by a Minister's Wife. Philadelphia: American Baptist Publication Society, [1853].

Wick, Peter, ed. *The Court of Flora. Les Fleurs Animées. Illustrations of J.-J. Grandville.* New York: George Braziller, 1981.

Wiebenson, Dora. *The Picturesque Garden in France.* Princeton, NJ: Princeton Univ. Press, 1978.

Wilhelm, James J. *The Cruelest Month—Spring, Nature, and Love in Classical and Medieval Lyrics.* New Haven, CT: Yale Univ. Press, 1965.

Wilson, Dorothy Clarke. *Stranger and Traveler: The Story of Dorothea Dix, American Reformer.* Boston: Little, Brown, 1975.

Wirt, Elizabeth Washington Gamble. *Flora's Dictionary.*

Wynne, John Huddleston. *Fables of Flowers for the Female Sex.*

Index

Victorian Literature and Culture Series

Karen Chase, Jerome J. McGann, *and* Herbert Tucker, *General Editors*

————••⟨∞⟩••————